TREES IN THE URBAN LANDSCAPE

TREES IN THE URBAN LANDSCAPE
Site Assessment, Design, and Installation

Peter J. Trowbridge
and
Nina L. Bassuk

WILEY

JOHN WILEY & SONS, INC.

This book is printed on acid-free paper. ∞

Copyright © 2004 by John Wiley & Sons, Inc. All rights reserved

Published by John Wiley & Sons, Inc., Hoboken, New Jersey
Published simultaneously in Canada

For general information on our other products and services or for technical support, please contact our Customer Care Department within the United States at 800-762-2974, outside the United States at (317) 572-3993 or fax (317) 572-4002.

Wiley also publishes its books in a variety of electronic formats. Some content that appears in print may not be available in electronic books.

Library of Congress Cataloging-in-Publication Data:
  Trowbridge, Peter J.
Trees in the urban landscape : site assessment, design, and
installation / Peter J. Trowbridge and Nina L. Bassuk.
     p. cm.
  ISBN 0-471-39246-4 (Cloth)
1. Trees in cities. 2. Urban landscape architecture I. Bassuk, Nina.
II. Title.
  SB436.T86 2004
  715'.2—dc22

                              2003017375

Printed in the United States of America

10 9 8 7 6 5 4 3 2 1

*To our family, friends, and colleagues who enabled us
to write this book*

CONTENTS

PREFACE xi

CHAPTER **1**
DOING IT RIGHT FROM THE START:
SUCCESSFUL URBAN PLANT ESTABLISHMENT 1

What Went Wrong? 2

Think Like a Tree: A Rational Process for Successful Plant Establishment 3

Back to Basics 4

Where is the Water Coming From? 4

Are There Enough Available Nutrients in the Soil? 4

Is There Enough Oxygen? 5

Is There Light for Tree Growth? 5

Are Temperatures Appropriate for Plant Growth? 5

A Process of Plant Establishment 6

Right Plant/Right Place/No Place 8

Nature or Nurture 10

Coming Full Circle 13

Reference Cited 14

CHAPTER **2**
SITE ASSESSMENT AND ANALYSIS: AN OVERVIEW 15

Above-Grade Factors 16

Legal Jurisdiction 16

Structural Limitations   18

Design Intentions   20

Microclimate Conditions   20

Existing Vegetation   21

Belowground Factors   25

What Is Soil?   28

Why Is Soil Structure Important?   30

How Do We Assess Texture in the Field?   32

How to Conduct a Percolation Test   32

Soil Density   35

Chemical Properties of Soils   38

Cation Exchange Capacity   41

Salt Content of the Soil   42

Root Growth and Soil Temperature   42

Soil Tests for Fertility   43

Decision Making Based on Site Assessment   43

Space   43

Hardiness and Microclimate   44

Wet and Dry Soil Conditions   45

Soil pH   46

Salt   47

Soil Density   47

References Cited   48

CHAPTER **3**
MODIFICATION OF SOILS 49

Background: Issues for Soil Modification   49

What Soil Should Be Brought in as a Replacement?   50

Burying Poor Soil and Creating Land Form   50

Amending Soils   52

Amending with Organic Matter   53

Drainage and Aeration Systems   55

Soil pH   57

Soil Nutrients and Salts   60

Soils Under Pavements: Structural Soils   61

Description of the Problem   61

Why Is This So?   61

Soil Density   62

What Is Proctor Density?   63

How Much Soil Volume Does a Tree Need?   64

Where Can One Find Enough Soil?   64

Structural Soils: How Do They Work?   65

Mixing Methods   67

Quality Control   67

Appropriate Usage   69

Soil Volume Calculations   73

Why Is an Adequate Soil Volume Important for Tree Growth?   73

How Much Soil Volume Does a Tree Need?   73

How Do We Calculate Soil Volumes for Trees at Their
Envisioned Design Size?   74

How Can This Information Be Used to Reduce Tree-Sidewalk
Conflicts?   81

Spatial Configuration of the Planting Area   83

Building Up   83

Shared Rooting Space   84

Surface Treatment over the Rooting Zone   85

Turf Grass   85

Mulch   86

Cantilever Surfaces over Planting Areas   91

Ameliorating the Effects of Grade Changes   92

Adding Fill Around Existing Trees   92

Lowering the Grade Around Trees   94

Renovation of Planting Areas Around Existing Trees   94

How to Do It   95

Remediating Poorly Draining Soils Around Existing Trees   98

Drainage Principles and Techniques   99

Purpose of Drainage   99

Effects of Soil Texture and Structure on Drainage   99

Basics of Drainage   99

Types of Drainage   101

References Cited   102

CHAPTER **4**
PLANT SELECTION **105**

What Functions Do Plants Serve in the Urban Environment?   105

Temperature Modification   106

Wind   106

Noise   110

Pollution   110

Plants Create Spaces   110

Erosion and Runoff 110

Recreation/Habitat 111

How Do We Begin Matching the Plant to the Site? 112

Space and Hardiness 112

Sun/Shade 113

Soil Moisture 113

Soil pH 115

Salts 116

Pests and Diseases 116

Transplanting 117

Cost and Availability 117

Maintenance Issues 117

Native or Non-native Plants 118

Diversity Versus Uniformity 118

Current Strategies 119

The Case for Visual Uniformity 119

The Case for Species Diversity 119

A Solution 120

Primary and Secondary Criteria 120

Recommended Groups of Visually Compatible Trees 121

Selecting and Using a Plant Group 122

Specifying Plants 124

Additional Recommended Tree Groups 131

Reference Cited 134

CHAPTER **5**
**TRANSPLANTING AND INITIAL CARE
IN THE LANDSCAPE** 135

Plant Quality and Nursery Production Practices 136

Methods of Production and Harvest 136

**Some Trees Are More Difficult to Transplant Successfully Than
Others 148**

Tree Size 148

The Process of Handling and Storage 156

Planting Procedure 157

References Cited 162

CHAPTER **6**
SITE PRESERVATION AND MANAGEMENT **165**

Preserving Existing Trees 165

Possible Construction Activities and Related Damage to Trees 166

Writing Specifications for Vegetation Protection During
Construction 171

Impact of Soil Compaction During Construction 176

Paving Around Trees 176

Remediation Techniques for Trees Situated in Recently
Compacted Soils 177

References Cited 178

Concluding Remarks 178

APPENDIX **I**
**Tree and Large Shrub Tolerance of Varying Soil Moisture, Soil pH,
and Salt Conditions 181**

APPENDIX **II**
Model Soil Specifications 195

APPENDIX **III**
Model Landscape/Planting Specification 199

INDEX **205**

PREFACE

Understanding the limitations and opportunities of a given landscape to sustain plant growth will ultimately determine the success or failure of any landscape design. In this book, our objectives are to empower landscape architects, horticulturists, and city foresters with tools so that they may make detailed assessments of sites that pose problems or present opportunities for proposed and existing plantings. In addition, subjects we engage in this text include understanding microclimates, soil texture, soil compaction, soil pH and nutrients, drainage, and spatial limitations to plant growth both above and below ground as well as evaluating existing vegetation. This sets the stage for appropriate plant selection and installation guidance to meet the design intent as well as point out the need to modify the planting design or the site conditions when feasible.

Detailed considerations of soil amendments, drainage and aeration, nutrients and innovative materials, methods, and details are provided. Critical step-by-step calculations to determine needed soil volumes to achieve envisioned designs are outlined. Associated with these calculations are strategies to design for planting areas and configurations that improve the success of plant establishment in urban areas.

The way in which we make plant selections for a given site based on documented site assessment is stressed in this text. Strategies for the consideration of biological diversity and visual similarity are considered, and some tree species that may be used to achieve such ideas are suggested. Essential considerations of planting techniques and maintenance are provided, as are techniques for site preservation and management during construction.

Many people have contributed to the science and art of urban tree establishment. In this text, we present their best ideas. We are grateful for the efforts of graduate students at Cornell University's Urban Horticulture Institute for their contributions over the years, many of which are presented here. We are especially appreciative of the research done by Louis Anella,

Michelle Buckstrup, Susan Day, Mathew Evans, Jason Grabosky, Carol Grohs, J. Roger Harris, Michael Haug, George Hawver, David Headley, John Jordan, Patricia Lindsey, Barbara Neal, Donald Rakow, Thomas Ranney, and Angela Rivenshield. We also appreciate the guiding expertise of Joann Gruttadaurio.

Design conceptualization through site assessment, soil remediation, detailing, plant selection, installation, and maintenance are all considered in detail and are accessible to the student and practitioner of landscape architecture as well as the horticulturalist and urban forester. It is our hope that the strategies, techniques, and best contemporary research and horticultural practices will advance and improve the success of establishing trees in cities.

Peter J. Trowbridge
Nina L. Bassuk

CHAPTER 1

DOING IT RIGHT FROM THE START:

Successful Urban Plant Establishment

Imagine this scenario. A town wants to upgrade its Main Street. To finance the job, a capital project is established by elected officials after two years of political arm-twisting. Almost another year goes by as designs are developed and evaluated, agreed upon, and sent out for bid. A contract is signed, and work commences to build new sidewalks and install new lights and street trees. Finally, after the long wait, everyone is looking forward to these community improvements. Six months later, all is complete, and the townspeople enjoy the new sidewalks and lights—but especially wait for the trees to grow; they look forward to experiencing the shade-lined streets depicted in the drawings. Three years later, even a semblance of this vision has not materialized. The trees look sickly and weak. The leaves are various shades of yellow or brown. Many trees have dead branches, and leaves drop much earlier in the fall than their counterparts in the nearby forest (Figure 1-1). As this is Main Street, extra efforts are made to care for the ailing trees. Trees that are already nearly dead are replaced, and extra watering is given to those that remain. Still, next year, things seem worse. More trees die and are replaced. Efforts are made to fertilize the trees. Nothing helps. By now a third of the trees have been replaced, but nothing that is done seems able to turn the situation around.

Figure 1-1 Newly installed and severely declining street trees planting in a small rural community.

In another city, in the Sunbelt, a different scenario is played out. Here, elected officials passed an ordinance requiring that new parking lots be planted so that eventually 20 percent of the surface area will be shaded by tree canopies. To accomplish this goal while taking out as few parking spaces as possible, trees with potentially large canopies are planted in small openings in the parking lot. After five years, the trees haven't grown much, and a few appear even smaller than when they were planted! The hoped-for shady canopy doesn't seem to be materializing, and the city is at a loss to explain why.

WHAT WENT WRONG?

Even with the best of intentions, anyone planting trees or creating a landscape in an urban context must have a firm understanding of environmental resources that allow trees to grow to their envisioned design size (Figure 1-2). Only through efforts that recognize and provide for the needs of the tree can we gain the benefits for which we planted it in the first place, whether for shade, pollution reduction, reduced stormwater runoff, increased property values, erosion control, habitats for wildlife, windbreaks, blocking undesirable views, creating parks for recreation, or providing a link between our increasingly urban existence and the natural world.

Most of the places in which we live, whether rural, suburban, or urban, have been significantly impacted by human activities—building houses or businesses, creating roads, or laying pavement for sidewalks or parking lots. These alterations are unquestionably more numerous in an inner city area than a rural village, yet they are fundamentally the same, pound for pound, in impact. A dying tree in a 4- by 5-foot cutout in the sidewalk in New York City is not fundamentally different than a dying tree in the same planting space in a rural village parking lot in northern New York State.

We need to approach planting trees in human-impacted landscapes as rigorously as we engineer those landscapes themselves. No one would think of building a house without adhering to the sound building principles that yield a solid foundation, walls with structural integrity, and a watertight roof. Building codes must be followed to reduce fire hazards and maintain the safety of potable water and electric service. We test our concrete and mortar to be sure they are strong and won't break apart before their lifespan is over. Yet with trees in the urban context, we seem to feel they will take care of themselves. After all, we don't have to think about planting a tree in a wilderness area. Forest regeneration generally takes care of that. The human-impacted urban landscape, however, is nothing like a wilderness area. Its soils

Figure 1-2 Envisioned design-size trees for a residential street.

are modified through the regrading, compaction, cutting and filling, and, sometimes, contamination that comes with creating buildings, roads and associated land uses.

All of these factors profoundly change the physical, chemical, and biological nature of soil, the substrate on which trees depend for so many of their vital resources. Urban soil may or may not be successful in providing the necessary resources for a tree's growth; after all, cities were not built with trees in mind. Trees are most often afterthoughts squeezed into a landscape built for pedestrians, cars, and buildings. However, there are methods that anticipate the requirements for healthy tree growth and thus lead to successful plantings.

THINK LIKE A TREE: A RATIONAL PROCESS FOR SUCCESSFUL PLANT ESTABLISHMENT

The first step in changing our attitudes toward planting and devising a rational plan of action is to acknowledge that the urban landscape bears little resemblance to the natural landscape where trees evolved. The urban landscape is so idiosyncratic and heterogeneous in form and function, it would be futile to generalize about what the urban landscape actually is (Figure 1-3).

Figure 1-3 Heterogeneous nature of the urban landscape. Two *Tilia cordata* planted at the same time, 20 feet apart.

In assessing urban landscapes, we find there are so many factors to consider that a process is necessary to methodically assess the many variables that will be encountered. Because of these variables in the urban environment, it is best to approach this investigation from the tree's point of view.

BACK TO BASICS

What do all plants need? There are six basics:

Air, with its components of *oxygen* and *carbon dioxide,* is critical to respiration and photosynthesis.

Light is necessary to provide energy for photosynthesis.

Water and *nutrients* are mined by plant roots from the soil.

Appropriate temperatures are needed to sustain all stages of plant growth.

These six factors—oxygen, carbon dioxide, light, water, nutrients, and appropriate temperatures—are the basics that sustain plant growth. Instead of analyzing the unique conditions that make up any proposed landscape site, we look at the site from the plant's point of view.

Where Is the Water Coming From?

Is there too little due to soil restrictions or too much due to lack of drainage or a high water table—or perhaps both alternating at different times of the year? Is the soil so dense that roots cannot grow and thus are limited in their ability to take up water in a restricted soil volume?

Are There Enough Available Nutrients in the Soil?

Soil pH—the acidity or alkalinity of the soil—can make nutrients more or less soluble and therefore more or less available to be taken up by plant roots. In urban environments, because of human debris incorporated into the soil, especially related to construction or industry, pH can vary significantly (Figure 1-4; see color insert). In parts of the world where hills of coal mine spoil have been developed for housing, the soil pH may be as low as 3.5, creating an aluminum toxicity problem that limits most plant growth. In other areas, the leachate from limestone contained in concrete and other building materials may raise the pH to 8.4 or higher, causing problems for some plants with reduced uptake of iron or manganese. In still other soils, toxic chemicals and salts interfere with normal plant growth.

Is There Enough Oxygen?

Plants, like animals, need oxygen for respiration. All parts of the plant—shoots and roots—need oxygen. If soil drainage is impaired and all soil pores are filled with water, oxygen won't be able to get to the roots, and they may die. If a gas leak displaces oxygen in the soil, plant roots likewise will die. Lack of oxygen in the root zone is one of the quickest killers of plants.

Is There Enough Light for Tree Growth?

Light is the driving force of photosynthesis. Many plants have evolved to take advantage of varying levels of light. However, trees, for the most part, being the tallest plants in the landscape, require full sun—estimated at about four to six hours per day in the growing season. Some smaller trees adapted as understory plants may tolerate lower levels of light. Urban environments with tall buildings that cause false horizons can limit the amount of direct sunlight that trees receive.

Carbon dioxide is rarely a limiting factor in the urban environment or elsewhere. It is the essential gas necessary for the production of carbohydrates during photosynthesis. Carbon dioxide diffuses into the leaves of the plant through leaf pores called *stomata*. Water vapor also exits the plant through stomata. If plants are under drought stress, their stomata close to prevent greater water loss. Low light levels also close stomata. As a result, carbon dioxide is prevented from coming into the leaf, and photosynthesis is reduced. Direct damage to leaves caused by insects or mechanical damage also will damage the photosynthesis apparatus.

Are Temperatures Appropriate for Plant Growth?

Large urban areas are found to create heat islands that can increase temperatures a few degrees from the surrounding countryside. This is generally not a problem for most plants. More important are the microclimate effects of building façades; these increase the reflected and reradiating heat from car tops and asphalt and can cause trees to lose water faster and, in extreme cases, directly damage leaves (Figure 1-5). For example, on a sunny 72°F day in Ithaca, New York, a 125°F surface temperature was measured on a south-facing brick wall within a few feet of green ash trees. The trees were in restricted soil conditions, so the increased demand for water caused by the leaves losing water so rapidly could not be met by increased water uptake from the roots (Figure 1-6). The trees defoliated two or three times each summer until modification to the soil around the tree roots no longer limited the water supply.

Figure 1-5 Reflected and reradiated heat from building façades and pavement.

Root zone temperatures can also be changed by urban microclimates. When a root system is raised out of the ground in a planter, root zone temperatures exhibit fluctuations similar to those of air temperature. Roots have evolved to grow in large masses of soil that are buffered from the day-to-day fluctuations in air temperature and are often not adapted to these extremes. The smaller the soil mass, the more damaging these fluctuations can be for root growth. The process of investigating the proposed planting site for plant suitability is called *site assessment*. Figure 1-7 characterizes the process of site assessment.

A PROCESS OF PLANT ESTABLISHMENT

With a good understanding of site conditions that provide opportunities for planting, it is possible to proceed to the plant establishment process. After site assessment, we can ask which plants are best adapted to the site. Aside from the six basic environmental factors that a plant requires and conditions that should

Figure 1-6 Roots restricted by compacted soil.

Figure 1-7 SITE ASSESSMENT CHECKLIST

Site Location _____

Site Description _____

_____

Climate

USDA Hardiness Zone
- 7a
- 6b
- 6a
- 5b
- 5a
- 4b
- 4a
- 3b
- 3a

Microclimate Factors
- Re-reflected heat load
- Frost pocket
- Wind
- Other _____

Soil Factors
Range of pH Levels_____
    (note actual reading on sketch)

Texture _____
- Clayey
- Loamy
- Sandy

Compaction Levels_____
- Severely compacted
- Moderately compacted
- Somewhat
- Uncompacted

Structural Factors
Limitations to Aboveground Space
- Overhead wire height _____
- Proximity to buildings/structures
- Other _____

Limitations to Belowground Space
- Utilities marked and noted on sketch
- Approximate rooting depth for site:

_____

_____

_____

Sunlight Levels
- Full sun (6 hr or more)
- Partial sun or filtered light
- Shade

Irrigation Levels
- No supplemental irrigation
- Automatic irrigation system
Irrigation amount and rate:

_____

Drainage Characteristics
- Presence of mottled soil
- Low-lying topography
Indicator plants suggest site drainage as:
- wet
- well-drained
- dry
Percolation test results (in./hr)
- poorly drained (<4"/hr)
- moderately drained (4"–8"/hr)
- excessively drained (>8"/hr)

Other Soil Considerations
- Indications of soil layer disturbance
- Evidence of recent construction
- Presence of construction debris likely
- Noxious weeds present _____

_____

- Evidence of excessive salt usage
- Erosion of soil evident
- Evidence of soil contamination
- Usage that compacts soil

Specific Soil Problems

_____

_____

_____

_____

Figure 1-7 *(Continued)*

VISUAL ASSESSMENT OF EXISTING PLANTS

Species	Size	Growth Rate	Visual Assessment

MAKE SKETCH OF SITE

Note north arrow; circulation patterns; pH readings; location of overhead wires, underground utilities, building and pavement, as well as problem drainage areas.

---

be assessed at the site, other constraints should be factored in, too. Are there physical barriers to plant growth underground or aboveground? For example, to integrate trees into streetscapes with overhead utilities, choose a tree that will mature without interfering with the primary electric lines. Otherwise, utility companies will be required to clear the primary power lines of branches, often causing disfigurement and injury to the tree (Figure 1-8). Less tangible site considerations such as legal factors, rights-of-way, easements, and historic districts should also be addressed before plant selection can occur.

RIGHT PLANT/RIGHT PLACE/NO PLACE

Matching the site constraints or opportunities to plant requirements is the important next step in plant establishment. However, in some cases, it is important to recognize when site limitations restrict plant choices such that the site must be modified before successful planting can occur (Figure 1-9). Generally speaking, the more the site can be modified toward ideal conditions, the greater potential exists for plants to do well. However, site modification is often labor- and cost-intensive. If plant selection alone can match the site conditions, then this should be the first choice.

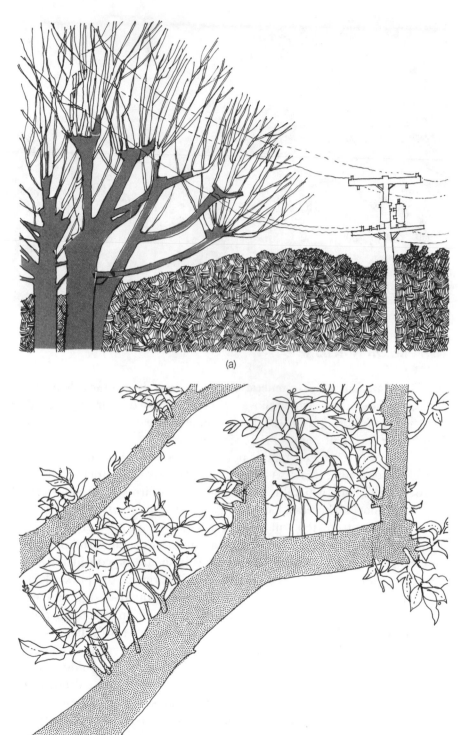

(a)

(b)

Figure 1-8 Inappropriate pruning associated with (a) overhead spatial limitations for a tree canopy and resultant regrowth, and (b) suckering caused by poor pruning methods.

Figure 1-9 Potentially large canopy trees planted under awnings of a building. The site is too restrictive to allow for tree growth.

NATURE OR NURTURE

All organisms come with genetic apparatus that determines their traits. However, the extent to which those traits are expressed is directly related to the environment (Figure 1-10). For example, a tree given optimal levels of light, water, nutrients, appropriate temperature, oxygen, and carbon dioxide will grow to its full or genetic potential. Optimal levels of the six basic factors differ among plants. A Pin Oak tree (*Quercus palustris*) will not tolerate a high soil pH, which limits the availability of iron in the soil, and will grow very poorly, whereas a Littleleaf Linden (*Tilia cordata*) has no trouble extracting iron from the soil even at a high pH and is therefore better adapted to high pH soils. Environmental conditions such as soil pH, light, and temperature are difficult to change; this should be considered when choosing plants to fit those conditions. Issues relating to soil physical characteristics are more complex and affect oxygen in the root zone and water availability. Depending on the severity of the condition, a combination of plant selection and site modification may give the best result. For instance, heavy clay soils often don't drain well (not enough oxygen), while some sandy or gravelly soils drain excessively (not enough water-holding capacity). Plants that tolerate poor drainage or those that are quite drought tolerant can be chosen for these opposite conditions. One could also amend sandy soil with organic matter to increase its water-holding capacity and assure more vigorous growth even for a tree that is drought tolerant. Modifying a clay soil to make it drain faster is more difficult. One can heavily amend the soil, or replace it, but amending clay soils is a substantial undertaking; one would still want to err on the side of choosing plant material that can withstand intermittent poor drainage. In both instances, installing underdrainage is essential (Figure 1-11).

(a)

(b)

Figure 1-10 (a) London Plane tree growing to its genetic potential in optimal conditions, and (b) London Plane tree on New York City street under difficult environmental conditions.

The one condition for which it is impossible to select plants is soil compaction. Soils may be compacted to densities that prevent roots from penetrating them. If this is the case, modifying the soil to reduce density, or replacing the compacted soil with new soil, or building up the soil profile and, in essence, burying the compacted soil are all options. In all cases, at the point where the modified soil meets the existing compacted soil, drainage must be installed to prevent water from backing up into the rooting zone.

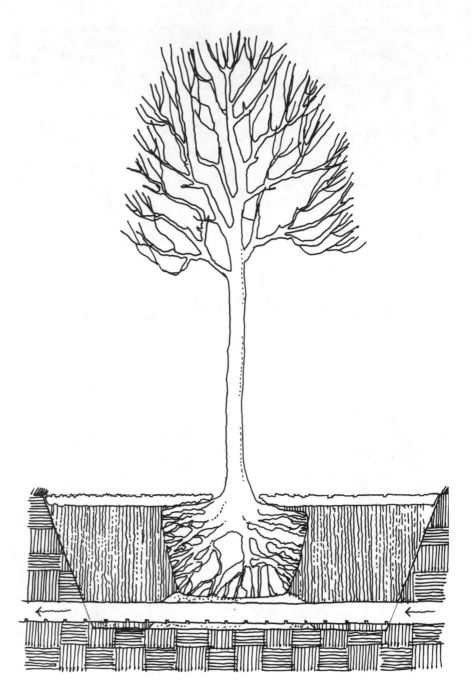

Figure 1-11 Underdrain detail in a typical tree pit. Perforated pipe is often used to drain away excess groundwater.

New research at Cornell University suggests that somewhere in the range between 25 and 33 percent organic amendment, by volume, is necessary to reduce the density of compacted sandy loam, while almost 50 percent organic amendment is necessary to reduce the density of compacted clay loam soil (Rivenshield, 2001). References reporting that plants can tolerate compacted soil are really referring to the plants' ability to withstand poor drainage, a concomitant feature of compacted soil (Figure 1-12).

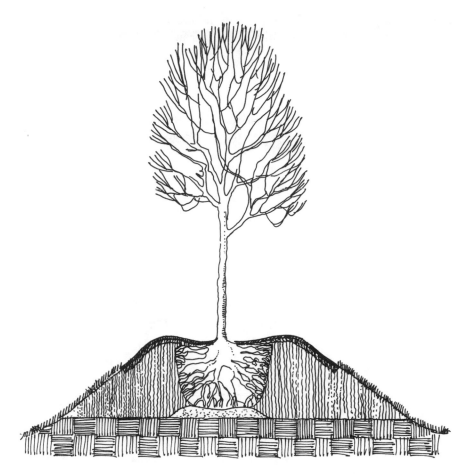

Figure 1-12 Built-up soils over a compacted base of preexisting soils, allowing root growth.

COMING FULL CIRCLE

The final steps in the plant establishment process are proper transplanting and early maintenance practices. Unfortunately, even when good decisions are made up to this point, the plants may still fail due to improper transplanting. Common problems such as allowing the plants to dry out before planting, planting too deep, overmulching (or no mulching), lack of water during the initial season growth, mechanical damage by mowers and string trimmers, overpruning, and other issues that affect plant establishment can set back or even kill plants that are already under considerable stress because of the elimination of part of their root system in the process of removing them from the nursery.

Using the process of (1) site assessment, (2) plant selection and/or site modification, and then (3) proper transplanting and initial maintenance, we can have a more successful planting.

In the most challenging situations, where numerous environmental stresses and design constraints overlap, a combination of site modification strategies and appropriate plant selection provides the best result. With what we now know, we can develop several creative solutions using all the strategies at our disposal to achieve a greener urban environment.

REFERENCE CITED

Rivenshield, Angela. 2001. Organic amendment to improve the physical qualities of compacted soils. Master's thesis, Cornell University.

CHAPTER 2

SITE ASSESSMENT AND ANALYSIS:

An Overview

One of the most important activities that must take place before either planting design or installation occurs is a comprehensive site assessment and the resultant analysis, as outlined in Chapter 1. This chapter presents the broad range of considerations that are part of any site exploration, both above and below the ground. How we synthesize the information to make informed decisions that may determine the ultimate health and vigor of trees and their growth is important. The critical analysis of site information may also determine what actions or interventions are needed to successfully execute design intentions. This may include modification to a site's features above grade as well as conditions below grade, including soil modification and soil amendment. Appropriate plant selection for known site conditions and the modification of those site conditions above and below the ground can mitigate problems related to planting trees in urban areas. The modification of site conditions identified during the site assessment can result in healthy, long-lived trees that express the intended design purpose.

ABOVE-GRADE FACTORS

While some of the most critical long-term factors affecting tree growth occur in the soil, the spatial limitations as well as spatial benefits of vegetation above the surface of the ground are what we primarily experience. Many site conditions that should be taken into account are readily visible such as nearness to buildings, related awnings, and overhangs as well as overhead utility lines, adjacent retaining walls, and pavements. However, many factors that limit tree placement as well as design and growth are invisible. These invisible factors include utility easements, vehicular rights-of-way, safe-driving regulations related to visibility along roads and at intersections, and other property restrictions.

This chapter explores in detail the apparent considerations of site assessment as well as the legal and jurisdictional aspects that influence design, plant selection, site modification, and plant establishment.

In urban areas, buildings create the most limiting factors for planting design. The most obvious limitation is the space they occupy, including their overhangs, such as awnings and arcades (see Figure 1-9). Tall buildings create localized microclimates, including wind tunnels, artificial solar horizons, and rain shadows, that limit the precipitation that actually reaches the ground. Extensions of buildings, including site walls and pavements, also restrict where broad-spreading canopy trees can be sited. In addition, pavements of all kinds—including sidewalks, plazas, roads, parking lots, and ancillary paved areas—limit tree locations. Much like buildings, pavements absorb, reflect, and reradiate heat as well as divert essential rainfall while limiting useful soil areas and volumes.

Overhead utility lines, while not inherently limiting to tree growth, limit normal canopy height and extension due to pruning and clearing around wires (see Figure 1-8). Unfortunately, overhead wires tend to parallel streets and occupy areas over tree lawns, the obvious place to plant large, shade-producing canopy trees.

Superficial utility locations below the surface of the ground also limit planting design and tree locations. Utilities that are not buried deep, such as telecommunication banks, gas lines, electric lines, and associated vaults, also may share tree lawns and compete for planting space (Figure 2-1).

Site assessment for these above-grade and superficial structures requires an accurate and up-to-date survey to determine the complex site conditions that occur in cities. Using the survey, a visible and jurisdictional assessment of limiting site features and planting opportunities can be identified.

Legal Jurisdiction

A well-developed site survey can assist in identifying those less visible aspects of a site that can limit or potentially enhance opportunities to establish trees. Legally defined easements and rights-of-way can influence a

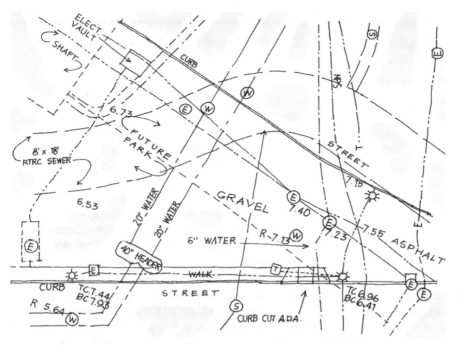

Figure 2-1
Complexity of below-grade utilities typical of many city streets.

planting proposal because of limits of planting space due to pedestrian or vehicular access or allowable maintenance practices that can occur under utility lines.

Maintenance easements held by utility companies or municipalities are among the invisible limitations to planting of particular sites. These easements may occur under power lines, along waterways, within designated greenways, trails, and greenbelts, and along highways and parkways. Local, state, and federal highways may have setbacks for vegetation establishment, especially trees within the highway right-of-way, which can be justifiably limited for safety reasons. This is done so that when vehicles leave the road, they will have a safe off-road area that reduces the potential of hitting trees. Vegetation also is limited at intersections and locations of critical decision making where clear vision with unobstructed views is needed.

Local sign ordinances and view rights to highway signs and billboards also limit the size and placement of trees (Figure 2-2). Once again, these limitations may not be readily visible on site. A survey that locates such easements and property rights is needed.

Development guidelines and ordinances can also direct where and how we engage in tree planting. Planting requirements should also be considered for a site during the assessment process. Contemporary design guidelines can be very prescriptive regarding the location, type, and size of trees to be used for a new project or renovation development. Equally, local property restrictions may limit the location and size of plants with respect to view corridors and scenic easements. In areas prone to wildfire, restrictions may be in place for selection of species that are known to be incendiary.

Figure 2-2   MODEL DESIGN GUIDELINE FOR USE OF VEGETATION AS
BUFFER OR SCREENING

Trees in vegetative buffers and screens should be of varying species, heights, and caliper when installed. One-third of the total number of trees should have a 1½-inch-caliper minimum or 10 feet in height; one-third of the total number of trees should have a 2-inch-caliper minimum or 12 feet in height; and one-third of the total number of trees should have a 2½-inch-caliper minimum or 14 feet in height. Species compositions of trees in buffer areas should have no less than 30 percent evergreens. Tree species selected should also have varying heights at maturity.

Vegetation in buffers and screens should be native and naturalizing plants compatible with soil conditions, including first-flush characteristics associated with drainage easements.

The Planning Board, during site plan review, will consider the placement of all buffers and vegetative screening so the views of developed areas from nearby parks, trails, green spaces, and residences will have as little impact as possible. Such buffers may be on an adjacent property under different ownership as negotiated and approved during site plan review. Buffers or vegetative screening will be paid for, constructed, and maintained by developers. Species selection for buffers shall be locally identified. Buffer plantings may be in drainage easements and wetlands when appropriate. Buffer plantings should appear natural both in their species composition and stature.

CHECKLIST CONSIDERATIONS

- Size and species composition as required for buffer planting or vegetative screen.
- Species composition of buffer/vegetative screen to mature at varying heights and appear to be natural.
- Vegetative screen between development and trails.
- Vegetative screen between development and parkland.

Also, clear, treeless areas may be required around buildings in fire-prone areas.

Local and regional requirements and limitations for removing or adding vegetation to greenways and significant identified landscapes should also be considered. Specific limitations for some sites may pertain, such as the selection of native species only for unique and environmentally sensitive sites. Historically significant or culturally important landscapes may also have planting guidelines relative to identified planting documents.

Structural Limitations

In urban areas, there are many conditions that require the consideration of structural limitations. When planting is installed on rooftops, the weight of soil, water, and plants can be calculated against the structural limitations of the building or roof deck structure. Less obvious in an urban area are the hidden limitations of structures such as underground vaults, subway roofs, telecommunication conduits, and other subterranean structures. Such limitations on planting over the many subsurface structures may be unknown. The advanced age and brittle nature of some subterranean structures can severely limit additional loading. As previously mentioned, these structures may be superficial, limiting planting depths (see Figure 2-1).

Planting next to structures such as retaining walls can also have limitations. Excessive loading behind retaining walls can cause them to rotate and fail unless this additional weight is calculated and planned for. Planting behind and topographically above site walls can cause a structure to fail due to a downward thrust that can cause wall rotation (Figure 2-3).

Figure 2-3
Retaining wall with
surcharging related
to tree planting.

Design Intentions

There are many reasons you might choose to plant trees. Based on an assessment of a site and expected needs, vegetation may be used to alter sun–shade patterns, provide an acoustical barrier or a visual buffer, or support wildlife habitat. In addition, planting might be considered as a human food source and apothecary, exploiting the nutritional medicinal benefits of carefully selected plants. Specific plants have special cultural meanings and uses for ethnic or religious groups (Figure 2-4; see color insert). A design might aim for a natural look or a highly symmetrical and formal plant layout. The aesthetic appeal of plants cannot be overstated. However, this should be balanced against the need for increased biological diversity. This would insure against a landscape potentially prone to devastation from a particular insect or disease.

Plants can assist in space and place-making. They can create edges, groves, and a wide variety of conditions historically used in urban areas around the world (Figure 2-5). An individual plant and assemblages of plants can have symbolic or cultural meaning. Planting strategies can be educational in nature, as in an arboretum, or simply an aesthetic display.

In cities, plants, and trees in particular, have been used to mitigate the scale, the material nature, and microclimates created by large groupings of buildings. Plantings are used, as is often said, to soften buildings, which is interpreted to mean balancing the architectural with the more natural conditions of the city.

Microclimate Conditions

Trees are used to both create desirable microclimates and to mitigate the effects of undesirable microclimates in complex urban areas. They are most

Figure 2-5 Plant material can create outdoor rooms and significant spaces in the landscape.

often planted to balance sun and shade, especially in areas where summer-time heating is extreme. Many urban areas have building material surfaces that absorb and reradiate heat. The reduction of the urban heat sink and reradiating material surfaces is generally desirable (Figure 2-6).

Plantings can also mitigate wind in urban areas. They can break up and lift as well as reduce long laminar wind flows that occur over broad expanses of flat, low-elevation buildings, topography, or open areas. Waterfront sites, common in significant cities around the world, are most susceptible to the full effects of wind.

Existing Vegetation

One of the most telling site assessments involves the critical analysis of existing vegetation. Several aspects of this vegetation, which give a general indication of plant health, include early fall coloration of foliage (Figure 2-7; see color insert), scorched edges of leaves (Figure 2-8; see color insert), or premature leaf drop and an unnatural yellowing of leaves called *inter-veinal chlorosis* (Figure 2-9; see color insert). All of these conditions can be readily seen at a distance and confirmed with close inspection. Another plant assessment observation relates to numerous dead branches. Declining vegetation is seen in what is characterized as *branch die-back* (Figure 2-10).

Figure 2-6 Shade and placemaking provided by a grove of trees in a small urban vest-pocket park.

Figure 2-10 Branch die-back and proliferating shoot growth on older wood.

This is diagnosed when the tips of branches appear dead, lacking leaves and healthy buds. This die-back can also happen in certain zones of the canopy, or one part of a canopy, due to mechanical damage to one side of a tree. Zonal branch die-back can occur with bud-kill from salt spray on one side of a tree or root and mechanical damage to a particular side of a tree. An example of zonal damage may occur with root elimination due to utility trenching along one side of a tree or surface damage to the cambium on the tree trunk. Other subtle indications of severe branch die-back can be seen when many branches have been repeatedly pruned off a tree, or many tips of branches have been pruned away. This may indicate that pruning occurred previously to remove dead or diseased branches. Suckering from the trunk base and roots may also be an indicator of plant stress (Figure 2-11).

Another technique for assessing the health and vigor of trees is evaluating the amount of growth a plant has achieved in any particular year. This is called the *increment of growth*. It is determined by measuring on a typical stem the length of a shoot from its tip backward to the prior year's terminal bud, thus isolating its annual growth. For most trees that have overcome transplant shock and have been in the ground for three or more years, the annual increment of growth can be from 6 inches to 2 feet or more per year. The first few years after transplanting can result in shorter increments of growth due to transplant shock (the shock of being moved from the nursery to the planting site). The short-term history of plant growth can be determined by documenting several years of increment of growth (see Figure 2-12).

Another plant assessment involves looking for mechanical damage on the trunk of a tree. This is seen mostly as deep gouges in the bark and deeper into the tissue of the plant. While the cause may not be apparent, look for the effects of mowing too close to the tree, string-trimmer damage, vehicular damage, and the effects of construction equipment on tree trunks, branches, and roots. Natural phenomena such as heavy ice and snow loading cause cracking and damage to trees and limbs. Wind damage and lightning strikes, which leave characteristic damage patterns on vegetation, are also important to document.

In some cases and related to particular species, a phenomenon called *included bark* can result in mechanical damage. This condition occurs when

Figure 2-11 While some species have greater potential to throw up root suckers, the condition is often a sign of plant stress.

two large branches grow very close to one another without actually fusing, even though they may look attached. Bark growing on two or more adjacent branches keeps the branches from attaching to one another. This can result in the branches splitting apart as they grow in weight. Other damage to trees may be caused by poor branch attachment to the trunk of a tree. This

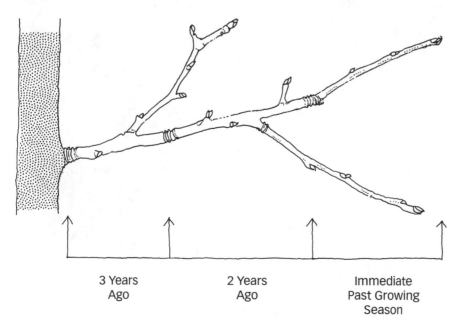

3 Years Ago   2 Years Ago   Immediate Past Growing Season

Figure 2-12 Sketch of an increment of growth on a tree branch.

problem is characteristic of some species or may be the result of poorly grown or pruned trees (Figure 2-13). The ultimate effect is branches that tear away from the trunk, resulting in severe damage to the tree and opening the way for pathogens, fungus, and rot. Mechanical damage may cause significant impairment to plant growth, depending on its severity.

Sometimes plants grow *too* well. The canopy can grow at such an excessive rate that the top is disproportionate to the size of the trunk, resulting in what is called *sail*. While this in and of itself is not a problem, it does make branches vulnerable to failure under wind, ice, or snow loads. While excessive sail is unusual, certain fast-growing species can develop this problem under optimum growing conditions.

Figure 2-13
Included bark and poor branching structure.

Another assessment of vegetation that should be considered is when trees are grown quite closely, as in a bosque. Over time, interior branches that do not get sufficient sunlight may decline, depending on species, and die, causing a falling branch hazard. Again, while this is not common in urban areas, it should be noted when present.

Insect infestation can be a seasonal problem without long-term effects on trees, or it may cause catastrophic death when the insects become a vector for another disease. In recent history, Dutch elm disease caused widespread tree death. Certain genera and species are especially susceptible to insect infestation. *Tilia cordata*, a widely used tree internationally, is susceptible to Japanese beetle and aphids. Maples on the east coast and central states of the United States have recently been threatened by the Asian long-horned beetle, which can have catastrophic results. Viburnum leaf beetle, gypsy moth caterpillar, and many other insects have had broad and negative effects on the vegetation in urban areas. The nature of insect infestation and damage is quite complex and may require the expertise of an entomologist, who can systematically assess the short- and long-term effects of insects on the urban forest.

When salt is used as a wintertime de-icer, it can cause both short-term problems and, in the worst cases, plant desiccation and death. Certain species within the genera of *Acer* and *Pinus* are highly susceptible to salt damage. However, all plants are affected to some degree. The timing and nature of the salt application can influence the extent of damage. For example, near highways and along ocean shorelines where buds and leaves are repeatedly exposed to a fine salt spray, the resulting severe desiccation over an extended period may cause bud death, leaf scorch, leaf drop, branch dieback, and plant death. One characteristic of repeated bud death is a witch's broom, a dense cluster of small branches resulting from terminal and lateral bud death over many seasons (Figure 2-14).

Salt damage can also occur when salt is taken up by the roots and deposited in plant tissue. This is most often seen as leaf scorch and, more severely, as leaf mortality and premature leaf drop. While leaves and plant tissue can be analyzed for salt content, observations on a site can be seen as cause and effect—that is, trees planted near a highway with one-sided leaf or bud damage directly associated with the highway.

Overall, many above-grade analyses should be carried out prior to either design or plant installation. Without adequate assessment and analysis, we are doomed to repeating the many problems that exist locally for any particular site.

BELOWGROUND FACTORS

It is widely held that the majority of a tree's problems come from the soil where it is planted, and indeed there is a strong consensus among urban horticulturists that soil largely determines the success of a landscape planting.

(a)

Figure 2-14 (a) Characteristic witch's broom due to repeated bud desiccation from de-icing salt spray, and (b) detailed view of a tip of a branch.

(b)

Soil assessment is the most critical part of the site assessment process and is the part that requires the most time. We need to understand the physical properties of the soil because they are key to allowing roots to grow and to that all-important balance between air and water in the soil. We also need to understand the depth and usable volume of the soil that is present as well as its chemical properties. Our focus for soils is, then, on volume, physical properties, and chemical properties.

Soil is the basic substrate on which all life depends, the weathered mantle of the earth. Over thousands of years, the earth's surface has experienced the action of plant and animal organisms, microorganisms, temperature changes, water, and wind; the result is the creation of soil. Soil is vital to plant establishment because it influences so many of the basic factors for plant growth: water, nutrients, oxygen, and its own temperature.

Soil is not solid. The ideal soil has about 45 percent mineral solids, 5 percent organic matter solids, and 25 percent each water and air (Figure 2-15). In undisturbed sites with no appreciable human impact, soils are arranged in layers, or horizons. A highly organic layer may be present on the surface and made up of the most recently deposited organic matter in partial states of decomposition. The next layer is the topsoil, which is defined only as the layer closest to the surface. Topsoil can have variable depths from many meters to virtually nothing. It generally contains higher levels of soil nutrients, organic matter, and microorganisms as compared to other soil profiles.

Below the topsoil is subsoil, which has less organic matter content and is generally denser than topsoil. Below the subsoil is the parent material, which consists of recently decomposed rock from the solid rock layer below.

In most urban areas, these otherwise typical profiles are rarely seen. Urban soils have the history and evidence of human activities written in them. In the process of constructing and demolishing buildings and other built forms of the city, we mix and change the way soils were laid down over centuries. We

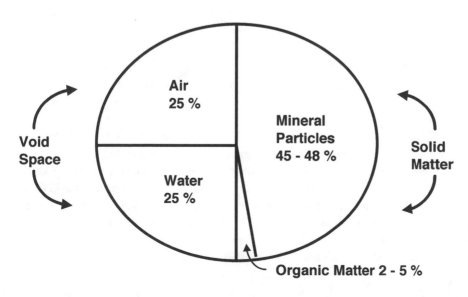

Figure 2-15
Diagram showing distribution of void space and solid matter in idealized soil.

fill in areas, flatten hills, bury debris, and forever change the soil on which we live. Phillip Craul, in his text *Urban Soil in Landscape Design* (1992), states that urban soils possess eight characteristics:

1. Soils have vertical variability caused by the cutting and filling that reflects human endeavors.

2. Soil structure has been changed in some areas so that the crumbly aggregation of soil particles is crushed into an undifferentiated mass.

3. Soils often have an impervious crust that sheds water. Compaction compounded with the lack of vegetative cover gives rise to this condition.

4. Soil pH may be changed due to contaminants and to the runoff from built surfaces.

5. Compaction destroys the macropores in the soil, thus impeding air and water drainage.

6. Soils often have interrupted nutrient and organic matter cycling due to the removal of decaying leaves and other vegetation.

7. Urban soils often contain human junk—nicely put, *anthropic matter*. It is always less costly to bury the rubble from a building than to take it away. The history of materials, foundations, basements, and utilities remains in urban soils.

8. Urban soils are often separated from the enormous mass that is the earth's soil. This occurs on rooftops and in containers and planters. These relatively small masses of soil can heat and cool much faster than the contiguous mass of earth's soil. These rapidly changing and extreme temperatures can be a challenge to plants that have adapted to much more modest changes.

Some or all of these factors can always be seen in urban soils. Use this list as a guide when developing a soils assessment in an urban area.

What Is Soil?

The solid mineral portion of soil is made up of three types of particles: sand, silt, and clay. Of these, sand particles are the largest. They are classified by size, ranging from very coarse (1–2 mm in diameter) to very fine (0.1–0.05 mm in diameter).

Silts have the next-smaller particle size, ranging from 0.05 to 0.002 mm in diameter. Clay particles are the smallest at less than 0.002 mm in diameter. Sometimes it is useful to picture the relative difference in size of these particles like this: If the midrange size of sand were the same as a basketball, silt would be the size of a golf ball and clay a mere kernel of corn. Whereas sands and silts are just smaller and smaller rocks, clays have a wafer shape (Figure 2-16).

The percentage of sand, silt, and clay in a given soil is said to make up the soil's *texture*. Soils are named based on their texture—for example, silty clay. *Loam* is a term given to soil that has intermediate properties of sands, silts, and clays.

Soils that have approximately 20 percent or more clay often have the word *clay* in their name. Likewise, soils that have 50 percent greater sands or 40 percent silts are so named. A smaller amount of clay is needed to impart the qualities of clay because of its tremendous surface area and chemical reactivity.

Using the United States Department of Agriculture (USDA) texture triangle, we can see how the percentages of sand, silt, and clay come together to determine the name and texture of a particular soil. Texture is important because it influences many properties of that soil, especially soil drainage (Figure 2-17).

Soil structure refers to the arrangement or aggregation of soil particles into larger clumps called *peds* (Figure 2-18). As microorganisms slowly eat organic matter, soil particles are glued together by means of the excretions of these microbes. Clays are also important in creating soil structure because of their charged surface and small size (Brady, 1990).

Figure 2-16
Relative sizes of clay (smallest), silt (medium), and sand (largest) mineral components of soil.

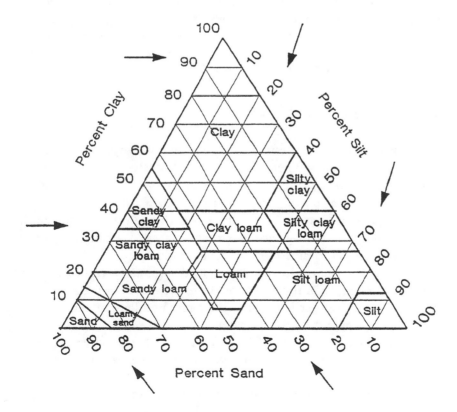

Figure 2-17 USDA Soil Triangle.

Figure 2-18 Soil showing aggregation of soil particles into peds.

Soils may be aggregated into peds of various shapes. Blocklike or granular shapes create a loose, open structure that maximizes water and air infiltration into the soil. Soils that form into horizontal plates are not as advantageous for water, air, and root movement. When soils have little structure or aggregation, the soil structure is said to be massive—one large block with no smaller units. Too often, urban soils have poor structure due to compaction. Compaction can crush soil peds and destroy structure.

Why Is Soil Structure Important?

The formation of peds creates larger aggregates of combined particles. When these large conglomerates are grouped together, they create large pores called *macropores* (Figure 2-19), which are essential for water and air drainage. Interpedal pores, when connected, allow excess water to drain away in response to gravity. After water moves through these pores, air follows. Aeration and drainage are inextricably linked. Poor drainage causes poor aeration; a well-drained soil has good aeration.

Within peds are much smaller pores called *intrapedal pores* or *micropores*. These pores do much of the water holding in the soil. Soils make good substrates for holding water because of the forces of adhesion and cohesion. *Adhesion* is the force that attracts water to any solid surface. *Cohesion* is the force that attracts water to itself. The interaction of soil texture and structure largely determines how much water is held by the soil and how much drains away.

The closer a solid surface is to water, as in a micropore, the stronger are

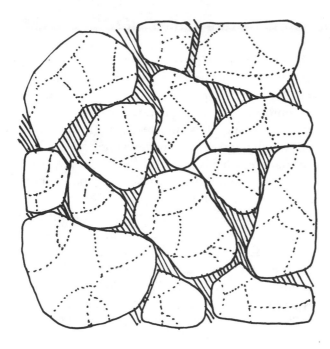

Figure 2-19 Sketch of macropores and micropores in soils.

the forces of adhesion holding the water against gravity. As pores get large, adhesive forces are weakened because water is farther from the solid surface. This allows water to be drawn away by gravity. If very little water is left on the soil surface, adhesive forces are very strong and the water unavailable for root uptake.

For each soil texture, from large pores to small pores, the amount of water held against gravity increases as the particle sizes get smaller. Sands have large particles and large pores, and thus the adhesive forces are weak and water is not held tightly. In clay soils, the small pores hold water very tightly due to the closeness of the particle surface and water. These soils hold a tremendous amount of water against the force of gravity.

The amount of water a soil can hold after the excess is allowed to drain away via gravity is called *field capacity*. At field capacity, water can begin to be taken up by plant roots or evaporated from the soil surface. The osmotic forces moving water into roots proceed until water cannot be taken up against the adhesive forces exerted by the soil particle on the thin film of water on its surface. At that point, when no more water can move into the root, the soil is said to be at the *permanent wilting point*. Between field capacity and the permanent wilting point is that portion of water called *plant-available water*. This amount of water differs among soil textures. Soils with good structure hold water intrapedally but allow water to drain through interpedally. This balance between aeration and water-holding capacity is ideal for plant growth. It is also what is almost uniformly lacking in urban soils that are compacted and lack structure.

How Do We Assess Texture in the Field?

It is possible, with practice, to learn to determine the texture of a soil by feel. Texture-by-feel techniques for assessing soil types are well founded and widely practiced. Texturing relies on the fact that a soil with more silt and clay can be made into a larger, more plastic ribbon than one with a greater amount of sand. The clay and silt is more readily molded than soil with large amounts of sand, which is granular by nature (Figure 2-20).

Another important test that integrates many of the physical characteristics of soils is the percolation test. How fast water moves through the soil profile is dependent on soil texture, structure, and level of compaction. A "perc" test is best done when the soil is moist, after a significant rain event. If it is not possible to do a perc test after a rainfall, then it is critical that the hole and its surroundings within a foot or two be as wet as possible. This is important because soil water will be pulled laterally by the adhesive forces of the dry soil, thus giving a falsely high indication of water drainage.

In a perc test, we want to test the rate of water flow through the soil profile by gravity. This is highly dependent on the macroporosity of the site soils. The greater the macropores moving the water down, the greater will be following aeration. In a saturated or near-saturated soil, a percolation result of 4 inches of drainage or less in 1 hour means drainage is very slow and will pose a problem for plant establishment.

Lack of drainage and concommittant poor aeration is the quickest killer of plants. As roots need oxygen to respire, the lack of it causes root death and subsequently whole plant death in fairly quick succession.

How to Conduct a Percolation Test

Evaluate your site by its history of use as much as possible. Make note of where the soil may have been regraded, compacted, or added to. More testing should be done in places where trees, shrubs, and herbaceous plants will be planted. Fewer tests need be made where turf is planned.

To conduct a perc test, remove the sod in an area, if it exists, of about 1 square foot and dig down 12 to 18 inches, removing the soil. Fill the hole with water several times if the soil is dry and thoroughly wet a 1-foot area around the hole (Figure 2-21). When you are convinced the soil is near saturation, fill the hole with water and immediately measure the water height in the hole with a yardstick. Fifteen minutes later, measure the height again. Subtract the second reading from the first to obtain inches lost in the last 15 minutes. Multiply this by 4 to get inches drained per hour. A slight overestimate of drainage is common because some water is pulled horizontally. Rate your soil for drainage as follows:

<4 inches/hour = poor drainage

4–8 inches/hour = moderate drainage

>8 inches/hour = excessive drainage

Figure 2-20 TWO METHODS FOR DETERMINING SOIL TEXTURE

METHOD 1 (After Steve J. Thien, "A Flow Diagram for Teaching Texture-by-Feel Analyses," *Journal of Agronomic Education* (Nov. 1979))

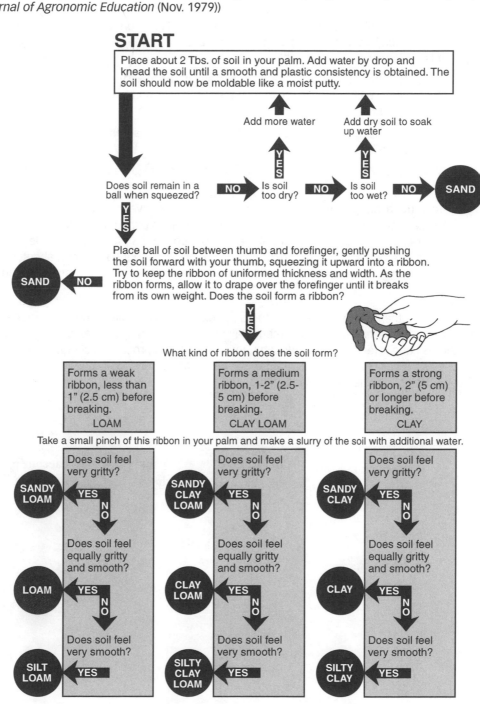

START

Place about 2 Tbs. of soil in your palm. Add water by drop and knead the soil until a smooth and plastic consistency is obtained. The soil should now be moldable like a moist putty.

Add more water

Add dry soil to soak up water

Does soil remain in a ball when squeezed? **NO** Is soil too dry? **NO** Is soil too wet? **NO** **SAND**

YES

Place ball of soil between thumb and forefinger, gently pushing the soil forward with your thumb, squeezing it upward into a ribbon. Try to keep the ribbon of uniformed thickness and width. As the ribbon forms, allow it to drape over the forefinger until it breaks from its own weight. Does the soil form a ribbon?

SAND ← **NO**

YES

What kind of ribbon does the soil form?

| Forms a weak ribbon, less than 1" (2.5 cm) before breaking. LOAM | Forms a medium ribbon, 1-2" (2.5-5 cm) before breaking. CLAY LOAM | Forms a strong ribbon, 2" (5 cm) or longer before breaking. CLAY |

Take a small pinch of this ribbon in your palm and make a slurry of the soil with additional water.

HI

SANDY LOAM ← **YES** Does soil feel very gritty? **NO**

SANDY CLAY LOAM ← **YES** Does soil feel very gritty? **NO**

SANDY CLAY ← **YES** Does soil feel very gritty? **NO**

%

LOAM ← **YES** Does soil feel equally gritty and smooth? **NO**

CLAY LOAM ← **YES** Does soil feel equally gritty and smooth? **NO**

CLAY ← **YES** Does soil feel equally gritty and smooth? **NO**

S
A
N
D

SILT LOAM ← **YES** Does soil feel very smooth?

SILTY CLAY LOAM ← **YES** Does soil feel very smooth?

SILTY CLAY ← **YES** Does soil feel very smooth?

LO ← % CLAY → HI

Figure 2-20 *(Continued)*

METHOD 2: SOIL TEXTURE (Modified from J. Galbraith, 1994)

1. First grab a full handful of soil, wet it, crush it, and pitch out rocks and roots. Make a big (baseball size) moist (not soup!) dirt ball and then squeeze it to mix and mold it so it is uniformly moist and pliable.

2. After cleaning your hands, pick up the ball again. The more water it needs to wet it up, the higher the clay and silt content. The scratchiness and loudness is correlated with sand content.

3. Make the thickest ribbon you can straight up in the air (about ½ to ¾ inch thick) (Step 1). Note the length when it falls over.

4. Now make a thick ribbon with your hand pointed straight sideways (Step 2). Check the length.

5. Take the average length from both directions and for every inch of length, assume 8 percent clay. Next, feel or listen for or look for sand percentage. Smear a very thin layer on your finger or in your palm and rub hard (Step 3). To keep it simple, guess it to be one of these classes: about 10 percent or less, about 25 percent, about 50 percent, about 75 percent, or about 90 percent. Now use a textural triangle to find the texture.

NOTE: Look at the pictures to see how to do ribbons. A smooth, shiny smeared surface with no skips or gaps means about 30 percent clay or more (Step 4). If you can push your thumb into the ball and it feels like pizza dough (Step 5 and 6), it is probably a silt loam. If it is very sandy, make a ball and drop it into your other hand (Steps 7 and 8). If it breaks, it is a loamy sand. If it holds together, it is a sandy loam.

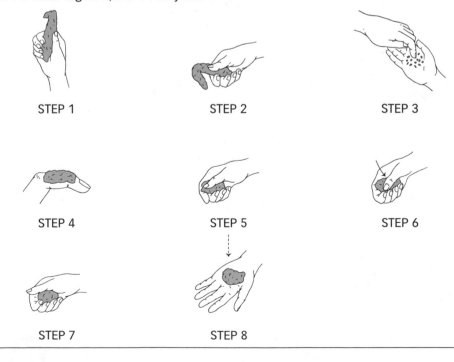

STEP 1   STEP 2   STEP 3

STEP 4   STEP 5   STEP 6

STEP 7   STEP 8

Figure 2-21 A field percolation test measuring in inches per hour.

Anything less than 4 inches/hour using this field method probably indicates poor drainage. Drainage much greater than 8 inches/hour may mean that the soil drains too rapidly. Be prepared to find unusual readings in urban areas. If you encounter a gravel seam or utility pipe, water may rush out of sight before you've had a chance to measure it. Try a nearby site to perform your perc test to check whether or not this is a widespread condition. Depending on the perc test reading, you may need to amend the soil. Methods for soil amendment are discussed in Chapter 3.

Soil Density

Soil density is the weight (or mass) of the material divided by its volume. With soils, we use the term *bulk density* or *dry density* to determine soil density. To determine bulk density, a known volume of soil is dried at 105°C for 48 hours and its weight is divided by that volume. Soil density is important, because some densities stop root elongation and root penetration through the soil. If roots cannot penetrate the soil, it might as well not exist beyond the root zone. The greater the usable soil volume, the greater the tree's growth potential (Day and Bassuk, 1994).

To measure bulk density, we use the two field methods found in Figure 2-22. It is important to know a soil's texture to interpret bulk density correctly. Sand has less total porosity than an equal volume of clay even though the macroporosity of the sand is greater. Therefore, sand weighs more than the same volume of clay. The bulk densities that inhibit root growth are texture-dependent because of soil porosity. In general, a sandy loam soil with a bulk density of 1.6–1.7 will inhibit root growth, while a clay loam with a bulk density of 1.4–1.5 will inhibit root growth (Figure 2-24).

An adequate volume of usable soil for the envisioned plant is key for design success. A thorough site assessment includes calculation of the square feet of soil and thorough bulk density and percolation tests determine the depth of usable soil. Another instrument we use to measure soil density and depth is a soil penetrometer (Figure 2–25). This reads out the pounds per square inch (psi) needed to force a probe into the soil to a certain depth. A sample field penetrometer is 1 yard long and divided into 3-inch increments on the shaft of the probe. As you press the probe into the soil, a pressure gauge measures the force needed to move the probe into the soil. Between 0 and 200 psi, roots will have no problem growing.

Figure 2-22 TWO METHODS FOR DETERMINING BULK DENSITY OF SOIL

METHOD 1

The Clod Method for Determining Bulk Density

Equipment Needed
- Vacuum-packing machine, commonly used for home packaging of foods.
- Several vacuum-proof plastic bags, big enough to fit around a soil clod approximately 4 by 4 by 2 inches.
- A small bucket large enough to submerge the wrapped soil clod.
- A scale able to weigh the soil to the nearest 0.5 ounce or 10 grams.
- An oven for drying the soil.

Procedure
- With a shovel or spade, dig in the site you want to test. Take an undisturbed soil clod unearthed in the digging process and vacuum-seal it in a plastic bag. Clods may be broken to fit the bags as long as they are not deformed in any other way. Very small clods should not be used. A 4- or 5-inch square is a reasonable size to aim for. Cut off any excess plastic bag, being careful not to puncture the vacuum seal.
- Submerge the sealed clod in a small bucket of water. Mark the water level when the clod is submerged.
- Remove the clod, take it out of the plastic bag, and break it up, spreading it into an oven-proof container. Be careful to keep all soil from the original clod in the container.
- Using a graduated cylinder or other volumetric measure, carefully pour water into the bucket to reach the water level mark in the bucket. This volume is the volume of the clod.
- Dry the soil in a very low oven 105°C (220°F) (or as low as your oven will go) for 8 or more hours.
- Weigh the dried soil.
- Calculate bulk density as the weight of soil divided by its volume (grams/milliliter).

Conversions: 28 grams = 1 ounce   30 milliliters = 1 fluid ounce

Figure 2-22 *(Continued)*

METHOD 2

Evaluating Soil Bulk Density Via the Saran Method (Figure 2-23)
(Adapted from Lichter and Costello, 1994)

Instructions
- Use a shovel or hand trowel to carefully cut away a patch of turf, if applicable, from above the intended sample site.
- The underlying soil surface needs to be approximately level.
- Use a large spoon to carefully dig a hole of approximately 15 centimeters in diameter and 15 centimeters in depth.

Great care should be taken during this step to create a hole with relatively smooth sides and without excessively disturbing the soil around it.
  When removing soil with the spoon, try not to compact the edges or bottom of the hole!

- All of the soil removed from the hole should be collected in a brown paper bag.
- Insert a sheet of Saran Wrap or a plastic bag into the hole.
- Fill a graduated cylinder to a known volume (for example, 250 milliliters) with water.
- Pour the water into the plastic-lined hole until it is filled just to grade level.
- Note the volume of water that remains in the graduated cylinder and calculate the volume of water used to fill the hole by subtraction.
- Dry the soil in an oven at 105°C (220°F) for at least 8 hours.
- Weigh the oven-dried soil.
- Calculate the soil sample's bulk density via the following formula:

Soil Bulk Density = Soil Dry Weight (g)/ Soil Volume (cm^3 or ml)
(Note that the volume of 1 cubic centimeter equals the volume of 1 milliliter)

The advantages of using the Saran Method instead of another method of bulk density estimation are that the tools required for the Saran Method are readily available and inexpensive, it is relatively easy to perform, and it can be used in stony soils. A disadvantage is that the Saran Method may be somewhat less accurate than other methods, such as the clod method.

However, between 200 and 300 psi, root growth will be inhibited. At 300 psi or greater, root growth is stopped. The penetrometer reading depends on the moisture status of the soil. A moist soil will allow the penetrometer to move more easily than will a dry soil. Make sure readings are compared using soils of similar moisture content. It is best to use the penetrometer in moist soil, as this is more characteristic of a soil conducive to root growth.

Figure 2-23 Field photograph of the Saran Method used for soil bulk density calculations.

Chemical Properties of Soils

Soils are the primary source of necessary nutrients for plant growth. By remembering the nonsensical phrase "See Hopkins Café, Might Go, Might Not, Cousin Mo Brings Claret," we remind ourselves of the essential elements or nutrients necessary for plant growth. When we decipher this mnemonic we find:

Figure 2-24 Heavily compacted soils with bulk density that would inhibit root growth.

Figure 2-25
Penetrometer and gauge.

Hydrogen Phosphorus Sulfur Calcium
Carbon — C HOPKNS café — IIron
Oxygen Potassium Nitrogen

[See Hopkins Café]

Magnesium — Mg Mn — Manganese

[Might go, Might not]

Zinc Boron
Copper — Cu Zn Mo B Cl — Chlorine
Molybdenum

[Cousin Mo Brings Claret]

or

C HOPKNS CaFe Mg Mn Cu Zn Mo B Cl

The first three elements—carbon, hydrogen, and oxygen—are available to plants in the atmosphere (carbon dioxide, water, and air), while all others are stored in the soil. Some plants can utilize atmospheric nitrogen with the aid of a beneficial bacterium in the roots. These few plants are said to be able to fix nitrogen from the air and bring it into the soil. These plants are the exception and are not typical of plants in general.

The essential nutrients are divided into two categories: the macronutrients and the micronutrients. Macronutrients include P, K, N, S, Ca, and Mg;

the micronutrients include Fe, Mn, Cu, Zn, Mo, B, and Cl. Macronutrients are required by plants in larger quantities, while micronutrients, although equally essential, are required by plants in smaller amounts (Brady, 1990).

A very small percentage of nutrients is taken up by plants from the soil because the nutrients must be in simple forms, broken down from complex compounds to simple ionic forms soluble in soil water. There is a strong correlation between soil pH and the solubility and therefore the availability of nutrients in the soil. The pH scale measures the acidity or alkalinity of the soil. It ranges from 0.0 to 14.0, with 7.0 being neutral. Values between 0.0 and 7.0 are considered acid, and those over 7.0 are considered alkaline or basic. The pH actually measures the concentration of hydrogen ions and hydroxyl ions in the soil. The greater the concentration of hydrogen ions (H^+), the more acid the soil; the greater the concentration of hydroxyl ions (OH^-), the more alkaline. When hydrogen and hydroxyls are in equal balance, the pH is 7.0, or neutral. Nutrient availability is largely determined by soil pH (Figure 2-26).

Between the pH values of 6.0 and 7.5, most nutrients are in abundant supply. However, when soils become very acidic, most nutrient availability falls off drastically. When soils are alkaline, certain nutrients such as iron, manganese, and zinc become less available.

The pH scale is logarithmic. Soil with a value of 6.0 is 10 times more acid than one with a pH of 7.0. However, a soil with a pH of 6.0 is 100 times more

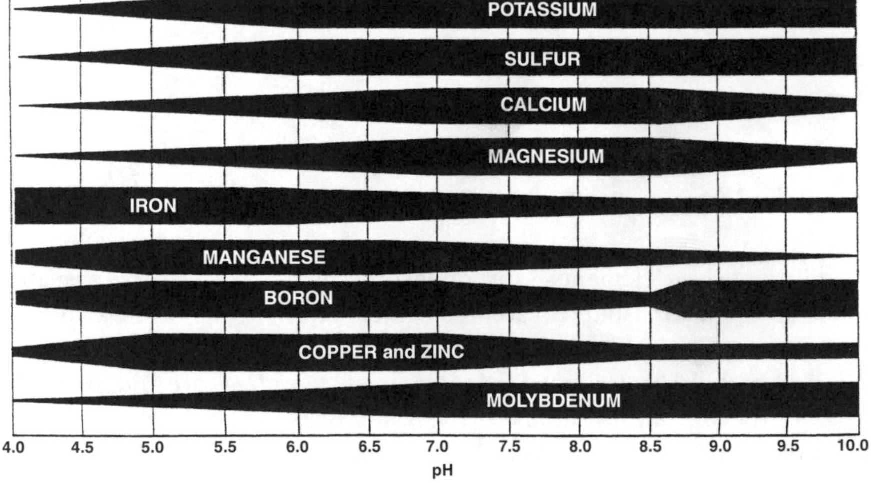

Figure 2-26
Nutrient availability relative to soil pH.

acid than one with a pH of 8.0. Soil pH readings are always given with one decimal place. Soils may have pH readings from 4.0 to 8.0, and occasionally some are found either lower than 4.0 (more acid) or higher than 8.0 (more alkaline).

Plants have evolved to grow in soils with varying pH. Some plants have a narrow pH range in which they grow well, while others can grow in a very wide range. Because it is difficult to change soil pH in a landscape setting, it is important to know the tolerances of various plants to soil pH. Planting a tree in an environment with an incompatible pH will result in nutrient deficiencies that may affect plant growth and survival.

In the urban environment, we often find soils with alkaline pH. This is due to all the limestone-containing building materials used in the built environment. When stucco, concrete, and mortar weather, they often raise the pH of a soil. We routinely note that soils near building foundations, sidewalks, and parking lots have a higher than neutral pH—as high as 8.2, in some cases.

Fortunately, many plants are adapted to high-pH soils and can get the iron, manganese, or zinc they need through a process that locally acidifies their root zone. If plants cannot do this, then they need to be planted in neutral to low-pH soil, where these micronutrients are normally more readily available. It is useful to group plants in three categories: those that require an acid soil (<7.0 pH), those that can tolerate into the neutral range (<7.5 pH), and those that can tolerate a high pH (<8.2 pH). Most plants that tolerate a neutral to high pH can also do well in more acid conditions. However, few plants can grow well in soil pH below 5.0 (see Appendix I).

Other factors affecting nutrient availability may have to do with the historical uses of a site. Open-pit coal mining, quarries, brickmaking, seashore locations, and various industrial uses and byproducts incorporated into soils can dramatically affect pH. The bedrock of a region, the parent material of a soil, most significantly affects soil pH.

Cation Exchange Capacity

Many of the nutrients plants require are in the form of positive ions (*cations*) such as calcium (Ca^{++}), magnesium (Mg^+), and iron (Fe^{++} or Fe^{+++}). These cations can be held by soils that have a negative charge. Both organic matter and clay are negatively charged and play a significant role in holding on to cations that otherwise would be leached away after rainfall or irrigation. The ability of soils to attract cations is called the *cation exchange capacity* (CEC) and is a measure of soil fertility. Very sandy or silty soils with low organic matter and clay have a poor ability to retain cations for plant use.

A high cation exchange capacity will also attract some heavy metals such as lead (Pb^+) and reduce its ability to move out of the soil. The easiest way to increase the CEC of a soil is to increase its organic matter content. Adding significant amounts of clay to a soil is difficult, but organic matter is easier to incorporate and has many beneficial properties in addition to a high CEC.

Salt Content of the Soil

Water and dissolved nutrients move into a root through osmosis. The root has a semipermeable membrane that allows water to move freely but retains nutrients once they are in the root. This generally makes the root more concentrated in nutrients than the surrounding soil; therefore, water will move from an area of lesser concentrated nutrients (the soil) to an area of greater concentrated nutrients (the root) through osmosis. Some conditions may reverse this. When a high concentration of salts is in the soil, as from de-icing salts or too much fertilizer, the soil nutrient concentration may be higher than the concentration of nutrients in the root. If this happens, water will move out of the root into the soil. The plant will experience water deficits, and its cells can desiccate. This condition is called *fertilizer burn* or *de-icing salt burn,* as the roots fail to grow and die back quickly.

If high salts are a problem in soil, copious leaching of the salts by flooding the root zone with water may reduce the problem as long as there is adequate drainage below the root zone.

Root Growth and Soil Temperature

The actively growing white roots are the most efficient at taking up nutrients. A plant with an impaired root system or one that is restricted will not be able to take up nutrients as effectively as one that is actively growing. The ability for some nutrients to be transported into roots also depends on specialized cells in the root that actively bring in nutrients through the semipermeable membrane. This active transport process also requires energy, which means that oxygen is required for respiration. In soils that are poorly drained and where oxygen is limiting, these processes cannot take place and nutrient uptake is reduced.

Soil temperature also has an important effect on root growth and nutrient uptake. At temperatures below 7.5°C, roots don't grow and nutrient uptake is curtailed. This can work positively for the plant; if de-icing salts are applied during the winter months, when little root activity is taking place, salt uptake is minimal. If salts are applied in the fall or spring when soils are warmer, then damage due to high salt concentrations is greater. During the spring or rainy months, free-flowing water can flush out high salt concentrations (Headley and Bassuk, 1991). This potential is affected by soil drainage characteristics. If the soil drains well, soil salts will have been leached away by the time temperatures warm up and salt can be taken up by the roots. If drainage is poor, salts will remain in the root zone and be available for uptake when soil temperatures rise. They will then be concentrated in leaves and plant tissue, causing desiccation and tissue damage.

Soil Tests for Fertility

A simple soil test can help determine if nutrients for plant growth are adequate. Missing nutrients may be added prior to planting or after the plants are in the ground. Each of the United States has an extension service that is familiar with soils in the region. Cooperating universities or institutions are thus excellent sources of local recommendations on fertilizer requirements for any particular soil. Moreover, because of the potential for overfertilizing and consequent high salts in the root zone, fertilization is often preferable only if plants show deficiency symptoms and after a soil test has been taken and recommendations for fertilization are received. It is common to see fertilizer burn caused by overzealous plant managers at transplanting. Transplantation is the most critical time for encouraging new root growth and water uptake. If too much fertilizer is given, water uptake may be impaired and root death might occur.

DECISION MAKING BASED ON SITE ASSESSMENT

Once you have finished a thorough site assessment, it is important to think about the information in a systematic way and apply it to the design process. The following questions must be answered before the next phase of the design process moves forward.

- Will the site support a thriving plant population, given good plant selections?
- Must changes be made to the design to accommodate environmental factors?
- Should the site be modified to reduce the environmental stresses found there?

While site assessment methods and procedures were outlined earlier in this chapter, it is useful to take a closer look at plant selection based on specific criteria. The following issues must be considered prior to design and plant selection.

Space

One of the most critical tasks is to evaluate the spatial envelope for planting. Be sure your design accounts for overhead wires. Do you need to plant a tree that would mature at a height below the wires, which are typically at a height of 30 feet? Are there narrow building setbacks or roadways where tall vehicles will prune the trees as they drive by? Do you therefore need to plant trees with a narrow oval or columnar shape? If trees with wide crown widths are chosen, can they eventually be pruned up to 13 or 14 feet—the necessary branching height that allows trucks and buses to pass by? Is sign visibility and clearance needed? Most trees near traffic signs need to branch up to at least 7 feet to give motorists clear visual access.

Choosing a tree size and shape is a good first step. Available rooting volume also must be evaluated. If the soil is too dense for root growth or drains poorly, decisions can be made about how to remediate those environmental problems. However, if the tree is on a rooftop and actual soil volume is limited, design alternatives should be evaluated to specify enough soil volume, or perhaps a smaller plant should be specified to match the soil volume available (Figure 2-27; see color insert).

Underground utilities are always a factor in tree placement in the urban environment. Try to avoid planting a tree directly over water and gas lines or electrical conduits. However, the situation must be evaluated on a case-by-case basis and determined in conjunction with local municipalities and agencies responsible for infrastructure. The urban environment may have so many underground obstacles that the desire for trees must be weighed against the potential for utility work in the future.

Limited rooting space almost always dictates planting of a tree of smaller stature because the limited soil volume can only support a tree with smaller leaf area. Sometimes it is possible to enlarge rooting volume by using structural soil or raised planters (Figure 2-28) where inadequate soil volume appears to be a problem. A more comprehensive discussion of and method for calculating soil volume is in Chapter 3.

Hardiness and Microclimate

Obviously, it is important to choose a plant that will be hardy in your zone. Sometimes in a particularly sheltered spot, you may be able to use plants that are a half-zone more tender. However, this should be well documented before you risk specifying a plant outside of a hardiness zone. Part of the site assessment should be to evaluate what plant species and cultivars are currently doing well in the area to be designed. In places where summer heat can be intense, it is even more important to evaluate plant performance in the area being considered for planting.

The USDA heat zone map is a useful tool, but since it is new, horticulturists have less experience in working with it than with the USDA cold hardiness map (Figure 2-29). Speaking with local specialists and university personnel and contacting municipal arborists in the area will help you to evaluate and determine the microclimate in a particular area.

Parking lots and street environments, where there is much reflected and reradiated heat, are areas where drought tolerance and heat tolerance of plant material should be among the foremost selection criteria (Bassuk and Whitlow, 1988). It is in these places where inadequate soil volume has the most detrimental effect on tree growth and longevity.

Sun and shade patterns can also play an important role in selecting plants for the urban environment. At least 4 to 6 hours a day of direct sunlight is

Figure 2-28
Masonry planters
providing needed
soil volume for trees
on a parking struc-
ture roof deck.

necessary for most tree growth. Some smaller trees will tolerate partial
shade. Many shrubs and perennials will tolerate or even prefer shaded
conditions.

Wet and Dry Soil Conditions

Soil texture and soil density are the two major factors that influence soil
water retention. The smaller the pores in the soil, the greater its water-
holding capacity. Usable depth and volume of soil also has a major effect on
water-holding capacity. A shallow and small volume of dense, heavy soil will
be intermittently wet and dry. Because this type of soil has poor drainage, it
remains wet initially after a rainfall, but as the soil dries, the small volume of
soil is inadequate to meet the needs of the tree growing there. Other soils
may be more uniformly wet (deep profiles of soil with a clayey texture and
little compaction) or dry (deep sandy soils with little compaction).

It is essential to look at trees' capacity to handle wet and dry soil conditions. Many trees tolerate a wide latitude of wet and dry soil conditions, but
others prefer only dry or wet conditions. Still others require the most difficult of all to achieve—consistently moist, well-drained soil conditions (see
Appendix I for trees that tolerate a wide range of site conditions).

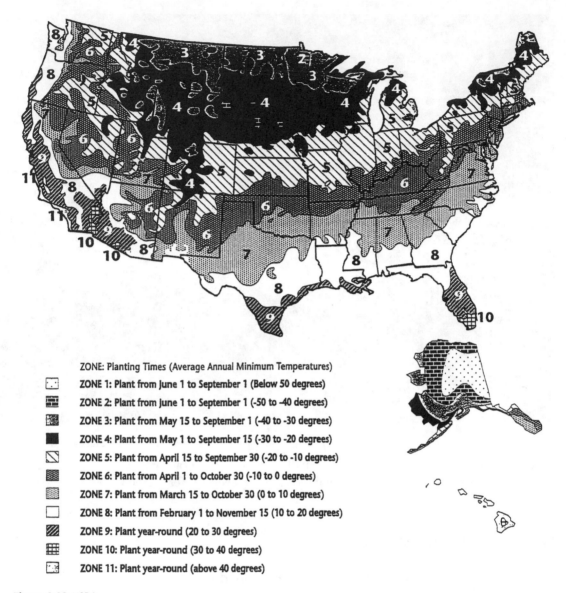

ZONE: Planting Times (Average Annual Minimum Temperatures)

ZONE 1: Plant from June 1 to September 1 (Below 50 degrees)

ZONE 2: Plant from June 1 to September 1 (-50 to -40 degrees)

ZONE 3: Plant from May 15 to September 1 (-40 to -30 degrees)

ZONE 4: Plant from May 1 to September 15 (-30 to -20 degrees)

ZONE 5: Plant from April 15 to September 30 (-20 to -10 degrees)

ZONE 6: Plant from April 1 to October 30 (-10 to 0 degrees)

ZONE 7: Plant from March 15 to October 30 (0 to 10 degrees)

ZONE 8: Plant from February 1 to November 15 (10 to 20 degrees)

ZONE 9: Plant year-round (20 to 30 degrees)

ZONE 10: Plant year-round (30 to 40 degrees)

ZONE 11: Plant year-round (above 40 degrees)

Figure 2-29 USDA Cold Hardiness Map.

Soil pH

The acidity or alkalinity of soil conditions is difficult to change in a permanent landscape. With an annual agricultural crop, where soils are tilled and amended every year, it is possible to continuously affect the soil pH by either adding sulfur to lower the pH or adding lime to raise it. In a landscape, there is only one time to effectively amend the soil, and that is at installation. Subsequently, it is difficult to make a continuous and permanent change in soil pH. Therefore, it is recommended that plants be chosen that tolerate the soil pH as measured instead of trying to change it. The only instance where changing the pH permanently might be attempted is with a small, contained soil volume where existing soil could be replaced and an appropriate new soil specified (see Appendix I for plants tolerant of variable pH). Nutrient availability to most plants is directly related to soil pH (see Figure 2-26). Subsequently, choosing plants with specific pH tolerance is critical to plant health, vigor, and growth.

Salt

Some plants tolerate being sprayed by salt from the sea or drenched with road salt. Choosing such plants can be important if salt is a major factor in your landscape. However, several other factors can make salt stress impacts more or less important. Soil drainage can have a profound effect on salt damage, especially from de-icing salts, as previously mentioned. De-icing salts such as NaCl or CaCl are readily soluble in water. With spring snow melt and seasonal rain, these chemicals can be leached lower in the soil profile to where they cannot affect tree roots, which are primarily within the first 3 feet of the surface. If drainage is impeded, then salts are likely to stay in the trees' root zone as the soil warms up in spring and root growth begins. Ensuring good drainage will lessen salt damage to plants. Also, avoiding applying salt when the soil temperature is above 7.5°C will also avoid root uptake. This generally occurs in late fall or late spring, two times of the year when warmer soil temperature will facilitate salt uptake in trees (see Appendix I for plants tolerant and sensitive to salt).

Soil Density

Soil densities greater than that which a root can penetrate immediately affect usable soil volume for the plant. This is an environmental stress that cannot be selected for with appropriate plant material. It is true that soil compaction also gives rise to poorly draining soil, which is a condition where appropriate plant selection has its place. However, when a soil is so dense that a root cannot penetrate it, it must be modified if *any* plant is to get the benefit of the surrounding soil.

Different textures of soils have different bulk densities at which root growth is restricted. As previously stated, root growth in a sandy soil may be restricted between 1.6 and 1.7 g/cubic centimeter, whereas root growth may be restricted at a bulk density of 1.4 in a clayey soil. It is important to know the soil texture and bulk density before making a decision about how much to change it or whether it needs changing at all (Craul, 1992).

After a thorough site assessment, plant selection should take into consideration available space above and below ground, hardiness zone and microclimate, sun and shade patterns, soil moisture, soil pH, and salt. Where bulk densities are limiting for root growth, the soil must be modified. Plant selection alone may not be adequate to overcome environmental stress factors.

REFERENCES CITED

Bassuk, N.L., and T.H. Whitlow. 1988. Environmental stress in street trees. *Arboricultural Journal* 12(2):195–201.

Brady, N.C. 1990. *The nature and properties of soils.* 10th ed. New York: Macmillan.

Craul, P.J. 1992. *Urban soil in landscape design.* New York: John Wiley and Sons.

Day, S.D., and N.L. Bassuk. 1994. Soil compaction: A review of the effects of soil compaction and amelioration treatments on landscape trees. *Journal of Arboriculture* 20(1):9–17.

Galbraith, J.M. 1994. Soil TaxES: An expert system for soil taxonomy. Cornell University Agronomy Bulletin R96-2. 50 pages.

Headley, D.B., and N.L. Bassuk. 1991. Effect of time of application of sodium chloride in the dormant season on selected tree species. *Journal of Environmental Horticulture* 9(3):130–136.

Lichter, J.M., and L.R. Costello. 1994. An evaluation of volume excavation and core sampling techniques for measuring soil bulk density. *Journal of Arboriculture* 20(3):160–164.

CHAPTER 3

MODIFICATION OF SOILS

O f the many factors that must be considered when planting trees in urban sites, soil modification is an essential one. Overcoming the limitations of heavily compacted or poor soils is the focus of this chapter. Recognizing and assessing soil conditions on a site is the first step in this process.

BACKGROUND: ISSUES FOR SOIL MODIFICATION

Once a site assessment is completed, it is important to reconcile the conceptual design intent with actual site conditions, whether those conditions prove to be limitations or opportunities. Many potential site limitations can be addressed with careful plant selection, as in the case of spatial limitations, soil pH, cold hardiness, sun and shade patterns, wet and dry soil conditions, and even salt contamination. However, there is one soil condition where plant selection is not a viable strategy, and that is soil compaction. The effects of soil compaction are twofold: increased soil density and decreased soil drainage. With any particular soil texture there are soil bulk density thresholds, as described in Chapter 2, beyond which roots cannot penetrate.

If that should be the case, the soil must be modified. Soil that cannot be penetrated by roots is simply no better than no soil at all.

There are several ways in which a soil can be modified. It can be (1) removed and replaced, (2) amended, or (3) buried under new soil with better growing characteristics.

The removal of soil and replacement with better soil is a drastic solution, but one that might be justified by the demands of the design. Most often, soil replacement is feasible if the amount to be replaced is not very large.

It is common to see topsoil brought onto a site and spread over an area so that 2 to 4 inches of new soil is added. This is most common on sites that have been the staging area for some large construction project. The added topsoil helps bury ruts and give a neater appearance. Its usual function is to aid in turfgrass establishment. This amount of soil is of little or no benefit to trees and shrubs (Figure 3-1). For these plants, at least 18 inches to 3 feet of new soil is necessary for good growth. Generally, the larger the plant and/or the more water it requires, the deeper and wider the replaced soil should be.

What Soil Should Be Brought in as a Replacement?

Although many might specify "topsoil" as the soil to use as a replacement, there is no standardized definition of the physical or chemical properties of topsoil. Topsoil can literally be any soil on top of the ground. It is necessary to specify the physical and chemical properties of replacement soil so that you bring in a soil that can sustain plant growth. To do this, a soil specification must be written that spells out the properties of an acceptable soil that a contractor can find or blend to meet the criteria. It is also necessary that the criteria for an acceptable soil can be laboratory tested and verified before acceptance by the landscape architect or designer (see Appendix II for a model soil specification).

Burying Poor Soil and Creating Land Form

Where it is not practical to remove soil and replace it, it is possible to bury the poor soil under a better specified soil. This is typically done where soils are heavy, poorly drained, or compacted, when a high water table approaches rooting depth, or where underground obstacles limit rooting depth. It may be done over a large, continuous area or in discrete areas corresponding to where large plants are to be established. The most common approach is to create berms, or raised planting areas. Too often, berms are created by scraping unspecified soil from an area to be leveled or lowered using a front-end loader or similar large machine. In this process, well-structured soil may become compacted. A better way to create land forms is to bring in specified, compaction-resistant soil and carefully place it on site. The depth of these forms should be no less than 18 inches and preferably closer to 3 feet if large plant material is to be established there (Figure 3-2).

There are several caveats concerning the design of berm shape and ori-

(a)

(b)

Figure 3-1 (a) Compacted soil showing poor drainage and rutted soil at time of planting. (b) Topsoil is spread over the soil, but underlying problems remain.

entation. A berm should have a minimum width of 2 feet, and the ratio of height to width should not exceed 1:3 for stability. The berm edge should slope gradually into the existing grade. Given the added elevation and slope, excess surface water will be shed off the sides of a berm. Make sure this water is not directed toward other plantings. Depending on the berm orientation to the site contours, excess water may be directed either around the berm or impounded on the site. If designed as part of a water conservation strategy, berming on the contour can decrease surface water runoff and increase infiltration.

Figure 3-2 Created berm providing usable soil volume over poor compacted soil.

Raised beds involve the construction of a retaining wall on one or all sides in order to contain the additional soil volume. This is most appropriate in a formal design, where space may be limited, or where a seating wall is a desirable feature. The goal of a well-designed berm or raised bed is to achieve greater rooting volume.

It is important that the existing soil under a created land form drains well. A technique called *subsurface soil sculpting* can aid in this process. With subsurface sculpting, the grade of the soil to be buried is graded in a way that moves excess water away from prepared planting zones before the new soil is brought in. Water should drain freely through the replaced soil and, when it reaches the old soil, it should be channeled away by the use of subsurface swales or drains via gravity. The grade or form of the replaced soil may look nothing like the shape of the sculpted buried soil that has been shaped for positive drainage (Figure 3-3).

Amending Soils

It is theoretically possible to amend an existing compacted soil so that its bulk density is below a root growth limiting level and its macroporosity is increased to allow for better drainage and aeration.

Seminal work done by Spomer (1983) showed that it would take a very large amount of an inorganic amendment, such as sand, to affect a positive change in bulk density and macroporosity. If sand were added to a soil containing only micropores, you would need to add approximately 75 percent by volume to effect a positive change in macroporosity. Adding less than that actually decreases the porosity of the soil. It is important, too, that any amendment be of a uniform size—preferably a large- to medium-diameter sand. If a well-graded sand is added, one with particles of all sizes, the smaller particles will nest within the larger ones, effectively reducing pore space. The best amendment has particles of nearly uniform size. When the uniform particles become so numerous in an amended soil that they begin to touch each other, macropores are formed (Figure 3-4). The designations and openings in Table 3-1 are important in understanding the relationship of sand and gravel size

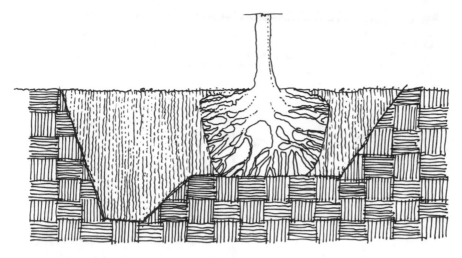

Figure 3-3 Sub-surface sculpting diagram of usable soil over shaped subsoil for drainage.

names common in the trade, the American Society for Testing Materials (ASTM) Sieve Designation, and related sieve or screen sizes. This information is essential when considering using sands or fine gravels as a soil amendment or evaluating sieve specifications of a soil analysis.

In practice, it is very difficult to amend a soil in the field with enough inorganic amendment to effect a meaningful improvement. So much must be added and tilled into 18 to 36 inches, that this may not be a viable option. Adding sand is useful if soils can be mixed away from the site and brought in and placed. This becomes the same technique as bringing in another soil to replace the old. Sand and gravel firms will blend a soil to specification. If a soil is required to be compaction resistant and freely draining, it is important that a soil specification be followed that will provide those qualities. A sand within a narrow particle size range, generally from coarse to medium (see Table 3-1), will provide the macropores for good drainage as well as root growth. By mixing so much sand into a heavy soil, the texture of the soil can be changed, but not without considerable effort.

Amending with Organic Matter

Although the practice of amending a soil with organic matter is an ancient agricultural practice, its application in landscape sites and especially in in-

Figure 3-4 Sand as a soil amendment. The effect of mixing sand with clay decreases pore space until the volume of sand exceeds 50 percent. (Source: *Arboriculture*, 4th edition, 2004, by Richard Harris, James Clark, and Nelda P. Methany, Prentice Hall, Upper Saddle River, NJ 07458)

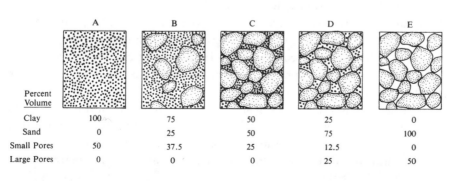

Percent Volume	A	B	C	D	E
Clay	100	75	50	25	0
Sand	0	25	50	75	100
Small Pores	50	37.5	25	12.5	0
Large Pores	0	0	0	25	50

TABLE 3-1   SIEVE DESIGNATIONS AND OPENINGS

ASTM Sieve Designation	Sieve Opening (mm)	Sieve Opening (inches)	Particle Name
0.265 in.	6.7	0.263	Gravel
0.25	6.3	0.250	Gravel
No. 4	4.76	0.185	Gravel
No. 6	3.36	0.131	Gravel
No. 8	2.38	0.093	Gravel
No. 10	2.00	0.078	Very coarse sand
No. 12	1.68	0.065	Very coarse sand
No. 14	1.41	0.055	Very coarse sand
No. 16	1.19	0.046	Very coarse sand
No. 18	1.00	0.039	Very coarse sand
No. 20	0.841	0.0328	Coarse sand
No. 30	0.595	0.0232	Coarse sand
No. 35	0.500	0.0195	Coarse sand
No. 40	0.420	0.0164	Medium sand
No. 45	0.354	0.0138	Medium sand
No. 50	0.297	0.0116	Medium sand
No. 60	0.250	0.0097	Medium sand
No. 70	0.210	0.0082	Fine sand
No. 80	0.177	0.0069	Fine sand
No. 100	0.149	0.0058	Fine sand
No. 120	0.125	0.0049	Fine sand
No. 140	0.105	0.0041	Fine sand
No. 170	0.088	0.0035	Very fine sand
No. 200	0.074	0.0029	Very fine sand
No. 230	0.063	0.0024	Very fine sand
No. 270	0.053	0.0021	Very fine sand
No. 325	0.044	0.0017	Silt

dividual planting holes has been questioned since the 1980s. Many researchers found that adding organic amendment to the backfill of a planting hole provided no useful benefits. An evaluation of this work shows clearly that no case was made in which the existing soil was limiting either by drainage or excessive bulk density. If there is no need for soil amendment, it is understandable why many researchers found its use unnecessary. However, when soils *are* compacted to root-limiting conditions, recent research has shown that organic amendment can have beneficial properties when applied in sufficient quantities.

Organic amendment to a soil should be attempted when it is possible to incorporate it over an entire planting site or bed and not just in a planting hole. It is possible that amending soil only in the planting hole can exacerbate a bathtub effect, where the loosened soil and organic matter in the planting hole, in an otherwise compacted soil, actually makes a wetter soil than one with no organic matter added.

The organic amendment should be tilled or dug in to a depth of 18 inches minimally and enough added to make a meaningful difference. With a compacted sandy loam, it is necessary to add at least 25 percent by volume to the entire 18-inch depth profile to make a positive change in bulk density and macroporosity. In a compacted, heavy, clayey soil, at least 50 percent of organic matter would have to be added to the same depth to decrease bulk density below root-limiting thresholds. Even with this level of organic matter, it is not clear whether macroporosity can be changed enough in a clay soil to remove that limiting factor in the planting site. Therefore, with a heavy soil, organic amendments should be added to reduce bulk density. However, plants should still be chosen that can tolerate wet soils (Rivenshield, 2001).

Many types of organic matter may be used to amend soils. Peat moss, peat humus, food waste compost, composted brewer's waste, and other composted organic material can be usefully employed as long as it is not too high in soluble salts (see Appendix II: Model Soil Specifications).

Other issues may need to be addressed when using compost. For example, pH should evaluated as part of the whole planting scheme. If the soil pH is already 7.8 and you are adding an amendment with a pH of 7.6, then this is not a concern. However, if you are amending an acid soil with an alkaline compost, this may affect your choice of plant materials.

Organic amendments should always be completely composted and a lab test run on them to verify pH, soluble salts, nutrient availability, and organic matter content. Moreover, if the amendment is too fresh and not well composted, the wood chips often used in it as a bulking agent can tie up some soil nitrogen while it continues to decompose. Moreover, poorly prepared compost may contain significant weed seeds that can cause a nuisance in the landscape.

Drainage and Aeration Systems

Whether you use amendments on or import good soil to a site, drainage should be acceptable within that depth of modified soil. Note, however, that below the improved soil there are often layers of poorly draining, compacted soil that can force excess water to back up into the plant's root zone. We've already seen how subsurface sculpting can aid in moving excess water away from newly created land forms. In tree planting areas, additional techniques may be used to move excess water away through *underdrainage*. Underdrainage must be used in conjunction with well-draining soil. A poorly drained soil will not be improved if a drain is added below. This is analogous to a wet sponge sitting over a sink; the sponge will not allow excess water to drain away until all of its pores are filled with water and water drains away in response to gravity. A dense, poorly draining soil will not drain until every pore is filled with water and additional water moves by saturated flow in response to gravity. If the forces of adhesion are too strong in a heavy soil, the soil will remain wet whether it is underdrained or not. Underdrains work only where there is a well-draining soil with plenty of macropores above it.

Two types of underdrainage systems are commonly used in landscape settings. The first is perforated plastic/PVC piping surrounded by uniformly graded gravel. A geo-textile or soil separator may be used in conjunction with the gravel to keep soil from migrating into the gravel and subsequently into the perforated pipe, reducing its effectiveness (Figure 3-5). The second common underdrainage system is the French drain. This device acts mechanically, much like the under drain using a perforated pipe described above. However, the French drain relies solely on the void space between uniformly graded gravel placed in a trench to move water out of a soil and away to a lower point on the site (Figure 3-6). In both of these underdrainage systems, it is essential that the drains be inclined, moving water downhill to another stormwater system or catchment area. Once again, these subsurface drainage systems function only with otherwise well-draining soils. For a more detailed discussion of drainage, see "Remediating Poorly Draining Soils Around Existing Trees," page 98.

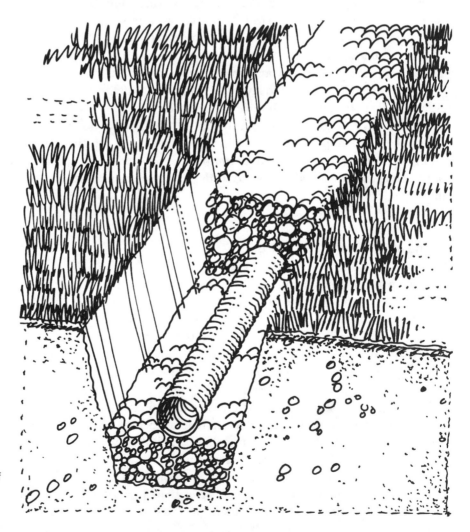

Figure 3-5 Detail of a perforated pipe drain in a gravel-filled trench.

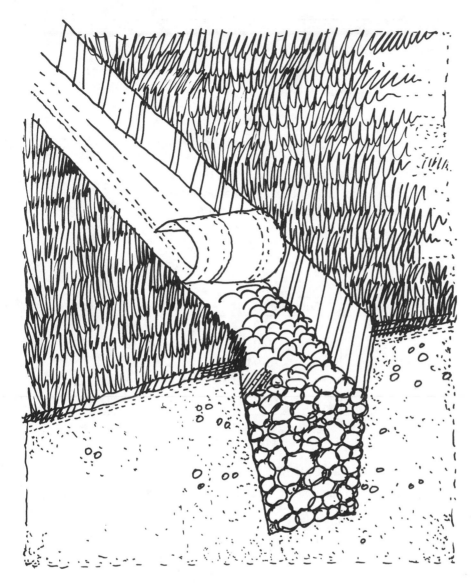

Figure 3-6 Detail of a French drain in a lawn area, with a geo-textile soil separator.

Soil pH

Several significant characteristics determine nutrient availability in soils. Soil pH is crucial in determining the availability of various nutrients as we saw in Chapter 2. Unfortunately, soil pH is difficult to alter over a large area in a landscape setting. In a field where a farmer grows an annually replanted crop, amendments can be added yearly to change soil pH. Sulfur is added to lower pH and lime is added to raise pH. But because soil parent material and long-term weathering are such strong determinants of soil pH, it is difficult to make a radical change. It is also true that raising pH is easier than lowering it, especially in the face of continuing deposition of alkalizing materials such as concrete and other limestone-containing building materials. Figure 3-7 provides critical information for raising and lowering pH in an existing soil.

Figure 3-7   CHANGING SOIL pH

A. TO RAISE SOIL pH: ADD LIMESTONE

Placement: must be in contact with soil
apply preplant
incorporate
finer > quicker reaction

Materials: know the properties of different liming materials, including
strength, rate of reaction, ease of use, economics

Time: before planting is always better

LIMING MATERIALS

Source	Calcium Carbonate* Equivalent%	Rate of pH Change
Burned lime	180	Very fast
Hydrated lime	140	Fast
Ground or pulverized limestone	75–94	Slow
Dolomitic limestone+	75–95	Slow
Pelletized limestone	75–95	Fast

*liming power of a material
+contains magnesium (recommended only if the pH is low and magnesium is low)

PREPLANT APPLICATION TO RAISE SOIL pH TO 6.5

Pounds of ground limestone/100 square feet—incorporate into upper 6 inches of soil

Existing pH	Sandy Loam	Loam	Clay
4.5	12.6	25.3	34.8
4.6	12.4	24.8	34.1
4.7	12.0	24.1	33.1
4.8	11.7	23.4	32.2
4.9	11.2	22.2	30.7
5.0	10.6	21.1	29.0
5.1	9.9	19.8	27.2
5.2	8.9	17.7	24.3
5.3	7.2	14.3	19.7
5.4	5.3	10.7	14.6
5.5	4.2	8.4	11.6
5.6	3.6	7.2	9.8
5.7	3.1	6.2	8.6
5.8	2.6	5.1	7.1
5.9	2.0	4.0	5.6
6.0	1.7	3.3	4.5

Figure 3-7 *(Continued)*

B. TO LOWER SOIL pH

- Use acidifying materials
- Note their rate of reaction
- Cost varies
- Ease of handling

ACIDIFYING MATERIALS

Sulfur—the recommended material (do not apply more than 5 pounds per 1,000 square feet on established turf). Avoid summer applications.

Aluminum Sulfate—concern about overapplication

Ammonium Sulfate—contains nitrogen

Iron Sulfate—expensive

Ferrous Sulfate—expensive

TO LOWER SOIL pH

Pounds of elemental sulfur/100 square feet—incorporate into upper 6 inches of soil

Existing pH	Desired pH	Sandy Loam	Loam	Clay
8.0	7.0	1.2	2.4	3.3
	6.5	1.7	3.4	4.7
	6.0	2.2	4.5	6.1
	5.5	3.1	6.1	8.4
	5.0	5.1	10.2	14.0
7.5	7.0	0.5	1.0	1.4
	6.5	1.0	2.0	2.7
	6.0	1.5	3.1	4.2
	5.5	2.4	4.7	6.5
	5.0	4.4	8.8	12.0
7.0	6.5	0.5	1.0	1.4
	6.0	1.0	2.1	2.8
	5.5	1.9	3.7	5.1
	5.0	3.9	7.8	10.7
6.5	6.0	0.5	1.1	1.5
	5.5	1.4	2.7	3.7
	5.0	3.4	6.8	9.3

While raising and lowering pH is possible to some degree, the best way to approach soil pH in the landscape is to choose plants that tolerate the existing pH. Extensive lists of plant pH tolerances are given in Appendix I.

Another important factor in maximizing plant nutrient uptake is to improve the physical qualities of the soil. Where roots can grow in a large volume of soil and where water is adequate, nutrient uptake will be maximized even where soil pH is not ideal. Consider, for example, *Ilex verticillata*, a plant that prefers moist acidic soil. A dry, compacted neutral pH soil may cause this *Ilex* to show symptoms of chlorosis, while uncompacted moist soil of the same pH will show fewer symptoms. Nutrients are taken up from the soil solution when adequate moisture is present.

Soil Nutrients and Salts

For landscape plants, if the soil is in the right nutrient range for a particular plant, little is accomplished by adding more nutrients. There is an advantage to providing nutrients to quickly grow the biggest plant in the nursery or greenhouse. However, it is often inadvisable to encourage excess growth in a landscape setting. Plants that grow very fast may do so at the expense of strong structural growth, leading to thin weak stems. Staking or pruning may be required to keep such rank growth in check.

The best way to determine if fertilization is required is to have a soil test done by a local testing agency or laboratory that knows the soils in your area. Your state's cooperative extension system can arrange for testing. Make sure the testing agency has the ability to interpret the test results and make recommendations.

Where existing soils have excessive accumulations of salts, it is important to identify the factor causing the high levels in order to successfully remedy the problem. Soils may be exposed to de-icing compounds used on sidewalks or roadways. The site may be on or near the seacoast. The salinity of the water occurring naturally on the site may be at issue, whether groundwater, surface water, or irrigation water. Salinity is also a problem in many arid regions where precipitation is low relative to evaporation from the soil surface; under these conditions salts accumulate in the soil instead of being leached out. Finally, overfertilization or the application of compost with a high salt level can also be problematic.

Salts, especially chloride, can be leached farther down into the soil profile with water. Water in excess of the amount needed to completely saturate the soil must be applied. If enough precipitation occurs at the right time, this process may occur naturally. If sufficient water is available, the salt levels can be managed with an intelligent irrigation regime. The success of leaching as a control method is highly dependent on the infiltration capacity and the internal drainage capabilities of the soil in question. If drainage is poor, leaching is not a viable option. When fertilizing, use materials with a low salt index, or incorporate a low-salt natural organic material. When applying salts for de-icing purposes, if the budget or aesthetics allow for it, use less toxic substitutes around trees; such substitutes include calcium magnesium acetate (CMA) and, simply, sand and cinders. Also, if possible, avoid applying salt at the early and late periods of snowfall, as the still-warm soil and active roots can take in more salt at these times, as mentioned in Chapter 2 (Headley and Bassuk, 1991).

SOILS UNDER PAVEMENTS: STRUCTURAL SOILS

Our next topic is finding usable soil volumes under pavements for root exploration and growth. Innovative new materials and methods for the installation of load-bearing materials that support root growth is discussed in the following section.

Description of the Problem

The fact that trees have difficulty surviving in urban and suburban environments is not a surprise. However, studies point out that trees surrounded by pavement in the most urban downtown centers (Figure 3-8) live for an average of 7 years (Moll, 1989), while those in tree lawns—those narrow strips of green running between the curb and sidewalk—live for up to 32 years. The same species might be expected to live from 60 to 200 years in a more hospitable setting.

Why Is This So?

Urban trees experience a laundry list of environmental insults such as increased heat loads, de-icing salts, soil and air pollution, and interference from

Figure 3-8 Typical planting pit in an urban area. The usable soil volume limits the life of street trees.

utilities, vehicles, and buildings (Bassuk and Whitlow, 1985). Yet the most significant problem they face is the scarcity of usable soil for root growth (Lindsey and Bassuk, 1992). A large volume of noncompacted soil with adequate drainage, aeration, and reasonable fertility is the key to the healthy growth of trees. Simply put, when soils are inadequate, plant growth suffers and trees die prematurely.

Soil Density

The process of building in a city, or even the installation of a sidewalk in an otherwise rural area, necessarily requires a high level of soil disturbance. Any construction effort requires soil excavation, cut and fill, regrading, and soil compaction (Figure 3-9). Often, highly efficient heavy machinery is brought on site to accomplish this work, increasing the potential for compaction of soils. Two critical effects of soil compaction directly impact plant growth: (1) Soil structure is destroyed, crushing the majority of large interconnected pores (macropores), which restricts water drainage and subsequent aeration, and (2) As the macropores are crushed, soils become denser, eventually posing a physical barrier to root penetration. There are numerous accounts of urban soils being literally as "dense as bricks" (Patterson, et al. 1980).

One method of evaluating relative compactness, or the severity of soil compaction, is to measure the soil's weight per volume, or its density. This measurement is communicated either by bulk density or by dry density. Dry density is the dry weight of soil per a given volume, often expressed as grams dry weight/cm^3 ($g\ cm^{-3}$ or $Mg\ m^{-3}$). Soils, depending on their texture, become limiting to root growth when their dry density approaches $1.4\ g\ cm^{-3}$ for clayey soils to $1.7\ g\ cm^{-3}$ for sandy soils, as noted in Chapter 2 (Morris and

Figure 3-9 Vibrating compactors and other equipment used to compact soils and structural fill materials under pavement.

Lowery, 1988). When roots encounter a soil so dense they cannot penetrate it, the roots may change direction, if that is possible, or stop growing altogether. Very often in the urban environment, roots coming out of a newly planted root ball into compacted soil will grow from a depth of about 12 inches up to where they remain just below the surface. This superficial rooting tends to make urban trees more sensitive to drought as soils dry out in the summer.

Conversely, when a tree is planted in compacted soil and drainage is impeded through the crushing of soil macropores, water may remain around the root zone, depriving the roots of needed oxygen. This can lead to root death and an impaired ability to take up water and nutrients necessary for tree growth.

Urban soils not covered by pavement may be broken up, amended, or replaced to make them more conducive to root growth. However, where soils are covered by pavement, the needs of the tree directly oppose specifications for a highly compacted base on which to construct pavement. All pavements must be laid on well-draining compacted bases so they do not subside, frost-heave, or otherwise prematurely require replacement.

What Is Proctor Density?

In order to create predictably compacted base course materials under pavements, the Proctor density or peak density test is typically used (Proctor, 1933). This assures that the base below the pavement is compacted sufficiently to meet the use and loading that it will receive. For any type of soil or aggregate, Proctor density can be characterized by the ASTM D-698 protocol. The soil type to be used is tested with the same amount of compactive effort (ASTM D-698-91 Method D), 56 blows from a 5.5 pound hammer free-falling 12 inches for each layer of aggregate or soil in a 6-inch-diameter mold of 4.6-inch depth. Testing is done with different aggregates at different soil moisture levels. As the soil moisture content increases, the standard Proctor effort will result in a higher soil bulk density as water in the soil acts as a lubricant, allowing soil particles to pack and nest more closely. The result is an increase in bulk density, or dry weight per volume, of the sample. Eventually, the water in the soil will reach a level where it actually holds the soil solids apart, resulting in a lower bulk density after the standardized compaction effort. This relationship of soil bulk density resultant from a standardized compact effort, over a range of moisture contents, can be graphed as a moisture–density curve. The peak of the moisture–density curve defines 100 percent Proctor density and the optimum moisture content for standard compaction (Figure 3-10).

The actual bulk density at 100 percent Proctor varies depending on soil texture or stone aggregate size distribution. In the field, it is often required that soils or bases under pavement be compacted to within 95 percent of peak Proctor density. This often results in soils with bulk densities greater than 1.8 or 1.9 g cm^{-3}. Thus, soils that must support pavement are often too dense for root growth. It is not surprising, then, that urban trees sur-

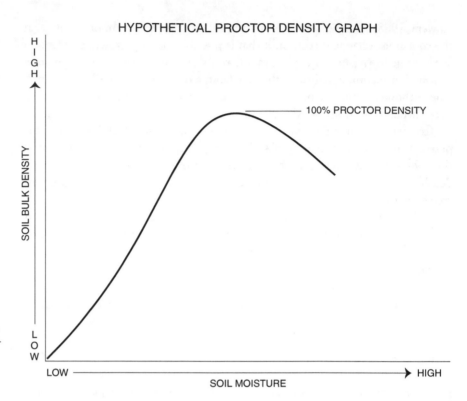

HYPOTHETICAL PROCTOR DENSITY GRAPH

Figure 3-10 Soil bulk density at varying soil moisture levels after a standard Proctor compactive effort.

rounded by pavement have the shortest lifespan in cities. Simultaneously, these paved areas tend to be those that most need trees to mitigate the heat island microclimates that exist in downtown areas.

How Much Soil Volume Does a Tree Need?

It is recognized that urban trees are desired and necessary to the health and livability of our cities. However, how much usable soil is necessary to allow them to fulfill their design functions? Research at Cornell's Urban Horticulture Institute has shown that a reasonable rule of thumb for most of the United States, except for the desert southwest, is to plan for 2 cubic feet of soil per square foot of crown projection. The crown projection is the area under the drip line of the tree (Lindsey and Bassuk, 1992). A complete description of soil volume calculation is given under "How Much Soil Volume Does a Tree Need?" page 73.

Where Can One Find Enough Soil?

Under the sidewalk is the potential for a large volume of soil that would be adequate to allow trees to reach their design size—as long as the soil volume for each tree is connected and continuous, giving each a chance to share soil with its neighbor. Looking at the forest as a model, trees may be spaced reasonably close together as long as they share a large common soil volume to support their needs (Bakker, 1983). Therefore, the task is to find a soil that meets pavement design requirements while simultaneously allowing for unimpeded root growth under the pavement. To do this, a gap-graded soil system has been developed that can be compacted to 100 percent Proctor density while still allowing roots to grow through it. The primary component of this soil system is a uniformly sized, highly angular crushed stone or crushed gravel that ranges from ¾ to 1½ inches in size, with no fine materials. If this nearly single-sized stone is compacted, the stones form an open stone structure with about a 40 percent porosity. For a single-sized spherical stone, a skeleton with 33 percent porosity would be produced (Shergold, 1953). Friction between the stones at contact points locks in, forming the load-bearing structure of the mixture. The second component of the mixture is a soil that partially fills the spaces between the stones' voids (Figure 3-11). As long as we do not prevent the stone structure from forming by adding too much soil, the soil in the voids will remain largely noncompacted, allowing good root penetration, aeration, and drainage.

Structural Soils: How Do They Work?

Structural soil mixes are two-part systems comprising a stone lattice for strength and soil for horticultural needs. Structural soils depend on a load-bearing stone lattice to support the pavement. The lattice provides stability through stone-to-stone contacts while allowing interconnected voids for root penetration, air, and water movement. The friction between the stones provides the strength. A narrow particle size distribution of the stone is chosen to provide a uniform system of high porosity after compaction. The

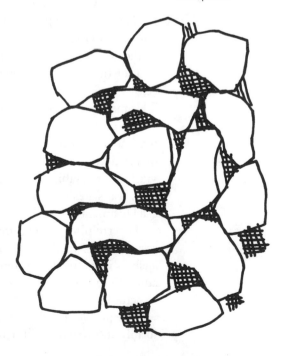

Figure 3-11 Structural soil profile showing stone-on-stone load-bearing system with soil in void spaces.

system assumes full compaction to construction standards, but angular stone is selected to increase the porosity of the compacted stone lattice. As the stone is the load-bearing component of the system, the aggregates should meet regional standards for aggregate soundness and durability requirements for pavement base aggregates.

The soil in the design mixture should be a loam to heavy clay loam with a minimum of 20 percent clay. It is critical that the soil nearly fill the large pores created by the stone lattice while not overfilling them. If the pores were overfilled, the soil would push aside the stone lattice and the load-bearing strength of the lattice would collapse. The interstitial clay loam soil itself should have about 5 percent organic matter content to help increase nutrient- and water-holding capacity while encouraging beneficial microbial activity. By carefully choosing the stone, soil, and mixing ratio, a gap-graded material able to provide the air and water balance and nutrients necessary for root growth and plant establishment can be created even after being compacted to meet engineers' specifications.

The objective is to partially fill the stone lattice voids with soil. The intention is to suspend the soil between the stones, which come together during compaction, producing a load-bearing compacted stone lattice with uncompacted soil in the voids. When properly designed and compacted, the system will have large voids that provide room for root growth and aeration of the root zone.

To develop both a base course that has high load-bearing ability and a medium for tree establishment, the ratio of soil to stone materials is a major consideration. If the stone voids are overly filled with soil, aeration and the bearing capacity of the system are compromised. Variability during the mixing process can occur, creating a mixture that is overfilled with soil. Too much soil will change the formation of the stone lattice. This change results in an unacceptable decrease in bearing capacity.

Any structural soil mix should assume the compaction normally expected in the construction of pavement sections. Compaction is often specified as a percentage of a peak density from a standard moisture–density curve (such as Proctor density) or a specified testing protocol (such as American Association of State Highway and Transportation Officials, or AASHTO T-99). Compacting to 95 percent peak density in this manner only gauges relative compactness and does not imply 5 percent porosity. This density measure gives a quality control mechanism to measure compactness and serves as a benchmark from which to evaluate the material for other engineering characteristics, such as bearing capacity, hydraulic conductivity, and plant-available moisture expected in the field.

The bearing capacity of the material is important, because the materials will be under large portions of pavement and may need to support vehicular traffic. The bearing capacity can also influence the thickness, and thus the cost, of the pavement. One criterion of use is the California Bearing Ratio (CBR), which can relate to other pavement design parameters (Atkins, 1997). This method gauges the bearing capacity of a material by comparing it to a standard material known to be acceptable. For ease in pavement design protocol, it is advisable to require a CBR greater than or equal to 50 in the design of a structural soil. The result is a material that can be compacted and provide a more stable base than found in many current sidewalk installations. This translates into a durable pavement design that can also support tree establishment.

Determining horticultural viability entails testing and observation of plant response over time. Collecting empirical data on plant response and growth analysis in controlled system applications remains the best method for evaluation. Research at Cornell University has shown that trees can grow well in structural soil mixtures (Grabosky et al., 1995, 1996, 1999, 2001).

One problem in designing the system is getting the mixture to blend uniformly and remain so during trucking, placement, and compaction. Due to

Figure 1-4 Urban soil with rubble incorporated.

Figure 2-4 Idealized street tree planting; broad, overarching tree canopies.

Figure 2-7 Tree showing early fall color in July.

Figure 2-8 Marginal leaf scorch on Red Maple.

Figure 2-9 Interveinal chlorosis in oak leaves due to nutritional deficiencies.

Figure 2-27 Planting beds on the rooftop of Rockefeller Center in New York City.

Figure 3-22 Planter areas built above the surrounding paving to provide more soil volume.

(a)

Figure 4-3 Culturally significant gardens as seen in (a) and (b) street tree planting, providing a distinctive sense of place.

(b)

Figure 3-23 Plants grow better when the soil is prepared as a large landscape bed.

Figure 4-5 Pleasing texture, color, and form are demonstrated in this landscape.

(a)

(b)

Figure 4-9 Photograph of different tree species with a similar appearance. (a) Two species of Maple and a Red Oak, and (b) a combination of Lindens and Callery Pears.

Figure 4-6 An example of the universal appeal of symmetrical plantings on an urban street.

Figure 4-10 Cultivar 'Autumn Blaze' of *Acer x freemani* showing superior vigor, form, and fall color.

mixing variation, it is not advisable to simply assign the maximum amount of soil possible. In fact, there is an observed loss in acceptable bearing capacity when the noncompacted soil fills the stone voids (Grabosky et al., 1999).

Cornell researchers found that the structural soil process benefits from the addition of a tackifying agent to stabilize the mixing process (Grabosky and Bassuk, 1995). The tackifier allows the stones and soil to mix more uniformly and prevents separation of the materials due to vibration in transit, dumping, and the working of the material in installation. A potassium propenoate-propenamide copolymer (an agricultural hydrogel) has been used successfully as a tackifier.

Mixing Methods

To determine the ratio of stone to soil, it is advisable to make three small test blends of slightly different ratios. A useful starting point is 18 percent to 22 percent soil by weight. We have found it best to define and control mixing ratios on a weight basis. This approach avoids the difficulties associated with variable volume-to-weight relationships and the changes in density of a given soil relative to its depth in a stockpile, moisture content, or handling. The hydrogel is included at very low rates and held at a constant rate relative to the stone for mix design purposes. These materials can then be tested to develop their respective moisture-density relationships (per AASHTO T-99 or ASTM D-698) and to provide a compaction protocol. The materials can then be tested for their respective CBR at the expected installed densities. The results give a baseline guide as to how much soil can be safely included in the mix design. Research trials have shown that structural soil meets the bearing capacity criterion of CBR greater than 50, at peak ASTM D-698 (AASHTO T-99) density, and that tree roots can penetrate and trees can be established successfully even at 100 percent peak density (Grabosky et al., 1996).

The material is mixed on the flat with a front-end loader. In this method, the stone is spread as a uniform 12-inch layer on a paved surface; the hydrogel is evenly spread onto the stone, followed by a moist soil layer. This layered approach can be repeated to develop a six-layer pile if the loader is large enough to effectively mix the material. Then the layered system is turned and mixed until uniformly blended. If the system is too dry, moisture may be uniformly added to assist in mixing. The hydrogel can also be distributed as a slurry to help in this regard. The material should not exceed its optimal moisture content for compaction determined from the moisture-density curve and sample trials.

Quality Control

The structural soil developed at Cornell University has been patented and licensed to ensure quality control. Its trademarked name is CU-Structural Soil or CU-Soil. By specifying this material, the designer or contractor is guaranteed to have the material mixed and tested to meet research-based specifications. Many individuals have employed systems termed *structural soils*. Indeed, the Cornell effort may have contributed to the term's popular usage. As all soils possess a structural component, the term *structural soil* is conceptually useful to identify a product. Many similar structural materials have been used representing a wide range of stone–soil ratios, with and without stabilizing materials, but very few have been formally tested with both pavements and plants. Hundreds of installations in Canada, the United States, Puerto Rico, Denmark, and Australia have demonstrated the viability of this approach (Figures 3-12 and 3-13). There have been several less successful efforts and outright failures with conceptually similar installations as well. The Danish Institute of Forest Research and the Cornell University Urban Horticulture Institute have independently reached many of the same conclusions (Kristofferson, 1998). The result is that many similar but different materials all fall under one conceptual term, *structural soil*—but not all of them work well.

Given the costs of failure, it is imperative to test any material appropriately with the involvement of the pavement design engineer. Our experience is that the system is more sensitive to pavement needs than to plant needs. As such, the most common miscues in the execution of a structural soil system are excessive soil and the inclusion of organic amendments without proper testing. Without thorough testing to define a compaction level or any control of compaction, installations may or may not be structurally sound or horticulturally viable. Without a compaction test during mix design, one cannot know what aeration and root-impeding issues lie ahead. Testing has shown little variation of plant establishment response over a wide mix ratio

Figure 3-12 Structural soil being installed in a continuous linear planting area between a sidewalk and a curb.

range. The root zone can be managed with irrigation and nutritional supplements over time, but it is expensive to lose and replace pavement prematurely.

Appropriate Usage

Structural soils, in the context of this discussion, have specific intended uses. The material supports pavement designed to withstand pedestrian and vehicular traffic. The materials can be designed for use under pedestrian malls, sidewalks, parking lots, and possibly some low-use access roads. The material is intended for use when no other design solutions provide adequate soil volumes for trees surrounded by pavement.

Structural soils are used as a base material under pavement. Our research has shown that tree roots in structural soil profiles grow deep into the material below the pavement (Figure 3-14). The same research shows a lack of root development in the surface 12 inches below the pavement surface (Grabosky et al., 2001). It is logical to assume that moving the roots down to the subgrade will distribute pressures generated from root expansion over a wider section of pavement, reducing or eliminating sidewalk cracking and heaving.

Figure 3-13 Porous pavers installed over the continuous tree pit of structural soil, as seen in Figure 3-12.

By design, structural soils are fully compacted with conventional equipment to standard relative compactness (full Proctor density). Also by design, they can serve as the base for the entire pavement section. Where a tree is to be installed, the material can be allowed to rise to surface grade, where the pavement opening for tree installation will be made. The opening provides an opportunity for watering and passive aeration systems at the surface.

Just below the pavement, if unit pavers are to be used, there can also be a setting bed material of narrowly graded sand aggregate that should possess no fine sands, silts, or clays. This standard setting bed layer can be to a depth normal for regional installation protocol. To discourage rooting in this layer, a geo-textile may be used between this material and the structural soil. The geo-textile should not restrict water movement. The structural soil material should have a minimum thickness of 24 inches, with 36 inches preferred (Figure 3-15).

Provision for an irrigation system may be considered. Given the large

Figure 3-14 Excavated structural soil showing root depth of a tree at a field study site. Roots are growing down and away from the surface.

volume of structural soil for tree roots to explore, the need for irrigation must be determined by region and management needs. While there is less moisture in a structural soil on a per-volume basis, the total root system occupies much of the pavement area. Fertilization can be dissolved into the irrigation water for nutritional management, if necessary, although to date nutrient deficiencies have not been found, probably due to the large volume of soil roots can grow into. There must also be positive drainage below the root system to prevent saturation. The subgrade below the structural soil may still be compacted and rendered essentially impermeable to moisture and roots. A perforated and wrapped drain connected to the storm drainage system should be placed between the structural soil material and the compacted subgrade.

The basis for plant selection for structural soils should aim toward alkaline-tolerant and drought-tolerant plant species. The stone used, whether limestone, granite, or other aggregates, will heavily influence pH. Structural soils made with limestone generally end up with a soil pH of about 8.0, regardless of the soil pH when the material was first mixed. For many parts of the country, this is not unusually high, even in normal soils and especially in urban areas. Using structural soil aggregates that do not influence pH, such as granite, may not affect pH as quickly, but the pH will continue to climb as the concrete slowly breaks down. A structural soil system provides an opportunity for choosing alkaline-tolerant species that require good drainage and are somewhat drought-tolerant. Table 3-2 lists trees that are both alkaline and somewhat drought-tolerant, making them possible choices when using a structural soil.

Planting a tree in structural soil is fairly simple. The pavement opening is expanded to allow for buttress root formation on older trees if possible. The wider opening could be paved in removable pavers or mulched. The tree is simply planted into the structural soil as it would be in a normal stony soil. The roots would be expected to immediately contact the structural soil and grow into the material. If there is a large unpaved opening around the

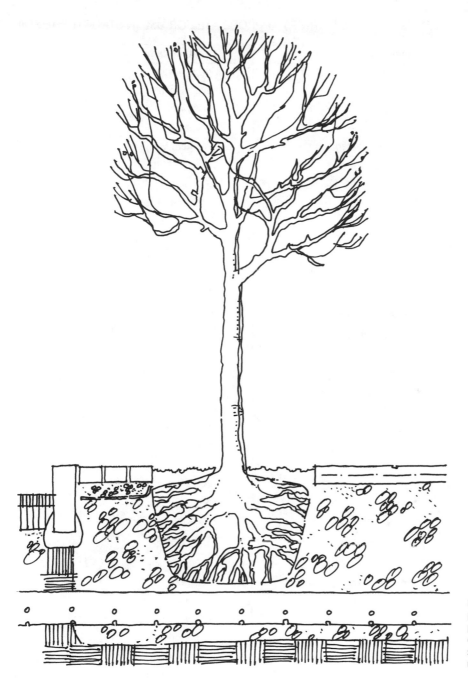

Figure 3-15 Typical paving detail for both pavers and rigid concrete over structural soil with a perforated underdrain.

tree (at least 8 by 8 feet), it is possible to use a good sand loam soil surrounding the root system and then structural soil under the pavement. It is presumed that supplemental watering will be provided during the first growing season, as would be expected for any newly planted tree. In regions where irrigation is necessary to grow trees, low-volume under-pavement irrigation systems have been used successfully.

TABLE 3-2   STREET TREES APPROPRIATE FOR USE IN STRUCTURAL SOIL

Botanic Name	Common Name
Acer campestre	Hedge Maple
Acer miyabei	Miyabei Maple
Acer nigrum	Black Maple
Acer platanoides	Norway Maple
Acer pseudoplatanus	Sycamore Maple
Acer truncatum	Shantung Maple
Carpinus betulus	European Hornbeam
Catalpa speciosa	Northern Catalpa
Celtis occidentalis	Hackberry
Cercis canadensis	Redbud
Cornus mas	Cornelian Cherry
Cornus racemosa	Gray Dogwood
Corylus colurna	Turkish Filbert
Crataegus crus-galli	Cockspur Hawthorn
Crataegus phaenopyrum	Washington Hawthorn
Crataegus punctata	Thicket Hawthorn
Crataegus viridis	Green Hawthorn
Eucommia ulmoides	Hardy Rubber Tree
Fraxinus americana	White Ash
Fraxinus excelsior	European Ash
Fraxinus pennsylvanica	Green Ash
Ginkgo biloba	Ginkgo
Gleditsia triacanthos	Honey Locust
Gymnocladus dioicus	Kentucky Coffee Tree
Koelreuteria paniculata	Goldenrain Tree
Maclura pomifera	Osage Orange
Malus spp.	Crabapple
Parrotia persica	Ironwood
Phellodendron amurense	Amur Cork Tree
Platanus x acerifolia	London Plane Tree
Populus alba	White Poplar
Populus deltoides	Northern Cottonwood
Populus tremuloides	Quaking Aspen
Pyrus calleryana	Callery Pear
Pyrus ussuriensis	Ussurian Pear
Quercus macrocarpa	Bur Oak
Quercus muehlenbergii	Chinkapin Oak
Quercus robur	English Oak
Robinia pseudoacacia	Black Locust
Sophora japonica (*Styphnolobium japonicus*)	Scholar Tree

TABLE 3-2 *(Continued)*

Botanic Name	Common Name
Sorbus alnifolia	Korean Mountain Ash
Sorbus thuringiaca	Oak-Leafed Mountain Ash
Syringa reticulata	Japanese Tree Lilac
Tilia americana	Basswood
Tilia cordata	Littleleaf Linden
Tilia tomentosa	Silver Linden
Tilia x euchlora	Crimean Linden
Ulmus americana	American Elm
Ulmus carpinifolia	Smooth-Leaf Elm
Ulmus parvifolia	Lace Bark Elm
Ulmus x hybrids	Elm hybrids
Zelkova serrata	Japanese Zelkova

SOIL VOLUME CALCULATIONS

It is imperative that available soil volumes for proposed tree plantings be known for tree establishment but also to allow for their envisioned design size. Adequate soil volumes allow for better tree growth in an urban setting.

Why Is an Adequate Soil Volume Important for Tree Growth?

The soil provides many resources for the tree, primary among them being water, oxygen, nutrients, and a medium for root growth. When soil volume is limited, tree growth suffers because so much of the top growth of the tree is dependent on what the roots can deliver, and that in turn depends on the size of the resource pool of soil. It is possible to grow trees in quite small containers as long as water, nutrients, and oxygen are supplemented, which is not easily done in urban areas. However, we are beginning to learn that roots not only are the conduits of resources to the tops of the trees but also produce growth factors necessary for shoot growth as well. Roots must grow themselves in order to produce these growth factors. Moreover, only new white roots efficiently take up nutrients. Therefore, if root growth is restricted, top growth will also be restricted even if water and nutrients are plentiful in the soil (Hawver, 1997).

How Much Soil Volume Does a Tree Need?

Several researchers have looked at this question. And although variables such as the size of the tree canopy, site conditions, and tree species have an enormous effect on determining an adequate soil volume, a few generalities can be drawn. Lindsey and Bassuk (1991) found that for much of the United States a soil volume of 2 cubic feet for every square foot of canopy crown projection is a good place to start. This is an overestimate if the tree is in the Northeast, where there is more rainfall, but works for drier areas of the Midwest and West. This research applies to mesophytic deciduous trees, not trees specially adapted to arid or swampy areas or evergreens. Most U.S. regions could apply this research, except for the desert southwest, where there is an extremely high atmospheric demand for water and very little replenishing precipitation. When we reinterpret other researchers' soil volume calculations, a similar relationship of between 1 and 3 cubic feet of soil volume per square foot of crown projection can be generated. It is easy to calculate the crown projection of an existing or envisioned tree by calculating the area under the drip line of the tree, which is the same as the crown projection. By using the formula for area of a circle (πr^2), the crown projection may be calculated. By doubling that figure and calling it cubic feet, we can come to a reasonable starting place to discuss adequate soil volumes for most urban trees.

How Do We Calculate Soil Volumes for Trees at Their Envisioned Design Size?

The most critical role of soil is to store water for tree growth. We can approach a soil volume calculation by asking how much water a tree needs and how large a volume of soil is needed to supply that water. Water is taken up by the roots, used by the tree, and lost from openings in the leaf, called *stomatal pores,* as water vapor. Factors external to the tree such as air temperature, wind speed, relative humidity, and light help determine how fast water is lost from the leaves. The hotter, drier, and windier a site is, the faster water is drawn from the leaf. This feature is called *atmospheric demand,* and it changes over the course of a day, a season, and a region. We can use long-term weather data for a site, collected by the National Oceanic and Atmospheric Administration (NOAA), in our calculations to respond to local conditions. If we were to have to collect all the data on air temperature, wind speed, and relative humidity from weather records and integrate them for our calculations, it would be a long and cumbersome task. Fortunately, data collected from a U.S. Weather Bureau Class A Evaporation Pan integrates all the factors contributing to atmospheric demand when measurements of water evaporation from the Pan are taken.

The other factor that contributes to water loss from trees is, of course, the tree itself. You might expect each species to have a different rate of water use. If this were so, we could not come up with a formula that would apply to many trees. Research by Lindsey and Bassuk showed that for trees that grow in mesophytic areas, neither swamplike nor desertlike, the most important factor determining water loss from a tree is the amount of leaf area it has—more particularly, the total amount of surface area the leaves have. Simply put, the more leaves a tree has, the more water it will lose through them. Nevertheless, individual species do differ in their response to water stress. Some trees are more tolerant of drought than others.

However, these differences are overshadowed by the consideration of the sheer number of leaves.

After we estimate leaf surface area for an actual or envisioned tree and access data from a local weather station and find the long-term Evaporation Pan measurements, we can estimate how much water will be lost from a tree. This enables us to determine how much soil will be needed to store and make available water over a given period. The following is a method for determining soil volume requirements for a tree envisioned in a site design.

Step 1: How Much Water Does a Tree Use over One Day?

Calculate crown projection of an envisioned tree at a reasonable maturity. Crown projection is the area under the drip line of the tree's canopy. We estimate this as a circle on the ground and calculate its area (πr^2) or the diameter of the canopy squared times 0.7854. For a hypothetical tree with a 20-foot canopy diameter, the crown projection would equal 314 feet squared (see Figure 3-16).

Tree canopies are not two-dimensional, however. Leaves are stacked on top of one another, each positioning itself to intercept light. This stacking of leaves in the canopy is called *leaf area index*—the ratio of total tree leaf surface area to crown projection. Another way of describing it is if you took off all the leaves on a tree and distributed them over the crown projection, how many leaves deep would they be? That number would be the leaf area index. Some trees, such as lindens (*Tilia*), are very dense, while others, such as honey locusts (*Gleditsia*), may be quite open. Based on research with a fairly dense tree, *Tilia cordata*, we found that a leaf area index of 4 would be a slight overestimate (Figure 3-17). In our calculations, the leaf area itself will be slightly overestimated. To estimate leaf area for a tree, simply multiply crown projection by leaf area index. In our hypothetical tree, 314 square feet × 4 = 1256 square feet.

Step 2: Determine the Local Atmospheric Demand or Evaporation Rate from the Site Where the Tree Is to Grow

We want to select the month with the highest mean monthly evaporation rate from the Evaporation Pan data. This ensures that the soil volume we eventually determine will be sufficient for the hottest and driest time of the year, the worst-case scenario. We use the 30-year average of the mean monthly evaporation data. That value for Ithaca, New York, for example, is 6.21 in July. This means that for every 1 square inch of surface water in the Pan, 6.21 cubic inches is typically evaporated out over the month of July. To obtain a daily evaporation rate, we divide the monthly rate by the number of days in that month (31) and come up with 0.20 cubic inch of water evaporated out of the Pan per day. Because we are going to use feet and not inches in further calculations, we multiply this daily value by 0.0833 to give us 0.0167 cubic foot of water evaporated per day.

So far we have an estimate of leaf area and an evaporation rate of the Evaporation Pan per day during the hottest month of the year. We need to relate the Evaporation Pan measurement to the leaves of the tree. We know that a leaf is not an open pan of water. Water is lost from pores or stomates

Figure 3-16 Diagram representing area of tree crown projection, or area under drip line.

in the leaf, while a pan of water has no resistance to evaporation. Through research, we have come up with an adjustment factor of 20 percent, which means that 1 square inch of leaf will lose only 20 percent, or one–fifth, of the water that 1 square inch of Pan will evaporate. This is called the *evaporation ratio.*

To yield the amount of water lost by our hypothetical tree, we multiply crown projection by leaf area index by evaporation rate by evaporation ratio:

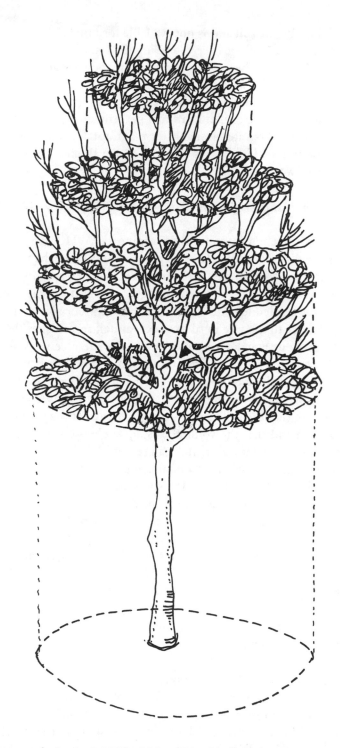

Figure 3-17 Diagram representing leaf area index calculations.

314 square feet × 4 × 0.0167 × 0.20 = 4.19 cubic feet of water (31 gallons)

Step 3: How Much Soil Is Necessary to Supply This Much Water to the Tree?

All soil holds varying amounts of water depending on its texture and structure. Not all of that water is available to plant roots, however. Some of it is held too tightly by the soil and is not available for uptake. A good analogy is a sponge full of water. Even after you wring the last bit of water from it, the sponge is still damp. The water remaining in the sponge is analogous to water unavailable for root uptake. In any given volume of soil, there is water that is available to the plant, water that is not available, and the solid soil particles themselves. Therefore, only a small percentage of the total volume of wet soil represents the water available for plant uptake. Soil available water-holding capacity (AWHC) varies between about 10 and 20 percent of the total volume of wet soil.

Step 4: Determining Available Water-Holding Capacity (AWHC) in Soils

The next step is to choose a soil and determine its AWHC. For our example, we choose a soil with an AWHC of 12 percent. If we take the water lost per day from our hypothetical tree 4.19 cubic feet (step 1), and divide it by the percentage AWHC, we come up with 34.9 cubic feet of soil necessary to store the water needed for one day. Ideally, we want our soil volume to supply enough water to the tree until the next rainfall replenishes the soil. It is possible to find out how long it takes before the site receives some specific amount of rainfall. If we choose to find the number of days between rainfall events of at least 0.10 inch, the average length of this dry period must be derived from the daily precipitation rates published by NOAA for each city. We're assuming that the soil starts out fully charged at the beginning of the growing season and that the volume of soil we choose will be sufficient to carry it through until natural rainfall can replenish it. This may be too great an assumption, particularly for containerized trees, for which limited rainfall interception and lack of potential soil water movement from the water table or from lateral sources can be assumed.

In our hypothetical example, in Ithaca, New York, 92 percent of all dry periods (less than 0.10 inch of rain) lasted 10 days or less. Thus, a rain-free period of 10 days can be factored into our soil volume equation:

34.9 cubic feet of soil (1-day volume) × 10 (rainfall frequency) = 349 cubic feet of soil

to provide enough water for our hypothetical tree for 10 days during the hottest part of the growing season.

Step 5: Calculating Bed Dimensions

The final step in the equation is calculating planting bed dimensions. The depth should be approximately 3 feet, give or take 6 inches. For 34.9 cubic feet, a bed roughly measuring 11 by 11 by 3 feet should be sufficient. Using a soil with a higher AWHC would make the bed dimensions smaller, as would using a smaller tree.

Table 3-3 gives examples of estimated critical soil volumes for a representative range of U.S. cities using the soil volume methodology. The tree used in this example has a crown diameter of 20 feet and is about 35 feet in height. Calculations were based on a tree with a crown projection of 314 square feet and an average leaf area ratio of 4.

This prior series of calculations (Table 3-3) assumes that there is no surface evaporation from the soil around the tree. If a mulch is used, these calculations will remain largely accurate. If grass or an understory planting is installed, you may account for it by raising the leaf area index to 5 or even 6 (if it's very dense) instead of 4 (Figures 3-18 and 3-19). Calculate a soil volume for a grove of trees as one very large tree, assuming there will be internal branching and leaf competition and that none of the trees will have a full canopy.

If a tree has a columnar shape and thus a small crown projection, account for that by raising the leaf area index by 1 or 2. The more narrowly columnar the tree, the greater the increase in leaf area index should be (Figure 3-20).

During plant establishment and after transplanting, trees may still need extra irrigation even if the soil volume is generous. Until tree roots have grown to occupy some of the soil and the trees have overcome transplant shock (see Chapter 5), they must be monitored for water stress.

Urban areas can be quite a bit hotter and drier than data from the nearest weather station may indicate. The urban heat island is a generalized effect whereby cities are several degrees hotter than the surrounding countryside. Our research has shown that in microsites, these differences can be

TABLE 3-3   EXAMPLES OF EVAPORATION, RAINFALL, AND SOIL VOLUME NEEDED TO SUSTAIN A 20-FOOT-DIAMETER CANOPY IN VARIOUS CITIES

City	Evaporation Pan Rate[a] Inches/Month	One-day Soil Volume[b] (Square feet)	Rainfall Frequency[c] (Days)	Total Soil Volume (Feet) If AWHC[d] of Soil Is Either 15% or 19%		
Ithaca, NY	6.21 July	28	10	300	220	(0.70 ft³/ft² CP)[e]
Seattle, WA	7.00 July	30	20	600	480	(1.5 ft³/ft² CP)
Mobile, AL	7.19 May	32	10	300	250	(0.80 ft³/ft² CP)
Indianapolis, IN	7.13 June	33	15	500	400	(1.2 ft³/ft² CP)
Minneapolis, MN	7.88 July	35	10	350	275	(0.87 ft³/ft² CP)
Miami, FL	8.03 July	36	10	350	282	(0.91 ft³/ft² CP)
Denver, CO	9.80 July	45	15	700	525	(1.7 ft³/ft² CP)
Phoenix, AZ	14.83 June	68	80	5400	4315	(14 ft³/ft² CP)

[a] The highest mean monthly pan evaporation value for 20 to 30 years of data recorded for each city divided by the days in the month and multiplied by 0.0833 to obtain daily water loss in feet.

[b] Assumes a soil available water-holding capacity of 15 percent.

[c] Defines the critical rainfall event. A minimum of 92 percent of all dry periods (less than 0.10 inch rainfall) lasted this number of days or fewer for each city. Derived from 10 years of data recorded for each city.

[d] AWHC = available water-holding capacity of the soil. This represents the fraction of the total water, on a volume basis, that is actually available for root uptake. Two available water-holding capacities are presented for comparison here: an average (15 percent) and a high (19 percent). AWHC of any soil mix can be ascertained in a lab test and specified for use on the tree pit.

[e] Derived cubic feet of soil per square foot of crown projection.

Figure 3-18   SOIL VOLUME METHODOLOGY CALCULATIONS

The following is an example of a soil volume calculation for an envisioned "design size" for a specific tree. The calculation is for a whole tree water loss and the subsequent soil volume needed to support a 20-foot-diameter crown tree in Ithaca, New York.

STEP ONE: DETERMINING DAILY WHOLE TREE WATER USE.

1. Calculate crown projection (πr^2).

$$(3.14) \times 10^2 = 314 \text{ ft}^2$$

2. Select the LA1 = 4.

3. Determine the evaporation rate.

Highest mean monthly evaporation rate is 6.21 inches for the month of July.

$$6.21 \text{ inches}/31 \text{ days} = 0.2 \text{ inch per day}$$

$$(0.2 \text{ inch per day}) \times 0.0833 = 0.0167 \text{ foot evaporated per day.}$$

4. The evaporation ratio is a constant = 20 percent.

Multiply all of above together to derive cubic feet of water per day.

314 cp × 4 LA1 × 0.0167 evaporation rate × 0.2 evaporation ratio =
4.19 cubic feet of water lost per day.

STEP TWO: DETERMINING AN ADEQUATE VOLUME OF SOIL.

5. Select the AWHC of the soil = 12%.

4.19 cubic feet of water lost per day/0.12 = 34.95 cubic feet of soil

6. Determine the rainfall frequency = 10 days.

34.95 cubic feet of soil × 10 days = 349 total cubic feet of soil
to meet the water demands of this size tree for a 10-day period.

STEP THREE: CALCULATING POSSIBLE BED DIMENSIONS.

11 by 10.5 by 3 feet in depth

6 by 19 by 3 feet in depth

Another example of soil volume calculation starts with a fixed volume of soil. The example will allow you to determine an optimum tree size given a known soil volume. How large of a tree in Ithaca, New York, will a typical 4 foot by 4 foot tree pit support?

Assumptions

Rooting depth of soil = 3 feet

AWHC of the soil = 12%

Figure 3-18   *(Continued)*

---

1. Calculate total rooting volume.

   3 depth × 4 width × 4 length = 48 cubic feet of soil

2. Calculate the amount of water held in this volume of soil.

   48 cubic feet of soil × 0.12% AWHC = 5.76 cubic feet of available water

3. Interval of precipitation = 10.

4. Cubic feet of available water 5.76 ÷ Interval of precipitation 10 = 0.576 cubic foot one day volume of water available.

5. One day volume of water ÷ evaporation ratio ÷ evaporation rate ÷ LAI = CP.

   0.576 ÷ 0.20 ÷ 0.0167 ÷ 4 = 42.1 ft²

6. √(CP ÷ π) = radius of canopy

   $$\frac{42.1}{3.14} = \sqrt{(13.7)} = 3.7 \text{ ft} = \text{radius of canopy } 7.4 \text{ ft (canopy spread)}$$

7. If the tree was irrigated every four days, how large a tree could this soil volume support? If irrigated every day?

   Change precipitation interval to 4 days or 1 day. Irrigated every 4 days = 11.7 feet canopy spread. Irrigated every day = 23.4 ft canopy spread.

---

quite large, especially when many reflecting and reradiating built surfaces impact the planting site. If this is the case in your planting site, increase the soil volume, if practical, use a species that is heat- and drought-tolerant, and have irrigation backup if necessary.

How Can This Information Be Used to Reduce Tree-Sidewalk Conflicts?

One might reasonably assume that soil under pavements may be accessed by tree roots in their search for water, nutrients, and oxygen. However, the need to compact the soil under pavements to give them strength and prevent subsidence often makes it impenetrable to tree roots. This purposeful compaction can severely limit the potential rooting space for a tree surrounded by pavement. For a middle-aged tree with a 20-foot canopy diameter, the crown projection is 314 square feet. Doubling that would indicate that about 600 cubic feet of soil is necessary to support it. Assuming that most roots grow within the first 2 to 3 feet of the surface, we require soil dimensions between 20 by 10 by 3 feet and 20 by 15 by 2 feet. This may be

Figure 3-19 Trees with ground-cover understory that increases the leaf area index.

achieved in a large tree lawn parallel to the curb on a street or in a specially designed plaza. But for trees growing in pavement cut-outs of 5 or 6 feet square, tree roots are necessarily going to grow under the pavement if they are to find the resources they need to grow.

Because soils under pavements are compacted, roots are generally relegated to growing up toward the surface of the soil, where the interface between the pavement and the aggregate base course allows for root growth exploitation. This sets them up for direct impact on pavements as the roots expand and grow radially. In a forest situation, large buttressing tree roots normally taper down as they grow away from the tree in the first 6 feet or so. It is these large roots near the base of the tree that cause the most damage to pavements.

One suggestion for reducing this problem is to leave a larger cut-out section of pavement so as not to interfere with these largest of tree roots. Another suggestion is to use a structural soil that can be compacted to meet engineers' specifications while still allowing tree roots to grow deeper. Structural soils could be used to channel roots safely under the pavement into an open grass area adjacent to the pavement or to be the sole rooting area. In either case, structural soils should be at least 24 inches deep, preferably 36 inches, and extend over an area at least equal in size to what the soil volume calculations predict (Figure 3-21).

SPATIAL CONFIGURATION OF THE PLANTING AREA

The designer has tremendous influence over how much soil plants will have to grow in. By understanding soil volume calculations and the potential use of supplements such as irrigation, it is possible to ensure that plants will fulfill their design potential in the newly created landscape. When soil volumes are constrained by surrounding pavement, as is so often the case in inner-city areas, and the designer cannot create an opening for the tree large enough to accommodate an adequate soil volume, modified soils or cantilevered sidewalks must be used to create an adequate soil volume. If an aboveground container will be used to grow a tree and soil volume is inadequate for its long-term health and growth, then planning for its replacement is the only reasonable option. The more one can match the size of the plant with the soil volume and the water it supplies, the longer the plant will live in that container.

Where the designer has considerable freedom to place plants in the landscape, several design options can maximize soil volume.

Figure 3-20 Columnar tree showing increase in leaf area index for crown projection.

Building Up

Creating a raised planting area is a useful way to achieve more soil volume in the same spatial footprint. Indeed, for rooftop or deck plantings where there is no connection to the earth, a raised-bed planting is the only option. In this case, all soil must be brought in and the designer has the greatest discretion as to the type of soil that is to be used. Raised soil volumes can also work well on grade where pedestrian passage doesn't prohibit the use of a berm or raised bed. It is useful to bring in this design idea when the soil at grade is either too compacted or poor for tree growth, or when the seasonal water table can inundate the root zone with water. Creating a raised planting area also affords the opportunity to develop complex planting arrangements, with understory and trees (Figure 3-22; see color insert). When pedestrian traffic in these spaces is prevented, soils will remain noncompacted.

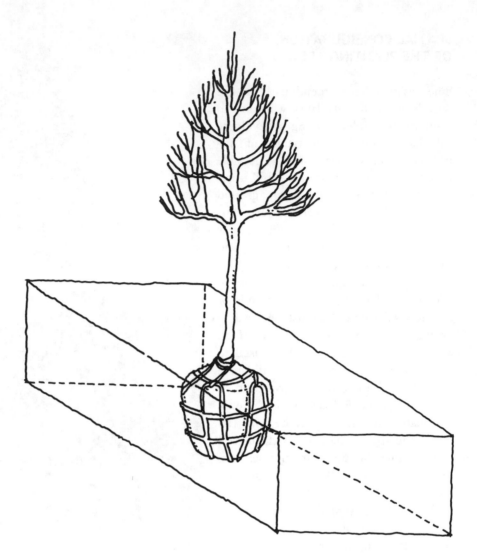

Figure 3-21 Diagram showing soil volume as determined from calculations.

Shared Rooting Space

In a natural setting, many plants share a common soil volume. It is reasonable to design with this idea in mind. For example, a tree that requires 600 cubic feet of soil to reach its envisioned design size will be at an advantage if a series of rooting spaces, each with 600 cubic feet, are connected so that each tree can "borrow" soil volume from the others. We don't know how much less soil volume can be specified if the soil volumes are contiguous, but undoubtedly the trees will grow more successfully for a longer period. When possible, it is always advantageous to plant in a continuous soil volume as opposed to a hole. This also applies to groupings of shrubs in the landscape. Instead of planting individual shrubs in a hole, planting shrubs in a large bed of cultivated soil will enable them to share a soil with a lower bulk density, reduce competition from grass, and avoid damage from lawn mowers (Figure 3–23; see color insert). Plants with their roots in a uniform soil mass will grow more uniformly and vigorously than those in soil with varying physical properties.

SURFACE TREATMENT OVER THE ROOTING ZONE

A tree's viability in an urban area is intimately related to soil volumes and the quality of soil that roots can explore. The material(s) that cover the soil modify the conditions below grade in a significant manner that influences the ability of roots to explore large soil areas and get the oxygen, water, and nutrients needed by the tree. In this section, we look at the influence of turf, mulch, pervious pavers, tree grates, and other surface treatments, such as cantilevered concrete slabs, on the longevity and viability of trees.

It is important to note that tree species tolerate conditions in the city and surface treatments in differing ways. However, all trees are affected in some way by the availability of water and oxygen levels afforded by various surface treatments.

Turf Grass

Turf grass is a common treatment of soil surfaces in urban areas. Most commonly, turf grass is used in parks and in many residential and, to some degree, commercial areas and on tree lawns adjacent to streets and sidewalks. In general, the direct effects of turf on tree roots and tree viability is minimal, especially with respect to mature trees. The turf keeps the soil from eroding and reduces the potential for surficial compaction while allowing for rainfall infiltration and oxygen to reach the root zone. Turf areas allow for the use of tree species that otherwise would not grow well in most temperate-climate cities. Species often referred to as *park trees*, such as sugar maples, American and European beech, many of the nut trees, and the more difficult to establish oaks, as well as many other species, do best planted in large soil volumes with turf or other ground cover surfaces. Such trees typically grow well in large turf areas off the street and away from the impact of winter de-icing salts and the potential for surficial compaction of soils.

By their physiological nature, turf and grass species are good competitors for available water and nutrients. While this may pose little problem for mature trees, it has been shown (Neely, 1984) that newly planted trees cannot compete as well for water and nutrients in lawn areas. Again, this varies by species, but all trees are affected to some degree, which is seen in growth, including shoot growth and trunk caliper. Nutrient deficiencies related to grass competition are specific to nitrogen and not potassium and phosphate.

Trees can benefit from some maintenance practices applied to turf, especially irrigation and high-nitrogen-level fertilizers as well as surficial aeration practices. However, certain herbicide applications to turf that impact broad-leaved plants can affect some trees and shrubs. Also, grass mowing with large equipment and string trimmers has been shown to damage trees, especially juveniles and thin-barked species. A common practice to keep mowing equipment away from trees is to establish a mulch ring around the trunk or stem. This application of mulch has the added benefit of eliminating the competition of grass on small-caliper trees.

Mulch

The use of mulch when trees are planted in grass as well as in open planters and planting pits has been well established, primarily in the United States. There are many mulch types, including organic mulches (bark, wood chips, compost, cocoa hulls, pine needles) and inorganic types (brick chips, gravel, crushed coral). While all mulches, properly installed, reduce soil compaction, erosion, and soil surface drying due to sun and wind, organic mulches have the added benefit of improving soil tilth, encouraging biotic activity, and providing limited nutrients to plants as they break down.

One of the great benefits of mulch is reducing soil temperature fluctuations. Mulch applications can reduce the possible extremes of soil temperatures, both hot and cold—but, more importantly, rapid change in temperature. In a forested environment, tree roots are annually mulched by leaf and needle litter. This naturally occurring mulch does not occur in urban areas. Even when leaf litter does develop in a park setting, it is often cleaned up or removed in the course of contemporary maintenance practice.

Mulches can also reduce (but not eliminate) weed growth around trees. This reduces annual maintenance near trees and in common planting beds and planters. Care must be taken in the amount of mulch used. The optimal depth for mulch applications is 3 to 4 inches. When mulch is deeper and applied around tree trunks and stems, constant moisture on the bark below the mulch level can occur, creating an environment for fungus and molds to form, affecting the bark layer and ultimately the health of the tree (Figure 3-24). Subsequently, it is important to pull mulch away from the plant trunk or stem to prevent this situation.

Tree roots quite naturally grow into the mulch layer, especially fibrous, superficial roots. Subsequently, as organic mulches decompose, it is essential to replenish them to protect these superficial roots. As plants are remulched, it is necessary not to apply too much, especially when annual applications are made. The cumulative depth of mulch should never exceed 4 inches. In this regard, it is important not to use weed mats below the organic mulch so that decomposed mulch is incorporated into the soil surface by earthworms and freeze-thaw mechanical action.

Be sure that organic mulches and compost do not negatively affect plants. This can occur when certain composts are not fully broken down or when large piles of mulch, not turned and exposed to air, give off a methane gas that can kill tender branches, leaves, and plants near the ground level where the fresh mulch is applied.

(a)

(b)

Figure 3-24 Too much mulch (a) placed against the tree trunk can result in (b) fungus and molds.

While pavement cannot be considered a mulch, very porous pavements can act like it. The most porous of pavements, referred to as *pervious pavements*, allow for water infiltration—and where water flows freely, air follows.

The United States alone paves over an astonishing amount of soil—"more each year than the Roman Empire paved in its entire existence" (Sorvig, 1993). Most of this pavement is bituminous concrete or asphalt, which is used primarily for roads and parking lots and also for walkways. While asphalt is not typically designed to be porous, there *are* pervious asphalts that are both structurally sound and porous. Asphalt's permeable quality was originally designed to eliminate surface puddling, but it also conveys the properties that allow roots to better explore compacted base material. Most of the fine gravels and sands typical of asphalt blends are eliminated in porous asphalt mixes, which are still bonded with bitumens. Even over densely compacted urban soils, porous asphalt used in combination with structural soil can provide the needed reservoir of water and air necessary for good plant growth. However, subsurface drainage will also be needed to ensure that roots don't get more water than is usable, leading to plant decline and, in the worst cases, plant death.

In addition to the benefits to urban plants, porous asphalt can reduce stormwater runoff and concentrated flow during rainfall events. Localized groundwater recharge is possible if water infiltrates urban soils and is held for future use and uptake.

The same characteristics of porous asphalt can also be achieved with unit paving profiles when porous jointing materials, setting beds, and base-course material are specified. A laboratory and field study of various installation procedures for unit pavers (Evans, et al., 1990) demonstrated that the following conditions should be considered (Figures 3-25 and 3-26):

1. Choose pavers that provide maximum joint opening without compromising structural integrity.

2. Use a permeable jointing material. Bituminous-bonded sand has been found more permeable than pure coarse sand (asphalt bituminous-bonded sand as the binder, with coarse sand rather than a gravel aggregate).

3. Use a bituminous-bonded sand as a paver bedding material to eliminate textural discontinuity and resultant slowing of downward water flow between jointing and bedding materials.

4. Install pavements with primary jointing running perpendicular to the surface flow of stormwater to capture as much as possible of a rainfall event.

In conjunction with these paver installation techniques, it is important to provide as large as possible an interconnected rooting medium, such as a structural soil or other well-draining soil, to retain moisture and provide the largest possible soil volume in the root zone. It is generally desirable to design for a combined rooting zone for trees on the street or in a planter. Incorporating subsurface drainage is always essential to ensure that optimal moisture occurs around the roots of the trees, as previously discussed.

When using porous pavers over the root zone of trees, determine use and loads due to pedestrians or greater live loads, such as vehicles, and select the thickness of the pavers accordingly. The greater the thickness of the paver, the more load will be distributed from one paver to another and the setting bed, whatever medium is selected. When using interlocking pavement, adjacent units are designed to collectively carry applied loads (Smith, 1991).

Compacting the subsoil below the paver base-course will increase uniform loading and reduce potential pavement settlement. Subsoils are typically compacted to 95 to 98 percent Proctor density (ASTM D-698) or a California Bearing Ratio standard (ASTM D-1883) (Smith, 1991). Base materials should also be compacted to a modified Proctor density of 95 to 100 percent. This is where structural soils (see "Soils Under Pavements,"

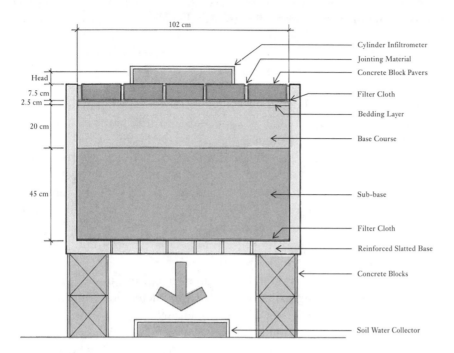

102 cm

Head

7.5 cm
2.5 cm

20 cm

45 cm

Cylinder Infiltrometer
Jointing Material
Concrete Block Pavers

Filter Cloth

Bedding Layer

Base Course

Sub-base

Filter Cloth

Reinforced Slatted Base

Concrete Blocks

Soil Water Collector

Section Through Box

Figure 3-25 Laboratory test box for testing pervious pavers in section.

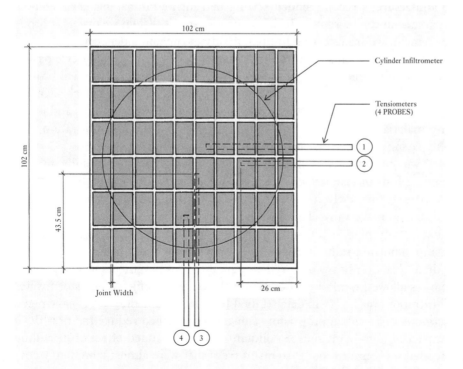

102 cm

Cylinder Infiltrometer

Tensiometers
(4 PROBES)

1

2

102 cm

43.5 cm

Joint Width

26 cm

4 3

Box, Top View

Figure 3-26 Laboratory test box (plan view) used for testing pervious paver pattern and jointing materials.

page 61) have an advantage in that they can be compacted to this degree and continue to allow roots to penetrate and explore the base course material. In general, to provide adequate rooting depth, the structural soil base course should be 24 inches to 3 feet deep. The paver setting bed on top of the structural soil base course should be bituminous sand. Typically, a common 3⅛-inch paver is set on a setting bed of 1 to 1½ inches. The setting bed should be screeded level within specified tolerances but should not be compacted prior to paver installation. Compaction of the paver profile should occur with a vibrating plate once the pavers are finally placed with edge restraining on all sides. This will allow the setting bed material to move up into the pavers' joints, eliminating a compaction interface between the setting bed and the jointing material. Only after the pavers are compacted should the jointing material be broomed into all joints. The jointing material may be coarse sand or bituminous sand. Cement sand or limestone screening reduces water and air infiltration into the paver profile and diminishes the subsequent potential value to trees.

Consistent joint widths should be maintained at 2 to 3 millimeters. Some manufacturers have designed pavers with 2-millimeter cleats on the sides to regularize paver jointing. This joint width ensures paver porosity and provides material to assist in the transfer of surface loads from one paver to another. Many manufacturers now produce "eco-pavers," which provide more open surface area, thus allowing oxygen and water infiltration into the subpaver soils (Figure 3-27).

In some instances, a semirigid pavement is desirable. In such cases, the manufacturer's recommended setting bed for a granular material such as coarse sand can be replaced with a porous asphalt. When we discuss porous pavement, we are referring to the porosity of the joints between pavers and not the pavers themselves. While "grass-crete" or "egg-crate"–style pavers have considerable openings to allow sod establishment, they have limited application in urban areas. Most concrete pavers and vitrified brick have low moisture absorption and high strength. The width of paver joints and jointing materials provide the only means for significant water infiltration into the paving profile from rainfall events.

Two studies have looked in detail at runoff coefficients for concrete pavers. Tests in a laboratory (see Figures 3-25 and 3-26) and in the field have been used for newly installed pavers in various patterns using simulated rainfall events (Evans, et al., 1990). In addition, field studies of heavily trafficked study plots in situ in a neighborhood setting were also investigated using simulated rainfall events (Hade, 1983). In these tests, it was determined that after heavy use, well-designed porous pavements using concrete pavers allowed rainfall to absorb into the paving profile. While stormwater infiltration was less than data studied for porous asphalt, porous pavements (concrete pavers), appropriately constructed, helped reduce the first flush impact of non–point source pollutants, with the added effect of providing needed moisture to root systems of trees that were almost completely covered by pavement.

Figure 3-27 Pavers used adjacent to tree pits.

Cantilever Surfaces over Planting Areas

Many unique and sometimes complex walking surfaces have been designed that cantilever over planting pits or planting areas. The great advantage of this approach is that the soil in the planting area does not have to be compacted around the tree roots to support surface paving. The walking (rarely driving) surface is supported on several sides by the surrounding pavement or other structures that span the root zone. Perhaps the most common of these systems is the tree grate, which typically come in two pieces that form a collar around the trunk of the tree. The grate sections are supported by thickened concrete/masonry and steel-reinforced rigid pavement, such as a subsurface concrete curb, or a grade beam. A grade beam is also a thickened section of concrete supporting the tree grate, but it allows the pavement to be a variable thickness, changing to some other pavement profile, usually thinner, away from the tree grate installation. The advantage of tree grates with respect to the health of the trees is that the area of soil immediately below the grate is uncompacted. Additionally, tree grates are manufactured by many suppliers and are easily purchased and installed. They are typically cast iron or cast aluminum but may be fabricated from reinforced concrete. One disadvantage is that a thickened edge or grade beam is needed at the perimeter of the tree grate, causing superficial roots to stop at the edge of the tree pit or grow down (Figure 3-28).

Tree grate installation can be expensive—sometimes much more so than the tree itself. This makes it a design solution that can be afforded only in special circumstances. Often, the opening available for the expanding girth of the tree trunk is limited. While many tree grates are designed to be cut around the center as the girth of the tree increases, this is often not done, resulting in the girdling of the tree. A maintenance program must be in place for modifying tree grates as the trees grow to avoid this problem. Another maintenance issue is cleaning out the debris, common to streets and sidewalks, that falls into the openings of the grates and is in full view. This maintenance task is rarely carried out because each segment of grate can weigh several hundred pounds and would need to be removed frequently.

The problem of debris falling into the open grates can be eliminated by cantilevering monolithic slabs over the tree pit opening. This, however, reduces the benefits of water freely falling into the tree pit and related air exchange. Substantial work has been done by several individuals to design large cantilever slabs that, like tree grates, eliminate the need for soil compaction around the tree roots. These construction techniques are so complex and expensive that they can be used only in rare and exceptional circumstances (Figure 3-29).

AMELIORATING THE EFFECTS OF GRADE CHANGES

Figure 3-28 Conventional tree grate installation, a standard detail for urban trees.

In any landscape, tree roots have adapted to grow at a certain depth in the soil where they can get enough water, oxygen, and space to physically grow through the soil. When we raise the grade over an existing root system, we may severely impact the availability of water and oxygen as well as change soil density.

Adding Fill Around Existing Trees

Some trees are more forgiving than others of having the grade raised over their existing roots. Typically, trees that tolerate poor drainage and can grow additional roots on the trunk above their old roots will fare better when filled around. Many problems may occur when the grade is raised above roots. Typically, these earthworks are built with heavy machinery that can compact the existing soil in the process of changing the grade. As new soil is added and regraded, it too can become quite compacted. The new soil also may be of a different texture than the original soil,

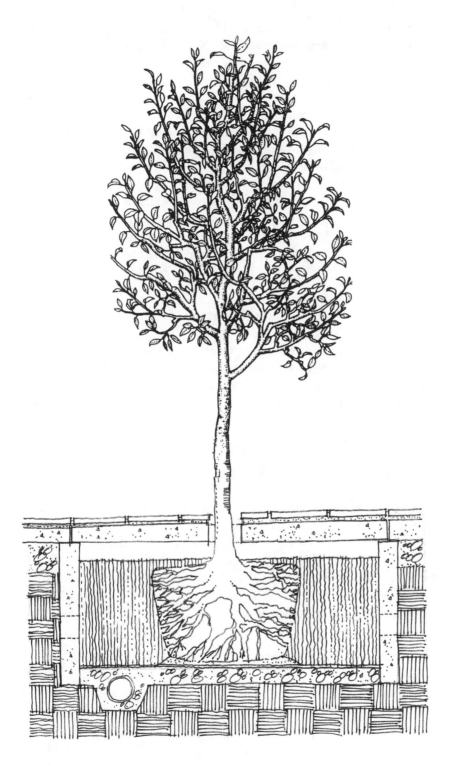

Figure 3-29 Sectional detail of cantilevered paver slab over a tree pit vault. Soils in vault are uncompacted.

which may lead to a perched water table on top of the existing root systems and, in turn, a soil with low oxygen levels. Even complex drainage systems that purport to bring oxygen to lower depths in a soil where the grade has been raised on top of roots often fail. This may be because the changes in soil texture and soil compaction may significantly alter the way water drains, depriving roots of oxygen. Little research addresses the question of how much of the root system can be covered before damage to the tree results.

Tree wells, where a retaining wall is built around the tree at some distance from the trunk and the grade raised to the top of the outside of the wall, are typically constructed of masonry materials (Figure 3-30). There are guidelines in the form of tree protection zones, based on trunk diameter, that specify a distance from the trunk within which no grade changes or root cutting should occur (see Figure 6-1). When a tree has been filled over only recently and is still growing well, the grade should be lowered to the original grade at least back to the edge of the tree protection zone, if not more.

Lowering the Grade Around Trees

The potential for tree damage must be assessed when lowering the grade or making cuts near tree roots. In such cases, much of the root system can be lost in this process. The same guidelines set out for tree protection zones pertain during grade lowering. However, this assumes a symmetrical root system. It is preferable to locate the tree's major roots using a nondestructive technique such as air or water excavation and avoid as many of the largest roots as possible when making cuts. The larger roots, or sinker roots, play an important role in tree stabilization and should not be disturbed if at all possible.

If a root is cut, care should be taken to make sure the cut ends do not dry out and are covered immediately. This will help speed the recovery process, whereby cut roots callus over and new roots are formed.

Special care should be given to trees that have had their roots cut by watering right after cutting takes place and thereafter during dry periods in the growing season. Remedial watering may be necessary for as long as 2 to 3 years after lowering the grade to enhance the tree's recovery from root loss.

Renovation of Planting Areas Around Existing Trees

It is much easier to renovate or modify soils before planting. However, there are many examples of trees that have been planted in compacted, poorly draining soil that can be renovated without destroying the trees in the process. Trees growing in dense, poorly draining soils may live, yet grow in a stunted and unsatisfactory way (Figure 3-31). Often, these trees' root systems have not grown beyond the original prepared planting hole and the roots remain, in effect, containerized, limiting root growth, and water and nutrient uptake.

Research conducted at Cornell University and elsewhere has shown that

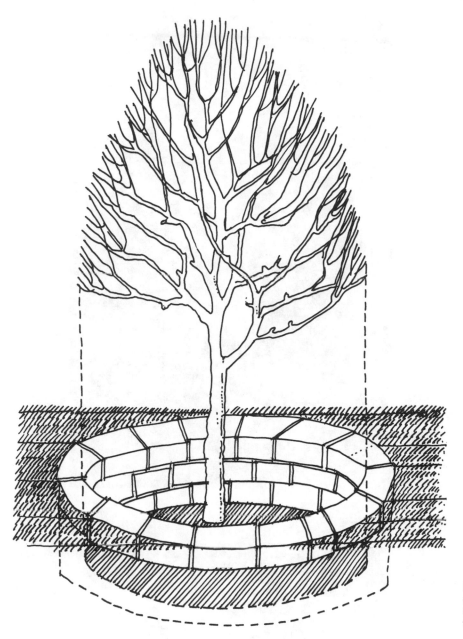

Figure 3-30 Detail of raising grades around an existing tree.

radial trenching around stunted trees can create an unrestricted soil area for roots to grow into, resulting in improved shoot growth.

How to Do It

Excavation around existing trees can be accomplished using several different soil removal methods. A backhoe bucket and air excavation tool are two of the more common digging tools.

After underground utilities are located, radial trenches can be mapped

(a)

Figure 3-31 Variable growth of the same species of tree due to heterogeneous soil conditions. (a) English Oaks on a small city street; (b) Willow Oaks on Pennsylvania Avenue, Washington, D.C.

(b)

out around the tree. The more trenches can be dug, the better for the tree. The trenches should be laid out symmetrically, if possible. The excavation then begins away from the tree, slowly digging toward it until roots are encountered. It is essential to intersect the roots of the tree without doing too much damage to them. Where the roots are encountered, the trench will radiate out from that point as far as is practical, but at least 10 feet. The trench should be dug at a depth of at least 12 inches, sloping downward and away from the tree to a depth of approximately 24 inches at the far end. All soil is removed from the trench and placed on a tarp. If the soil can be modified sufficiently to reduce its bulk density, it should be so amended and replaced. Compacted sandy soils respond well to this method. If the soils are clayey in texture, it may be more efficient to replace the soil in the trench with an uncompacted sandy loam. If it is not possible to replace the trench soil with better soil, organic amendments can be incorporated at a minimum of 50 percent by volume to reduce the density of heavier soils.

When all the trenches are dug, soil should be replaced in the trenches as soon as possible to minimize the time any intersected roots are exposed to the air. To further improve this situation and reduce recompaction of soil in the trenches, all turf competition should be removed within the radii of the trenches and the entire area mulched with 2 to 3 inches of shredded bark. No mulch should touch the tree trunk. The trenches should be watered initially and subsequently if natural rainfall is limited (Figures 3-32 and 3-33).

This method of soil amelioration can be undertaken at any time of year as long as intersected roots are not allowed to dry out. During periods of active tree growth, special care is needed to prevent root desiccation. Research at Cornell shows that new root growth in the trenches will precede any improvement in top growth. Depending on when the trenching is done, it may take up to a year to see improvement in top growth. Preventing recompaction of the soil through vehicular or pedestrian traffic is beneficial to the trenching process, as is providing adequate soil moisture in the trenches.

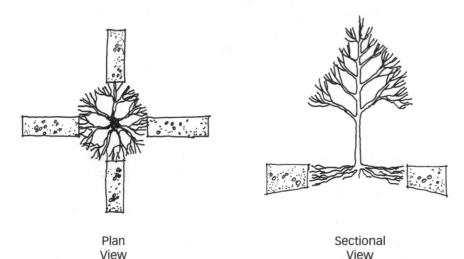

Plan
View

Sectional
View

Figure 3-32
Diagram showing radial trenching in plan and section.

(a)

(b)

Figure 3-33 Radial trenching around existing trees. (a) Using a backhoe to locate edge of root system, and (b) backfilling trenches with amended soil.

Remediating Poorly Draining Soils Around Existing Trees

It is easier to reduce the bulk density of a soil than to increase its macroporosity, or drainage. If soils are poorly draining and of a clayey texture, the results are less certain, especially if the tree is sensitive to wet soils. As discussed earlier in this chapter, large volumes of coarse sand amendment, as much as 75 percent by volume, are necessary to increase macroporosity. Moreover, at least 50 percent by volume of organic matter must be added to increase the macroporosity of poorly draining soils.

Radial trenching to increase drainage can be accomplished if the trenches intersect the lowest depths of the existing root zone and radiate away from the tree at still lower depths. At the farthest and lowest end of the trench, a sump drain can be added to provide more stormwater storage and to improve the drainage by gravity.

If there is a slope near the tree, a gravel-filled French drain can be incorporated into the trenching array to reduce standing water in the bottom of the tree planting hole and trench. It is critical that the French drain begin at the lowest part of the planting hole so excess water can drain away via gravity.

Although a trenching treatment may improve drainage and bulk density away from the existing root zone and encourage new roots, it is more problematic to improve drainage within the existing root system near the tree.

A vertical sump drain can be augered into the existing root system to move water to a lower grade. This assumes that drainage occurs at a lower grade, which may not be true. Sump drains are in the best instance a technique that can buy time for the root system, moving water away until the water backs up into the root zone. If the species planted is intolerant of standing water, the better option may be to remove the tree and start again with a more tolerant species and a better engineered drainage system that daylights subsurface water away from the root system of the tree.

DRAINAGE PRINCIPLES AND TECHNIQUES

It is essential to understand drainage principles when initiating planting, especially in urban areas or sites where soil compaction, high water tables, or otherwise poorly draining soils exist. This section explores drainage strategies associated with plant establishment and contemporary research that supports best new practices.

Purpose of Drainage

Very poor drainage creates unlivable conditions for most tree species. At times, drainage may be impeded by a soil hardpan, an old foundation, or other impermeable layer. In this case, breaking up the obstructing layer may be sufficient to improve the situation. Often, however, water must be diverted and removed by means of a drainage system. Surface drainage can be used to remove surface water and runoff so as to prevent water from collecting in undesirable spots and to reduce the amount of water that infiltrates the soil surface. Subsurface drainage can remove excess water that has already moved into the soil profile. This type of drainage essentially lowers the level of the water table in the vicinity of the drain, preventing roots from being flooded.

Effects of Soil Texture and Structure on Drainage

Soil texture (the proportions of sand, silt, and clay) is related to a soil's ability to drain. A sandy loam, for instance, usually drains better than a silt loam. It is not precisely the presence of the sand itself, however, that makes a sandy loam drain well. In essence, it drains quickly because it has a high proportion of large soil pores. Soil pores are the spaces between the soil solids. Small pores retain water, while large pores allow drainage. Pore size distribution, then, is the determining factor in questions of drainage.

Most sandy loams drain well because the large amount of sand (generally over of 50 percent), creates many large pores. It does not follow, however, that adding sand to soil always improves drainage. Drainage is improved only if the proportion of large pores is increased, which generally does not occur until a soil is over half sand. In fact, adding smaller amounts of sand can reduce drainage, as the smaller-sized clay and silt particles pack between the grains of sand, reducing pore space. A soil need not be high in sand content to maintain the large pores needed for drainage. Other factors besides texture influence soil pore size.

Soil structure also has a profound effect on pore size and, consequently, on drainage. *Soil structure* refers to the way in which soil particles are cemented into aggregates by organic matter and clay through biological activity and physical changes such as freezing and thawing cycles. Aggregates are huge when compacted with individual soil particles and can maintain large pore spaces and thus good drainage. The damage to soil structure caused by compaction is the primary reason that water movement is so restricted in compacted soils. Even a moderate weight on a very moist clay soil, for example, will crush soil aggregates. The macropores created by these aggregates are then lost, and poor drainage results.

The effects of soil texture and structure on drainage are a result of their effects on soil pore size distribution. Disturbed urban soils, however, often present a more complicated picture. It is not uncommon to have a compacted clay subsoil, perhaps sculpted with berms, overlaid with a topsoil of a different texture and structure. The picture could be further complicated by old submerged pavement, runoff from an adjacent paved area, or even by the act of digging planting holes. Clearly, we need to understand how water will move in this and other such complicated situations if we intend to provide adequate drainage for our landscape.

Basics of Drainage

Water moves through soil in two ways: unsaturated (capillary) flow and saturated flow. These two types of water movement more or less govern how any drainage system works.

Unsaturated flow: When water is not under pressure (as with standing water) and soil is not saturated, capillary forces govern water movement. Essentially, this means that smaller-diameter pores exert a greater attractive force, and water will move into these pores rather than enter the larger pores, which remain filled with air. This is why if you have clay (more small pores) laid over a layer of sand (more large pores), water will move through the clay soil and stop at the sand layer. It will not penetrate the sand layer at all until conditions of saturated flow take over—that is, until so much water has soaked into the clay that its pores are filled and water can flow through the large pores where it is not tightly held.

Saturated flow: Saturated flow occurs when soil pores are entirely filled with water. Under these conditions, the force of gravity (plus pressure, if there is standing water on the surface) primarily governs water movement. Because water flows exponentially faster through larger pores, most of the saturated flow is through the largest pores. This is why uniformly graded sandy soils (more large pores) drain faster than clayey soils (more small pores).

These basic principles of water movement explain some uses and limitations of drainage systems, as described below.

- Gravel in the bottom of a planting hole does not improve drainage; rather, it reduces the usable rooting space. Water flow will stop at the gravel (a "perched" water table) until the soil above is saturated.

- Internal drainage must be connected to an outlet if the water table is to be lowered. Sump drains under a planting hole will not improve site drainage but may, when the planting hole is completely saturated, serve as a temporary reservoir away from roots for water that would otherwise collect in the bottom of the hole.

- Water movement is strongly influenced by soil texture and structure regardless of the underdrainage supplied. An analogy can be made to holding a wet sponge over a sink. The sink will drain away the water that drips from the sponge. However, it will not suck the water out of the sponge, which holds the water tightly in its pores. Eventually the sponge will stop dripping, just as the soil will stop draining, although it may still be very wet. Proper underdrainage will, however, prevent roots from being flooded by high water tables.

- Surface drains must be open to the air in order to collect water. Otherwise, water may actually avoid the drain much as it avoids entering the gravel in the bottom of the planting hole—that is, until the surrounding soil is saturated.

- Soil interfaces restrict water flow. An *interface* is any place where soil texture abruptly changes, such as between the soil mix of a container plant and a typical site soil.

Types of Drainage

Site grading: Surface drainage can be achieved through site grading. Swales (wide, shallow trenches) can be formed in the soil to direct surface runoff. Runoff can be diverted to an outlet for removal from the site or simply collected on site. Low areas that might collect water in undesirable locations can be eliminated.

Sump drains: When connected to the surface, these provide limited surface drainage. As there is no outlet, water simply collects in the drain and then seeps into the ground.

Underdrainage: This type of drain lowers the water table to the level of the drain, or somewhat above that in the areas between drains. Usually, perforated plastic pipe is laid horizontally well below the rooting zone and covered with geo-textile to reduce clogging of the drain with silt. The drain must be connected to an outlet and laid at the proper gradient to conduct water to the outlet. Insufficient slope or an unprotected outlet may result in the drain clogging with silt because of slow water movement. This system may have connecting drain lines with inlets leading to the surface, adding at-grade drainage.

REFERENCES CITED

American Association of Highway and Transportation Officials. 1995. *Standard specifications for transportation materials and methods of sampling and testing.* 17th ed. Washington, D.C.: AASHTO.

American Society of Testing and Materials. 1997a. Section 4: Construction. In *Annual book of ASTM standards.* Philadelphia: American Society for Testing and Materials. 04.08 Soil and Rock (I) D 420-D4914.

————. 1997b. Section 4: Construction. In *Annual book of ASTM standards.* Philadelphia: American Society for Testing and Materials. 04.02 Concretes and Aggregates.

Atkins, Harold N. 1997. *Highway materials, soils, and concretes.* 3rd ed. Columbus, Ohio: Prentice Hall.

Bakker, J.W. 1983. Growing site and water supply of street trees. *Groen* 39(6): 205–207.

Bassuk, N., and T. Whitlow. 1985. Evaluating street tree microclimates in New York City. In *METRIA 5: Selecting and preparing sites for urban trees,* edited by L.G. Kuhns and J.C. Patterson. U.S. Forest Service, Northeastern Area.

Craul, Phillip J. 1992. *Urban soil in landscape design.* New York: John Wiley and Sons.

Day, S.D., N.L. Bassuk, and H. van Es. 1995. Effects of four compaction remediation methods for landscape trees on soil aeration, mechanical impedance and tree establishment. *Journal of Environmental Horticulture* 13(2): 64–71.

Evans, M., N. Bassuk, and P. Trowbridge. March 1990. Sidewalk design for tree survival. *Landscape Architecture* 80(3): 102–103.

Grabosky, J. 1996. Developing a structural soil material with high bearing strength and increased rooting volumes for street trees under sidewalks. Master's thesis, Cornell University.

Grabosky, J., and N. Bassuk. 1995. A new urban tree soil to safely increase rooting volumes under sidewalks. *Journal of Arboriculture* 21(4): 187–201.

————. 1998. An urban tree soil to safely increase rooting volumes. *U.S. Patent No. 5,849,069.* Ithaca, N.Y.: Cornell University.

Grabosky, J., N. Bassuk, and M. Marranca. 2002. Preliminary findings from measuring street tree shoot growth in two skeletal soil installations compared to tree lawn plantings. *Journal of Arboriculture* 28(2): 106–108.

Grabosky, J., N. Bassuk, and H. van Es. 1996. Further testing of rigid urban tree materials for use under pavement to increase street tree rooting volumes. *Journal of Arboriculture* 22(6): 255–263.

Grabosky, J., N. Bassuk, L. Irwin, and H. van Es. 1999. Pilot study of structural soil materials in pavement profiles. *The landscape below ground II: Proceedings of an international workshop on tree root development in urban soils.* San Francisco, Calif: International Society of Arboriculture.

————. 1999. An urban soil to safely increase rooting volumes. *The landscape below ground II: Proceedings of an international workshop on tree root development in urban soils.* San Francisco, Calif: International Society of Arboriculture.

————. 2001. Shoot and root growth of three tree species in sidewalks. *Journal of Environmental Horticulture* 19(4): 206–211.

Hade, J. May/June 1983. Runoff coefficients for compressed concrete block pavements. *Landscape Architecture* 72(4).

Hawver, G. 1997. Influence of root restriction and drought stress on container grown trees: Impacts on plant morphology and physiology. Master's thesis, Cornell University.

Headley, D.B., and N.L. Bassuk. 1991. Effect of time on application of sodium chloride in the dormant season on selected tree species. *Journal of Environmental Horticulture* 9(3): 130–136.

Kristofferson, Pella. 1998. Designing urban pavement sub-bases to support trees. *Journal of Arboriculture* 24(3): 121–126.

Lindsey, P., and N. Bassuk. 1991. Specifying soil volumes to meet the water needs of mature urban street trees and trees in containers. *Journal of Arboriculture* 17(6): 141–149.

Lindsey, Patricia, and Nina Bassuk. 1992. Redesigning the urban forest from the ground below: A new approach to specifying adequate soil volumes for street trees. *Journal of Arboriculture* 16: 25–39.

Moll, Gary. November/December 1989. The state of our urban forest. *American Forests,* Nov./Dec. 95 (11 and 12): 61–63.

Morris, L.A., and R.F. Lowery. 1988. Influence of site preparation on soil conditions affecting stand establishment and tree growth. *Southern Journal of Applied Forestry* 12(3): 170–178.

Neely, D. 1984. Grass competition for nitrogen around landscape trees. *Journal of Environmental Horticulture* 2: 86–87.

Patterson, J.C., J.J. Murray, and J.R. Short. 1980. The impact of urban soils on vegetation. *Proceedings of the third conference of the Metropolitan Tree Improvement Alliance (METRIA).* 3: 33–56.

Proctor, R.R., 1933. Fundamental principles of soil compaction. *Engineering News Record* 111(9): 245–248.

Rivenshield, A. 2001. Organic amendment to improve the physical qualities of compacted soils. Master's thesis, Cornell University.

Shergold, F.A. August 1953. The percentage voids in compacted gravel as a measure of its angularity. *Magazine of Road Research* 13: 3–10.

Smith, D. August 1991. Interlocking concrete pavers: Guidelines for design and installation. *Landscape Architecture* 81(8): 72–74.

Sorvig, Kim. February 1993. Porous paving. *Landscape Architecture* 83(2): 66–69.

Spomer, L. Art. 1983. Physical amendment of landscape soils. *Journal of Environmental Horticulture* 1(3): 77–80.

Taylor, H.M. 1971. Root behavior as affected by soil structure and strength. In *The plant root and its environment,* edited by W. Carson. Charlottesville, Va.: University of Virginia Press.

U.S. Army, Engineer Waterways Experiment Station. 1959. *Developing a set of CBR design curves.* Instruction Report #4. Washington, D.C.: United States Government Printing Office.

———. 1960. *The unified soil classification system and appendix.* Technical Memorandum No. 3-357 with Appendix A. Washington, D.C.: United States Government Printing Office.

U.S. Department of the Interior Bureau of Reclamation. 1974. *Earth manual.* 2nd ed. Washington, D.C.: United State Government Printing Office.

Whiteley, G.M., and A.R. Dexter. 1983. Behavior of roots in cracks between soil peds. *Plant and Soil* 74: 153–162.

CHAPTER 4

PLANT SELECTION

E very landscape design must start with the germ of a vision for the site in question and an understanding of how the site will be used and what functions the plants will serve in it. There is no one correct vision, of course. Landscape design is an art form precisely because of its infinite possibilities.

WHAT FUNCTIONS DO PLANTS SERVE IN THE URBAN ENVIRONMENT?

People who regard the use of plants in the urban environment as an aesthetic nicety are not seeing the whole picture. It will be increasingly incumbent on professionals to recognize and quantify the many functions that plants serve in order to justify the need for continued funding of the green urban environment in times of restricted budgets. The functions of trees have been empirically measured. These data are essential in mitigating the many environmental aspects of the urban environment that result in more livable cities.

Temperature Modification

Where summer temperatures are very high, plants, especially trees, provide shade and reduce air temperatures. The actual reduction in temperature may vary from a few degrees to more than 20°F. Improved human comfort levels and a reduced need for air conditioning are the direct result of the knowledgeable placement of appropriate-sized trees in urban spaces, especially adjacent to buildings. To have the greatest effect on cooling a building in the Northern Hemisphere, deciduous trees should be planted primarily on its west side and secondarily on its east side. The leaves will have their cooling effect in the summer heat but let most of the winter sun in after leaf-fall. Trees are most effective at shading people and buildings from the sun's rays as well as reflecting radiation back into the atmosphere.

Wind

Tree planting to reduce wind speeds has long been practiced around the world. Research shows that semiporous windscreens that include trees and shrubs can have a profound wind-reducing effect. A barrier of approximately 35 percent transparent material (Trowbridge, Mudrak et al., 1988) can create a long calm zone that can improve human comfort levels by decreasing wind chilling. Reduced wind speeds can also improve human mobility, including walking and riding bicycles, in places where wind tunneling impairs outdoor activities (Figure 4-1).

*Wind Mitigation Measures (see Figure 4-2)**

Vegetative barrier plantings are perhaps the most often considered form of wind shelter. The vegetative shelterbelts of the Central Plains states are a well-known example of effective windbreaks. Yet, unlike berms or walls, vegetation is a living material with dynamic qualities. This simple fact has unique implications for the way vegetation may be used as a wind-sheltering device.

Some of the vegetation shapes evaluated in wind tunnel tests included single and double rows of trees in straight lines like those found traditionally in farm windbreaks and in formal landscape designs. Based on the field study results, a limited number of naturally occurring vegetation shapes of massings found in shrub clones (e.g., sumac species) and forest edge conditions (e.g., deciduous trees bordered by shrubs) were also tested.

Wind tunnel tests were conducted on scale models (1 inch equaled 8 feet) of trees and shrubs in full leaf with relatively dense canopies (e.g., maple species). However, the models were more uniform in branching pattern and homogeneous in overall shape than their full-scale counterparts. Thus, there may have been some discrepancy between the porosity of the model and of full-scale conditions, which

---

*From Trowbridge, Mudrak et al., 1988.

Figure 4-1 Vegetative windbreak providing a hedge with approximately 30 percent transparency.

in turn may have affected the sizes of resulting mitigation zones. The research team concurred that the variation, although untested, was well within the 30 to 50 percent porosity range so widely documented in the literature. Thus they were confident that the mitigation zone results shown in the template were generally sound.

Five vegetation templates are described in this research. A comparison of these templates showed that the height and length of the calm zones varied with the height and structure of the vegetation tested. In general, vegetation filtered the force of the wind and created long mitigation zones in much the same way as perforated walls do. The wind tunnel setup did not allow mitigation zones to be recorded much beyond 280 feet. In the tests of vegetation, it was clear that the zones continued for an undetermined distance beyond 280 feet. Therefore, on the vegetation templates, the touchdown or terminations of the mitigation zones were not documented.

Shrubs 12 feet tall, the shortest plants tested, produced substantial mitigation zones. However, as was found for berms and walls, it was likely that a minimum plant height (probably 8 to 12 feet) is required to produce a mitigation zone 6 feet tall.

Of all the landscape forms tested, vegetation offered the richest palette of shape and material that can be used to effectively mitigate winds. Plants offer interesting and aesthetic forms that operate in the landscape on both large and small scales. Because plants are alive and

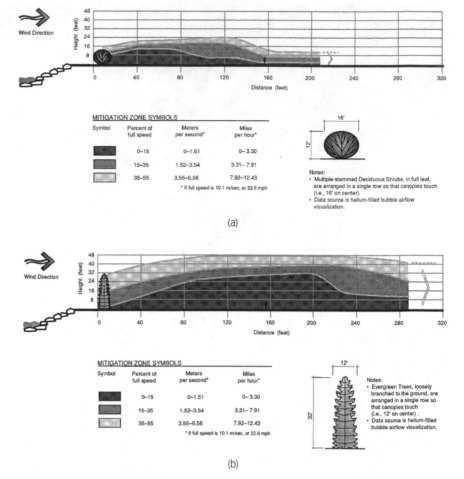

Figure 4-2 Two models of mitigation zones provided by (a) multistemmed deciduous shrubs, and (b) loosely branched evergreen trees.

change through time, however, their effective use is predicated on understanding and working with the major considerations of plant selection, plant establishment, and long-term growth and maintenance.

Plant selection is critical. Plants are dynamic, living organisms that must have appropriate soil, water, and sunlight to mature into specimens with sizes and shapes that can effectively mitigate winds.

When selecting plants, the needs of particular species should be matched to environmental conditions on the site. Only those that are hardy in the region should be chosen. Plants adapted to withstand both the mechanical and thermal effects of wind should be located at the leading edge of the windbreak. Mechanical effects of wind can include leaf loss and tatter, deformation of plant shape, breakage and loss of branches, and abrasion of trunks and leaves from the grinding action of wind-driven sand, ice crystals, or soil particles. Thermal effects of wind can include the increased loss of moisture from soil and leaf surfaces (particularly those which have been tattered or abraded), which results in plant desiccation.

The establishment period of young landscape trees and shrubs is of key importance. Soils must be adequately prepared to support plant growth. Then, sheltering elements may have to be provided to protect tender plants from the mechanical effects of wind. These protective shelters, or "nurse conditions," can be obtained through a variety of techniques such as snow fences. In addition, irrigation may have to be provided in the nonwinter months to protect young plants from desiccation.

Achieving wind mitigation with plants must be considered within a long time frame. Issues of seasonal variation, plant growth and decline, and ongoing maintenance affect how vegetative windbreaks perform over time. The seasonal nature of foliage makes some windbreaks effective for only parts of the year. Evergreen trees offer a continuous mitigating impact, whereas deciduous vegetation is mainly effective from late spring to early fall. Plant growth also affects how well a vegetative windbreak operates. Plants should be chosen so that their rates of growth are compatible with projected program needs. Although all of the vegetative trials assumed that canopies of trees and shrubs were touching, in actual application, it may take years for a vegetative barrier to reach this stage and thus become fully effective.

As a living material, vegetation declines more predictably over time than either berms or walls. Maintenance of vegetative windbreaks should be anticipated and planned in advance. Plant replacements will be required to extend the life of the windbreak beyond that of individual plants and should be regularly incorporated so that large gaps do not occur. Plants can also be selected, however, so that they better withstand the stress of the site as they age. For instance, selection of a variety of species as opposed to a monoculture is desirable because it helps to ward off attack by disease or pests over the years. Furthermore, selecting plants that are "willowy" rather than brittle helps to avoid structural damage from the physical force of the wind.

The possible applications of vegetation as a device to mitigate wind are wide ranging. Each form and corresponding pattern of sheltered zones implies different uses in the landscape. It is important to consider the growth of vegetation as well as the value of different plant characteristics when comparing coniferous with deciduous species, trees with shrubs, and low-branching with high-canopy structures which offer a significant palette.

Vegetation offers a natural and benign device to mitigate wind. It occupies a small amount of land for its relative effectiveness. Plant materials offer a range of aesthetic characteristics that can soften hard landscapes and animate dull environments. A vegetative windbreak not only creates calm spaces for activity, but also contributes appealing detail to site-scale environments.

A designer may also apply a range of styles when planning vegetative barriers. Both formal single-species rows of trees and an informal massing of mixed-species trees and shrubs serve as effective mitigation devices. Boulevards of trees, naturalistic mass plantings, and more conventional hedgerows all provide different stylistic opportunities for wind mitigation.

The lengths and heights of the calm zones suggest the scale of land use that can be sheltered. Tall and relatively dense vegetative barriers, such as evergreen trees, create a calm zone that may provide wind-sheltering for buildings up to four to five stories high and also for outdoor activities that require high, vertical, calm space. In comparison, a lower vegetative barrier like the multiple-stemmed deciduous shrubs creates a calm zone that is suitable for low-scale use, such as gardens and residential landscapes.

Noise

A few plants alone do a poor job of reducing noise. However, dense planting, especially combined with solid barriers or land forms, can reduce noise significantly. As cities become denser, reduction of noise pollution becomes a significant factor in increasing human well-being and reducing stress. Contemporary work has focused along busy highways near residential and retail development where noise pollution creates the greatest negative impacts.

Pollution

Plants play a role in reducing air pollution, both particulate and gaseous. Research has quantified this effect, which is just beginning to be studied in depth. Trees act as natural filters, removing not only particulate matter but also gaseous pollutants including carbon monoxide (CO) and sulfur dioxide (SO_2) by absorbing them through leaves and other plant parts. The particulate matter that clings to trunks, twigs, and leaves is usually washed into the soil by rainfall. However, trees do have the ability to absorb low levels of noxious fumes without related damage to the tree. More research is needed into the effectiveness of certain species in the reduction of airborne pollutants in urban areas.

Plants Create Spaces

Plants may be used to create physical barriers, directing foot traffic or screening unsightly views. Private spaces or places that mitigate a wide array of urban conditions can be created with the use of vegetation. Such places are increasingly prized in dense urban areas. Plants can change the sense of scale to a more human dimension. Notable features and architectural lines can be enhanced with appropriate planting. Historic neighborhoods often have culturally appropriate landscapes that are intrinsic to the historical experience and sense of place (Figure 4–3; see color insert).

Erosion and Runoff

Plants play a crucial role in reducing soil erosion as well as trapping and slowing stormwater runoff. Incorporating plants that can significantly reduce our reliance on stormwater abatement systems, improve natural water infiltration, and reduce the velocity of water moving over a landscape is important in contemporary design. Allowing for water evaporation, evapotranspiration, and infiltration as well as the replenishment of urban groundwater are universally critical aspects of landscape design. Plants can provide the ability to reduce runoff on highly erodable soils as well as areas of steep topography. Plants with a highly fibrous root system that yield a more complete ground cover with their stems and leaves work best in this regard.

Recreation/Habitat

Urban green spaces provide necessary animal habitat and are the places where most of the human population connects with the natural world as well as actively pursues recreation. These areas represent critical habitat in which humans can interact with animals in natural settings. Cities with well-tended parks are always listed as desirable places to live. Property values are significantly higher near well-tended green spaces as well as for properties considered well landscaped. The green urban environment provides an essential link to the natural world, marking seasonal changes and the enduring human need to be connected with nature (Figure 4-4).

The vast aesthetic possibilities plants offer can be overwhelming to the

Figure 4-4 People and their relationship to tree plantings in a plaza setting.

landscape designer. Yet, by embracing this diversity of seasonal interest, form, color, and texture we can create wonderfully inventive landscapes (Figure 4–5; see color insert). The realization of a design vision for a site and the ultimate success of a built landscape require more than creative elements of space, line, and form. They require a thorough understanding of how the site will be used by people and how it may or may not support the long-term biological needs of plants growing there.

All plants have a genetic potential to grow to a certain size and shape at a given rate under optimal conditions. Knowing the plant's potential and matching its needs to the site's ability to meet those needs is the key to achieving the realization of a design vision. Rarely do site conditions enable a plant to grow to its full genetic potential. However, if enough of a plant's needs are met (especially the appropriate levels of the basic six factors: light, water, nutrients, temperatures, oxygen, and carbon dioxide), the landscape designer can be confident that the proposed planting will develop into what was originally envisioned.

With all the potential choices in plant materials, developing the knowledge of plant adaptability to site conditions can seem to be an overwhelming task. Moreover, it is important to know the conditions under which plants will grow satisfactorily, if not optimally. Appendix I is one source of information about plant site preferences. Another is the extensive list of excellent references available to help the designer match the plant to the site. Learning how to use plants in various landscapes is a never-ending process. Designers who engage in this process will produce designs clearly distinguishable from those relying on a limited palette of plants that may be used almost anywhere within a climatic zone.

HOW DO WE BEGIN MATCHING THE PLANT TO THE SITE?

In earlier chapters, methods for detailed site assessment were provided. The results of a site assessment will provide information about many issues pertaining to effective plant growth. This section expands on matters that must be considered for successful plant establishment.

Space and Hardiness

The two most limiting factors for successful plant growth are how that plant can fit into its envisioned space and its ability to persist on the site given the extremes of heat and cold. Given the vast number of plant choices, coming up with the desired spatial envelope for plant growth on the site is a good place to make the first cut. All potential barriers to unimpeded growth mentioned in the material on site assessment should be examined as well as the size and shape of the envisioned plant. If there are impediments such as utilities or compacted soil that may be modified to provide adequate space for plant growth, the feasibility of such strategies must be explored with the client. Can the soil be modified to provide adequate volume for root growth? Can aboveground utilities be moved below ground to provide more unimpeded overhead space? Or does the design vision have to change to accommodate site limitations that cannot be remediated?

Planting a large red oak in a soil with only 12 inches of usable depth is not a realistic way to achieve a vision. Can greater depth be achieved by building up the planting area above grade, or should another plant choice be made? Will there be a sustained commitment to pruning tree branches so they will not interfere with aboveground utility lines, or should a tree be chosen that will not mature to a height that will interfere with the wires?

As previously described, a thorough site assessment is critical to correct choices in plant selection. In the urban environment, clear sightlines for visual access can be key for pedestrian and vehicular safety. Be sure to consider whether or not the tree you choose will branch to meet these conditions. Will the natural form of the tree be so altered to fit into a particular space that its aesthetic appeal is lost?

Plant adaptability to extremes of heat and cold is the next most important limitation on plant choices. Knowing the USDA heat and cold hardiness zone of your site is essential. It is also important to know about microclimatic factors such as reradiated heat, wind, rain shadows caused by buildings, and frost pockets. Often, the urban environment offers sheltered areas that enable a wider range of plants to be grown than would be possible in surrounding rural areas. This is because of the temperature-, light-, and wind-altering effects of buildings and built surfaces. Localized microclimates regularly occur in cities, sometimes because of building-created wind tunnels that channel the wind. However, raised planters can cause a relatively small amount of soil to change temperature as drastically as air temperatures. In addition, references sometimes don't agree on the hardiness parameters of plants. A good idea is to consult several references as well as local professionals. When there is a discrepancy, choose conservatively. Cultivars may also have different hardiness ratings compared to the species.

Sun/Shade

Most trees require four to six hours of full sun daily to grow to their envisioned size and form. Occasionally, a few smaller trees may tolerate partial shade (see Table 4-1). This can be a significant issue in many landscapes. When it comes to shrubs or perennials however, there are many more choices for plants that prefer partial or heavy shade.

Soil Moisture

In the natural environment, plants are often grouped by their ability to tolerate similar soil conditions such as soil moisture and pH. These are important parameters that should be used to choose plants. Some plants can

TABLE 4-1   TREES THAT TOLERATE PARTIAL SHADE

Botanic Name	Common Name
Acer tataricum spp. ginnala	Amur Maple
*Acer griseum	Paperbark Maple
Acer miyabei	Miyabei Maple
*Acer palmatum	Japanese Maple
Acer pensylvanicum	Moosewood
Amelanchier spp.	Serviceberry
*Asimina triloba	Pawpaw
*Betula alleghaniensis	Yellow Birch
*Betula lenta	Sweet Birch
Betula nigra	River Birch
Betula papyrifera	Paper Birch
Betula pendula	Weeping Birch
*Carpinus caroliniana	Musclewood
Cercidiphyllum japonicum	Katsura Tree
Cercis canadensis	Redbud
Chamaecyparis nootkatensis	Alaska Cedar
Chamaecyparis obtusa	Hinoki False Cypress
Chamaecyparis pisifera	Sawara False Cypress
Chamaecyparis thyoides	Atlantic White Cedar
Chionanthus virginicus	Fringetree
*Cornus alternifolia	Pagoda Dogwood
*Cornus florida	Flowering Dogwood
Cornus kousa	Kousa Dogwood
Cornus mas	Cornelian Cherry
Cornus racemosa	Gray Dogwood
Cryptomeria japonica	Japanese Cryptomeria
Davidia involucrata	Handkerchief Tree
Franklinia alatamaha	Franklinia
*Halesia tetraptera	Carolina Silverbell
Hamamelis mollis	Chinese Witch Hazel
Hamamelis virginiana	Common Witch Hazel
Laburnum anagyroides	Goldenchain Tree
Ostrya virginiana	American Hop Hornbeam
*Oxydendrum arboreum	Sourwood
Parrotia persica	Ironwood
Sciadopitys verticillata	Umbrella Pine
Sorbus alnifolia	Korean Mountain Ash
Sorbus aucuparia	European Mountain Ash
Sorbus thuringiaca	Oak-Leafed Mountain Ash
Stewartia pseudocamellia	Japanese Stewartia
Styrax japonicus	Japanese Snowbell

TABLE 4-1 *(Continued)*

Botanic Name	Common Name
Syringa reticulata	Japanese Tree Lilac
Thuja occidentalis	Eastern Arborvitae
Thuja plicata	Western Arborvitae
Tsuga canadensis	Eastern Hemlock
Tsuga caroliniana	Carolina Hemlock
Viburnum lentago	Nannyberry
Viburnum sieboldii	Siebold Viburnum

* Trees that prefer some shade

tolerate a wide range of soil moisture conditions from flooding on the one extreme to drought on the other. Where soil volumes are limited, it is common for plants to experience alternating periods of too wet and too dry soil conditions. This may be due to the shallowness of the soil. When it rains, water does not drain away and the roots experience oxygen deprivation. When the soil eventually dries out, the roots are in such a small area that there is too little water to support plant growth.

Where soil volumes are large and drainage is good, it is possible to grow a large number of plants, including those that cannot adapt to alternating soil moisture extremes. Knowing the conditions that determine moisture and oxygen availability in the soil are the keys to good design and successful plant establishment. Soil texture, depth, volume, density, drainage, and the presence of irrigation determine the availability of water and air in the soil.

Soils that are seasonably wet but otherwise well drained will accommodate a larger number of plants than those that are continually wet during the growing season or those that alternate between very wet and very dry. Sites that are dry most of the growing season also pose challenges in plant selection. It might be necessary to modify these soil conditions to provide a better balance between wet and dry conditions in order to grow plants successfully on the site. If little soil modification is possible to overcome these limitations, the number of plant choices for the site is severely limited (see Appendix I).

Soil pH

Testing soil pH is a simple, inexpensive technique that provides vital information about nutrient availability. Although most plants grow best at a slightly acid pH, many plants will grow well in pH's as high as 8.2. Fewer plants will grow well in extremely acid soils of pH 3.5 to 4.5, but there are some selections for this range too. It is important that plants be chosen that will do well in the existing soil pH. It is much more difficult to change soil pH, especially when making a permanent change. Regular monitoring of a site under consideration and frequent soil additions are often called for. If these are impractical, it is better to choose plants that tolerate the existing soils. Most reference books are quite conservative about the pH tolerances ascribed to many plants. Our research shows that there is generally a wider range of acceptable pH tolerance in many plants that will have acceptable growth (see Appendix I).

Salts

Consider plants that tolerate de-icing salts or general saline conditions such as seashore sites when developing a planting plan. Watch for places where salts drift in aerially, such as along the seashore and on highway roadsides during winter in northern climates, for soil-related conditions as in arid areas, and for saltwater intrusions into soils from seawater. There are few woody plants that will not be killed by some level of salts, but there are many that have *some* tolerance. Other site factors can exacerbate salt contamination, notably poor soil drainage. Most salts are quite water-soluble and will wash through the root zone after a good rain if soils are well drained.

Winter de-icing salts are generally applied when the plant is dormant and unable to take up much salt. Consequently, damage is greater when salts are applied at the end or the beginning of the growing season when the soil is warm enough (>40°F or 7°C) and salt uptake occurs. If salts are applied in the winter and drainage is impeded, roots may experience high levels of salts when the soil begins to warm up. Providing well-drained soil reduces most damaging effects of de-icing salts, as does choosing salt-tolerant plants (see Appendix I).

Beyond environmental factors, there are other management concerns that are important in plant selection, including plant susceptibility to pests and pathogens, the ability to be transplanted, availability in the trade, and maintenance requirements.

Pests and Diseases

Susceptibility of plants to insect and disease attack is a significant factor in plant selection. Plants that do not require pesticides to enable them to grow well should always be a first choice. It is worthwhile checking with local growers to find out about locally troublesome pests for a particular plant. Most plants have some pest problems. However, some species attract fewer pests. Excellent information is available on both species and cultivars that are resistant to particular pests and diseases. Also, when planted in sites to which it is well adapted, a species generally suffers fewer pest problems or is able to recover from an attack more rapidly. Woody plants that suffer from a lack of water are more susceptible to boring insects, which can do tremendous damage. Usually there are reasonable substitutions for plants that are particularly troubled by a certain disease or insect.

Transplanting

Several trees and shrubs are notably difficult to transplant. Certain practices help ensure greater success in transplanting, yet some species remain difficult even when appropriate transplanting measures are taken. It is only reasonable not to choose too many troublesome plants for any one installation. Refer to Chapter 5, page 156, for lists of plants and their relative difficulty in transplanting.

Cost and Availability

Many desirable plants are not available in appropriate sizes or are too costly to be specified for a landscape planting. Increasingly, plants can be found to meet specifications due to a diversified nursery industry. Timing is always important when transplanting. The designer may want to consider the availability of plants and consult with the contractor to be sure that species and sizes specified can be located. Alternatively, horticultural brokers may be hired to find plants that otherwise would be difficult to obtain. Having gone through the process of site assessment and making the best selections, it is worth trying to find the best plants before accepting contractor substitutions.

Maintenance Issues

Some plants produce an unacceptable amount of fruit or leaf litter under certain circumstances, or require regular pruning for appropriate appearance. Small-fruited or fruitless alternatives that present less of a litter problem may be available. If there is no regular maintenance, shrubs and trees that need little pruning should be selected.

Thorns may also be an issue in settings where people are likely to be in direct contact with the plants, such as a playground or a narrow street or alley planting. *Weak-woodedness* is a term that refers to the propensity of trees to break up or drop limbs in high winds or during snow and ice storms. Fast-growing trees are the most frequent offenders. Place such weak-wooded trees away from areas people frequent or property that may be damaged. Plants that may be perfectly acceptable in a natural area may not be suited to certain urban conditions.

Some examples of trees with fruits that may become a nuisance are:

Malus (Crabapple) cultivars with fruit > 1 inch in diameter

Malus 'Almey'

Malus 'Baskatong'

Malus 'Brandywine'

Malus 'Callaway'

Malus 'Centennial'

Malus 'Dolgo'

Malus 'Evelyn'

Malus 'Golden Hornet'

Malus 'Henry Kohankie'

Malus ioensis

Malus tschonoskii

Liquidambar styraciflua Sweetgum: numerous spiny ball-shaped fruits

Maclura pomifera Osage Orange: large, green orange-sized fruits (female trees only)

Ginkgo biloba Ginkgo: Female trees have abundant stinking fruits

Some examples of trees with thorns:

Crataegus crus-galli Cockspur Hawthorn

Crataegus phaenopyrum Washington Hawthorn

Note that all trees with *inermis* in their name denotes thornlessness

Native or Non-native Plants

The most important factor for the success of a plant in the landscape is its adaptability to the site and not its geographic origin. Most urban sites are altered so as to make a plant's native site conditions, prior to centuries of development, irrelevant. If a tree were native to parts of New York City in the sixteenth century, it still may not be the right tree for a particular site in New York City today. Non-native introductions represent a very small proportion of weedy plants that become a nuisance in nearby natural areas. Clearly, these invasive plants should be avoided. It is important to remember that the tendency of a plant to become invasive is a function of the particular plant and its environment. Local authorities know which plants are problematic in a particular area. Lists of invasive plants encompassing a very large area or defined by a specific political boundary are generally inaccurate or not detailed enough for a particular site.

Diversity Versus Uniformity

The selection and placement of trees in the urban environment is a complex task requiring the consideration of many factors. Issues such as visual access, spatial constraints, and disease and insect resistance can sometimes conflict with design objectives. Perhaps the most troubling conflict arises between the preference for visual uniformity and the practical need for biological and species diversity. Until recently, a typical street tree planting consisted of uniform rows of a single species, generally selected for its attractive appearance and high tolerance to urban stresses. However, as overplanting has brought about the decline of a number of such favorite species, it is clear that design objectives must be balanced against the practical need for species diversity in street tree plantings.

CURRENT STRATEGIES

Faced with the difficulty of balancing aesthetic and ecological concerns, designers all too often shortchange or even abandon one or the other. Where they may have once planted an entire neighborhood with the same species, those favoring uniformity might now plant a single species for one or two blocks of a given street. Although this sort of compromise may feel like a bow to diversity, it isn't a true solution to the problem. Planting trees in somewhat smaller same-species blocks will not necessarily prevent the kinds of devastation associated with monocultures, particularly if the species selected are already heavily planted in the community.

For those favoring an ecologically sensible approach, the alternative to monocultures is sometimes to plant wonderfully diverse selections of trees that share no common characteristics whatsoever. The results of such efforts can be aesthetically disappointing and have, in a number of cases, led to public outcry. Unfortunately, this approach to plant selection has served to fuel the idea that the only way to achieve uniformity in design is through the exclusive use of one species.

THE CASE FOR VISUAL UNIFORMITY

What makes uniform plantings so appealing in the first place? What makes them so difficult to give up? The advantages to uniformity are primarily aesthetic. A street lined with rows of identical trees brings to most observers a sense of order and tranquillity (Figure 4-6; see color insert). Even in the most heterogeneous of neighborhoods, a uniform street of trees can have a cohesive influence, tying together diverse elements and creating a sense of neighborhood identity. At a more political level, what could be more democratic than a uniform planting of trees that does nothing to reflect differences in the people, lawns, homes, and businesses just beyond the sidewalk? Street trees can even soften the potentially jarring transitions from residential to commercial areas.

THE CASE FOR SPECIES DIVERSITY

Unfortunately, the appeal of same-species plantings is ultimately outweighed by disadvantages. Even if aesthetics were the only consideration, the fact that unhealthy or dying trees are unattractive makes the need to diversify unavoidable. A quick review of disease and pest problems in street tree populations reveals numerous cases of devastation due to overplanting or the exclusive planting of a single species. Some of the most notable examples include the American elm (Dutch Elm disease), American Chestnut (chestnut blight), Honey Locust (honey locust plant bug), Norway Maple (giant tar spot and verticillium wilt), London Plane tree (anthracnose), and Crabapple (scab, fireblight, cedar apple rust, and powdery mildew). Overplanting of some popular species can also lead to serious maintenance problems. Species with characteristics such as weak wood, a tendency to develop chlorosis, girdling roots, and messy fruits can certainly be used in street tree plantings, but they are manageable only when planted in moderation. Examples include Norway Maple (girdling roots) and Silver Maple (weak wood).

Another factor that makes monocultures impractical is the tremendous diversity inherent in the urban environment. The challenges and stresses for trees can change dramatically within very small spaces, often making it impossible for a single species to thrive uniformly throughout a given area. Variables such as light, temperature, drainage, soil compaction, root space, soil pH, availability of water, exposure to salt, and restrictions to crown development can vary tremendously even from one tree space to the next. A careful assessment of site conditions prior to plant selection rarely points to the selection of a single species. Even designers who are aware of this often make the mistake of selecting one species that will purportedly survive under any and all difficult conditions. Such widely adaptable species dominate the aforementioned list of overplanted trees that have suffered decline, become unmanageable, or both.

A SOLUTION

To avoid similar problems in the future, it is clear that uniform plantings of a limited number of species must be avoided. But is it possible to gain the practical advantages of diversity without giving up the aesthetic advantages of uniformity? Fortunately, the answer is yes. Through careful selection and grouping of plants, communities of trees can be created that, despite their genetic diversity, satisfy our desire for visual uniformity.

Primary and Secondary Criteria

By breaking down into basic categories the visual characteristics that distinguish one species or cultivar from another, we have selected four criteria for putting trees into aesthetically compatible groups. The first two criteria, size and shape (Figure 4-7), are of primary importance in grouping trees because they have greater and more immediate impact on the visual impression individual trees make. This is particularly true as a tree matures or as the distance from the tree to the observer increases. The other two criteria—branching density (Figure 4-8) and foliage texture—are given *secondary* consideration because they generally are not as obvious to the casual observer and can even become difficult to distinguish as the distance from the observer increases.

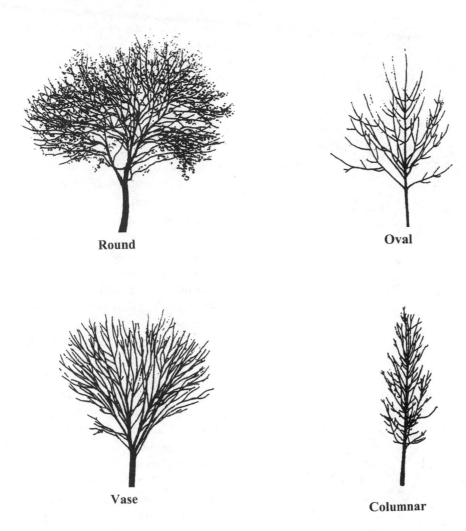

Round

Oval

Vase

Columnar

Figure 4-7 Sketches of variable tree canopy shapes.

Clearly, these categories are broad, but when applied with a measure of subjective analysis and common sense, they yield practical and appealing groups of trees. Trees with medium or borderline characteristics are placed subjectively on the basis of their subtle characteristics. For example, trees of the genus *Fraxinus* have medium-textured foliage, but because of the narrow apexes of their leaflets, they are placed in the fine-textured group. In some cases, the basic groups are presented with subgroups that work particularly well together. In other cases, a special characteristic shared by a number of trees called for the creation of an additional recommended group (Figure 4-9; see color insert)

RECOMMENDED GROUPS OF VISUALLY COMPATIBLE TREES

Tables 4-2 through 4-18 contain lists of trees that the public perceives as visually compatible. The lists provide a starting point for considering visual similarity together with biological diversity. It is imperative,

Figure 4-8 Sketches of variable tree branching density.

however, that trees of similar appearance be matched to site conditions through comprehensive site analyses.

SELECTING AND USING A PLANT GROUP

Before selecting a group of trees to work with, it is important that a thorough assessment be made of the planting site. Spatial constraints such as overhead wires, narrow setbacks, and limited soil volume may limit the size or shape options, as previously mentioned. Other factors to consider in selecting a group of trees include the desired visual effect and the intended practical function of the planting. Is the objective simply visual appeal, or will the trees be expected to provide shade, break wind, or shield sights or sounds? What is the scale of surrounding buildings, gardens, or parks? Is a formal or informal appearance more appropriate? Table 4–19 provides some examples of how various factors may lead to the selection of a group appropriate to a given situation.

In making tree selections, it is advisable to take into account the breakdown of species in the population around the site. Even if a wide variety of species is planted, individual trees could be at risk if they are of a species that is already overplanted in the area. Ideally, any one species should not make up more than 5 to 10 percent of the total tree population for a town, small city, or neighborhood. In general, the greater the number of genera used, the lower the risk of serious pest or disease problems.

In the simplest situations, where site conditions and requirements are more or less consistent, trees from one group may be selected and used uniformly throughout an area. However, the groups can also be useful in more complex situations. By changing only one characteristic at a time, trees from different groups may be blended together as site conditions or the desired

TABLE 4-2   CHARACTERISTICS OF VISUAL SIMILARITY OF TREES

1	Size	Large	Greater than 30 feet at 30 years
		Small	Less than 30 feet at 30 years
			Height to first branch
2	Shape	Round	Width > or = height of canopy
		Oval	Width < height
		Vase	Narrow at the base, becoming distinctly wider at the top
		Columnar	Width distinctly < height
3	Branching Density	Dense	Greater than 30 feet at 30 years
		Open	Less than 30 feet at 30 years
4	Foliage Texture	Coarse	Large leaves (or leaflets) with blunt ends or lobes
		Fine	Smaller leaves (or leaflets) with acute apexes

effect changes from one area to another. For example, if a cohesive planting is desired on a block where overhead wires limit the selection of trees on one side of the street, instead of simply planting all small trees with matching characteristics on both sides of the street, a designer could choose to plant small trees of a given shape, branching density, and foliage texture on the side with overhead wires and large trees with those same characteristics on the other. Other site factors that might call for such a blending technique include narrow setbacks, frequent truck traffic, and signage. Even within a

TABLE 4-3   LARGE TREES WITH ROUND CANOPIES, DENSE BRANCHING, AND COARSE-TEXTURED FOLIAGE

		Cold Hardy to Zone
Acer platanoides 'Emerald Queen'	Emerald Queen Norway Maple	4a
Acer platanoides 'Summershade'	Summershade Norway Maple	4a
Acer platanoides 'Superform'	Superform Norway Maple	4a
Acer rubrum 'Autumn Flame'	Autumn Flame Red Maple	3b
Acer rubrum 'Northwood'	Northwood Red Maple	3b
Acer rubrum 'October Glory'	October Glory Red Maple	4b
Platanus x acerifolia 'Bloodgood'	Bloodgood London Plane Tree	5b
Platanus x acerifolia 'Columbia'	Columbia London Plane Tree	5b
Platanus x acerifolia 'Liberty'	Liberty London Plane Tree	5b

TABLE 4-4   LARGE TREES WITH ROUND CANOPIES, OPEN
BRANCHING, AND FINE-TEXTURED FOLIAGE

Group 1		Cold Hardy to Zone
Celtis laevigata 'All Seasons'	All Season Sugar Hackberry	5b
Celtis laevigata 'Magnifica'	Magnifica Sugar Hackberry	5b
Celtis occidentalis 'Prairie Pride'	Prairie Pride Hackberry	3b
Eucommia ulmoides	Hardy Rubber Tree	5b
Maclura pomifera 'Park'	Park Osage Orange	5b
Maclura pomifera 'Wichita'	Wichita Osage Orange	5b
Group 2		
Cladrastis kentukea	Yellow Wood	4b
Fraxinus americana 'Autumn Purple'	Autumn Purple White Ash	4a
Fraxinus pennsylvanica 'Emerald'	Emerald Green Ash	3a
Gymnocladus dioicus	Kentucky Coffee Tree	4a
Phellodendron amurense	Amur Cork Tree	4b
Phellodendron amurense 'Macho'	Macho Amur Cork Tree	4b
Group 3		
Gleditsia triacanthos var. inermis	Thornless Honey Locust	4b
Gleditsia triacanthos var. inermis 'Halka'	Halka Honey Locust	4b
Gleditsia triacanthos var. inermis 'Moraine'	Moraine Honey Locust	4b
Gleditsia triacanthos var. inermis 'Shademaster'	Shademaster Honey Locust	4b
Sophora japonica 'Princeton Upright'	Scholar Tree	5b

given group, trees may need to be used selectively as factors such as pH and moisture change throughout the site.

The strategies presented here for selecting and grouping street trees provide the designer with many options for creating healthy and visually appealing tree plantings for streets. The recommendations are based on careful consideration of both aesthetic and practical concerns.

Specifying Plants

When specifying plants, it is important to use botanical names that are universally understood and accepted. Common names can be limited to regional use and subsequently are not definitive when specifying plants. Many trees are known by three or four different common names across the country. Consequently, it is imperative that plants are specified by their genus, species, and, when appropriate, cultivar and variety.

TABLE 4-5   LARGE TREES WITH ROUND CANOPIES, OPEN
BRANCHING, AND COARSE-TEXTURED FOLIAGE

		Cold Hardy to Zone
Quercus macrocarpa	Bur Oak	3a
Quercus muehlenbergii	Chinkapin Oak	5a
Quercus rubra	Red Oak	3b
Quercus robur	English Oak	5b

TABLE 4-6   LARGE TREES WITH OVAL CANOPIES, DENSE BRANCHING,
AND FINE-TEXTURED FOLIAGE

		Cold Hardy to Zone
*Metasequoia glyptostroboides	Dawn Redwood	5b
*Taxodium distichum	Bald Cypress	5a
*Taxodium distichum 'Shawnee Brave'	Shawnee Brave Bald Cypress	5a
Cercidiphyllum japonicum	Katsura Tree	5a
Corylus colurna	Turkish Filbert	5a
Fraxinus pennsylvanica 'Bergeson'	Bergeson Green Ash	2a
Fraxinus pennsylvanica 'Cimmaron'	Cimmaron Green Ash	2a
Fraxinus pennsylvanica 'Newport'	Newport Green Ash	2a
Fraxinus pennsylvanica 'Patmore'	Patmore Green Ash	2a
Fraxinus pennsylvanica 'Summit'	Summit Green Ash	2a
Fraxinus pennsylvanica 'Urbanite'	Urbanite Green Ash	5b
Nyssa sylvatica	Tupelo	5a
Ostrya virginiana	American Hop Hornbeam	3b
Pyrus calleryana 'Autumn Blaze'	Autumn Blaze Callery Pear	5a
Pyrus calleryana 'Whitehouse'	Whitehouse Callery Pear	5a
Sorbus alnifolia	Korean Mountain Ash	4b
Tilia cordata 'Chancellor'	Chancellor Littleleaf Linden	3b
Tilia cordata 'Glenleven'	Glenleven Littleleaf Linden	3b
Tilia cordata 'Greenspire'	Greenspire Littleleaf Linden	3b
Tilia cordata 'Olympic'	Olympic Littleleaf Linden	3b
Tilia cordata 'Rancho'	Rancho Littleleaf Linden	3b
Tilia x euchlora	Crimean Linden	4b

* Conifers

TABLE 4-7   LARGE TREES WITH OVAL CANOPIES, DENSE BRANCHING, AND COARSE-TEXTURED FOLIAGE

		Cold Hardy to Zone
Acer x freemanii 'Autumn Blaze'	Autumn Blaze Maple	4
Acer x freemanii 'Autumn Fantasy'	Autumn Fantasy Maple	4
Acer x freemanii 'Celebration'	Celebration Maple	4
Acer x freemanii 'Marmo'	Marmo Maple	4
Acer x freemanii 'Morgan'	Morgan Maple	4
Acer x freemanii 'Scarlet Sentinel'	Scarlet Sentinel Maple	4
Acer pseudoplatanus 'Spaethii'	Spaethii Sycamore Maple	5b
Acer platanoides 'Cleveland'	Cleveland Norway Maple	4a
Acer platanoides 'Parkway'	Parkway Norway Maple	4a
Acer rubrum 'Red Sunset'	Red Sunset Maple	3b
Acer saccharum 'Caddo'	Caddo Sugar Maple	3b
Acer saccharum 'Commemoration'	Commemoration Sugar Maple	3b
Acer saccharum 'Green Mountain'	Green Mountain Sugar Maple	3b
Acer saccharum 'Legacy'	Legacy Sugar Maple	3b
Acer saccharum 'Majesty'	Majesty Sugar Maple	3b
Tilia americana 'Redmond'	Redmond Basswood	3a
Tilia tomentosa	Silver Linden	5a

Species, Varieties, and Cultivars

The *species* is the most important unit in plant specification.

The species is written as two words: the genus, as in *Cornus,* the genus for dogwood, and *florida,* the specific epithet. Together, *Cornus florida* is the species name for Flowering Dogwood.

A species is a group of plants that share many of the same characteristics that are passed along from generation to generation. Each member of the species is genetically distinct. Some species may exhibit considerable variation among individuals in terms of leaf shape and color, flower color, fruit size, growth habit, and vigor, while others may show little variation.

When a particular variation within a species can be inherited from generation to generation, it is said to be a *variety* or *subspecies.*

Cornus florida var. rubra describes a variety of Flowering Dogwood, Pink Flowering Dogwood. It can be written *Cornus florida var. rubra* or *Cornus florida rubra.* Both are correct.

A *cultivar* (for *cultivated variety*) is a tremendously important designation in horticulture. A cultivar is chosen because of distinctly superior or notable traits such as form, autumn leaf coloration, flower color or size, vigor, cold hardiness, or disease resistance, to name a few (Figure 4–10; see color insert). Most of the time, cultivars are genetically identical or clonal. It is possible to

TABLE 4-8   LARGE TREES WITH OVAL CANOPIES, OPEN BRANCHING, AND FINE-TEXTURED FOLIAGE

		Cold Hardy to Zone
Alnus glutinosa	European Alder	4a
Alnus glutinosa 'Pyramidalis'	Pyramidal Black Alder	4a
Alnus glutinosa 'Fastigiata'	Upright Black Alder	4a
Betula nigra 'Heritage'	Heritage River Birch	4a
Betula platyphylla 'Japonica'	Asian White Birch	2b
Betula populifolia 'Whitespire'	Whitespire Birch	2b
Fraxinus americana 'Autumn Applause'	Autumn Applause White Ash	4a
Fraxinus americana 'Champaign County'	Champaign County White Ash	4a
Fraxinus americana 'Rose Hill'	Rose Hill White Ash	4a
Fraxinus americana 'Skyline'	Skyline White Ash	4a
Fraxinus excelsior 'Hessei'	Hess European Ash	4a
Ginkgo biloba 'Autumn Gold'	Autumn Gold Ginkgo	4b
Gleditsia triacanthos inermis 'Skyline'	Skyline Honey Locust	4b
Pyrus calleryana 'Aristocrat'	Aristocrat Callery Pear	5a
Quercus imbricaria	Shingle Oak	5a
Quercus phellos	Willow Oak	6b
Robinia pseudoacacia	Black Locust	4b
Ulmus carpinifolia x parvifolia 'Frontier'	Frontier Elm	5b
Ulmus 'Homestead'	Homestead Elm	5a
Ulmus 'Pioneer'	Pioneer Elm	5a
Ulmus 'Urban'	Urban Elm	5a

TABLE 4-9   LARGE TREES WITH OVAL CANOPIES, OPEN BRANCHING, AND COARSE-TEXTURED FOLIAGE

		Cold Hardy to Zone
Aesculus x carnea 'Briotti'	Briotti Red Horse Chestnut	5a
Aesculus x camea 'O'Neill'	O'Neill Red Horse Chestnut	5a
Catalpa speciosa	Northern Catalpa	4a
Liquidambar styraciflua	Sweetgum	5b
Liquidambar styraciflua 'Moraine'	Moraine Sweetgum	5b
Liriodendron tulipifera	Tulip Poplar	5a
Quercus acutissima	Sawtooth Oak	5b
Quercus bicolor	Swamp White Oak	4a
Quercus coccinea	Scarlet Oak	5a
Quercus schumardii	Schumard Oak	5b

TABLE 4-10   LARGE TREES WITH VASE-SHAPED CANOPIES AND FINE-TEXTURED FOLIAGE

		Cold Hardy to Zone
Prunus sargentii 'Columnaris'	Upright Sargent Cherry	5a
Ulmus americana 'Delaware #2'	Delaware American Elm	2b
Ulmus americana 'New Harmony'	New Harmony Elm	5
Ulmus americana 'Princeton'	Princeton American Elm	2b
Ulmus americana 'Valley Forge'	Valley Forge Elm	5
Ulmus americana 'Washington'	Washington American Elm	2b
Ulmus parvifolia 'Dynasty'	Dynasty Chinese Elm	5b
Ulmus parvifolia 'Ohio'	Ohio Chinese Elm	5
Ulmus parvifolia 'Prospector'	Prospector Chinese Elm	4
Ulmus parvifolia 'Pathfinder'	Pathfinder Elm	5a
Ulmus x 'Patriot'	Patriot Elm	4
Ulmus x 'Sapporo Autumn Gold'	Sapporo Autumn Gold Hybrid Elm	5a
Zelkova serrata 'Green Vase'	Green Vase Zelkova	5b
Zelkova serrata 'Halka'	Halka Zelkova	5b
Zelkova serrata 'Village Green'	Village Green Zelkova	5b

have a cultivar of a variety or of a species. *Cornus florida rubra* 'Cherokee Chief' is an example of a particularly well-formed, red flowering selection of *Cornus florida rubra*, which is perpetuated by asexual propagation in order to maintain its genetic character. The cultivar name is always capitalized and put in single quotes. When the species derivation is complex, cultivar names can

TABLE 4-11   LARGE TREES WITH COLUMNAR CANOPIES

		Cold Hardy to Zone
Acer x freemanii 'Armstrong'	Armstrong Hybrid Maple	4
Acer nigrum 'Green Column'	Green Column Black Maple	5
Acer platanoides 'Columnare'	Columnar Norway Maple	4a
Acer rubrum 'Bowhall'	Bowhall Red Maple	3b
Acer rubrum 'Columnar'	Columnar Red Maple	3b
Acer rubrum 'Karpick'	Karpick Red Maple	3b
Carpinus betulus 'Fastigiata'	Upright European Hornbeam	5a
Ginkgo biloba 'Lakeview'	Lakeview Ginkgo	4b
Ginkgo biloba 'Princeton Sentry'	Princeton Sentry Gingko	4b
Pyrus calleryana 'Capital'	Capital Callery pear	5a
Pyrus calleryana 'Chanticleer'	Chanticleer Callery Pear	5a
Quercus robur 'Attention'	Attention English Oak	5a
Quercus robur 'Fastigiata'	Upright English Oak	5a

TABLE 4-12 SMALL TREES WITH ROUND CANOPIES

		Cold Hardy to Zone
Acer buergeranum	Trident Maple	6a
Acer campestre	Hedge Maple	5a
Acer tataricum ssp. ginnala	Amur Maple	3a
Acer tataricum	Tatarian Maple	3a
Acer truncatum	Shantung Maple	4a
Carpinus caroliniana	Musclewood	3b
Cornus mas	Cornelian Cherry	5a
Crataegus phaenopyrum	Washington Hawthorn	4b
Crataegus punctata inermis 'Ohio Pioneer'	Thornless Ohio Pioneer Hawthorn	4a
Crataegus viridis 'Winter King'	Winter King Hawthorn	5a
Koelreuteria paniculata	Goldenrain Tree	5b
Malus baccata 'Jackii'	Jackii Crabapple	3a
Malus 'Donald Wyman'	Donald Wyman Crabapple	4
Malus floribunda	Flowering Crabapple	4b
Malus 'Henry Kohankie'	Henry Kohankie Crabapple	4
Malus 'Professor Sprenger'	Professor Sprenger Crabapple	4
Malus 'Sugartyme'	Sugartyme Crabapple	4
Malus 'White Angel'	White Angel Crabapple	4a
Malus x zumi 'Calocarpa'	Calocarpa Crabapple	4a
Sorbus intermedia	Swedish Mountain Ash	5
Syringa reticulata 'Summer Snow'	Summer Snow Japanese Tree Lilac	3a

be added to the genus name directly, as in *Malus* 'Adirondack' (Adirondack Crabapple) or *Crataegus* 'Vaughn' (Vaughn Hawthorn).

Plants are generally specified using a technical planting key when they are to be installed by a contractor; this key is included in construction documents. A planting plan is always accompanied by a technical planting key. This includes the plant type, represented as plant initials (for example, *Pinus strobus*-ps), the number of plants of a certain species (including cultivars), the botanical name, the common name, the size and root type, and any special comments that would help the contractor order those plants.

PLANTING KEY

Plant Type	No.	Botanical Name	Common Name	Size	Root Type	Comments
ps	3	*Pinus strobus*	White Pine	8–10 feet	B&B	Not sheared

TABLE 4-13   SMALL TREES WITH OVAL CANOPIES AND DENSE
BRANCHING

		Cold Hardy to Zone
Acer platanoides x truncatum 'Norwegian Sunset'	Norwegian Sunset Maple	4a
Acer platanoides x truncatum 'Pacific Sunset'	Pacific Sunset Maple	4a
Acer campestre 'Deborah'	Deborah Hedge Maple	5a
Amelanchier 'Autumn Brilliance'	Autumn Brilliance Serviceberry	3b
Amelanchier 'Autumn Sunset'	Autumn Sunset Serviceberry	3b
Amelanchier 'Cumulus'	Cumulus Serviceberry	3b
Amelanchier 'Majestic'	Majestic Serviceberry	3b
Amelanchier 'Princess Diana'	Princess Diana Serviceberry	3b
Amelanchier 'Robin Hill'	Robin Hill Serviceberry	3b
Amelanchier 'Tradition'	Tradition Serviceberry	3b
Cornus kousa	Chinese or Kousa Dogwood	5a
*Malus 'Adams'	Adams Crabapple	4a
*Malus 'Baskatong'	Baskatong Crabapple	4
Malus 'Centennial'	Centennial Crabapple	4
*Malus 'Centurion'	Centurion Crabapple	4
Malus 'Dolgo'	Dolgo Crabapple	3b
Malus 'Doubloons'	Doubloons Crabapple	4
Malus 'Harvest Gold'	Harvest Gold Crabapple	4
*Malus 'Indian Summer'	Indian Summer Crabapple	4a
*Malus 'Liset'	Liset Crabapple	4a
Malus 'Madonna'	Madonna Crabapple	4
Malus 'Ormiston Roy'	Ormiston Roy Crabapple	4a
*Malus 'Prairie Fire'	Prairie Fire Crabapple	4
*Malus 'Purple Prince'	Purple Prince Crabapple	4
*Malus 'Robinson'	Robinson Crabapple	4
Malus 'Silver Moon'	Silver Moon Crabapple	4
Malus 'Zumirang'	Zumirang Crabapple	4
*Prunus virginiana 'Canada Red'	Canada Red Chokecherry	3a
Sorbus thuringiaca 'Fastigiata'	Oak-Leafed Mountain Ash	3b
Syringa reticulata 'Ivory Silk'	Ivory Silk Japanese Tree Lilac	3a
Syringa reticulata 'Regent'	Regent Japanese Tree Lilac	3a

* May have a purplish or bronze tint to the foliage

TABLE 4-14   SMALL TREES WITH VASE-SHAPED CANOPIES

		Cold Hardy to Zone
Malus 'Adirondack'	Adirondack Crabapple	4
Malus 'Sentinel'	Sentinel Crabapple	4
*Malus 'Strawberry Parfait'	Strawberry Parfait Crabapple	4
Prunus 'Accolade'	Accolade Flowering Cherry	5

* May have a purplish or bronze tint to the foliage

Sizes of plants for purchase are ordered differently depending on the type of plant. Wide-growing shrubs are ordered by width in inches. Evergreen trees, upright shrubs, multistemmed trees, trees less than an inch in caliper or under 6 feet tall, and trees branched to the ground are ordered by height in feet. Single-stemmed trees with clearly defined single trunks and measuring 1 inch or more in caliper are specified by caliper. Caliper is the diameter of the trunk at 6 inches from the ground for trees up to and including 4 inches in caliper and at 12 inches from the ground for trees greater than 4 inches in caliper. The technical planting key cross-references to the proposed planting plan the number, plant type, size, root type or condition (Balled and Burlapped, Bare Root, Container), and other special characteristics or comments that may be atypical or not covered in ANSI Standards.

Root type refers to the way the plant is harvested in the nursery. Bare-

Additional Recommended Tree Groups

TABLE 4-15   LARGE ROUND TREES WITH MAPLE-LIKE LEAVES

		Cold Hardy to Zone
Acer platanoides 'Emerald Queen'	Emerald Queen Norway Maple	4a
Acer platanoides 'Summershade'	Summershade Norway Maple	4a
Acer platanoides 'Superform'	Superform Norway Maple	4a
Acer rubrum 'Autumn Flame'	Autumn Flame Red Maple	3b
Acer rubrum 'Northwood'	Northwood Red Maple	3b
Acer rubrum 'October Glory'	October Glory Red Maple	3b
Platanus x acerifolia 'Bloodgood'	Bloodgood London Plane Tree	5b
Platanus x acerifolia 'Columbia'	Columbia London Plane Tree	5b
Platanus x acerifolia 'Liberty'	Liberty London Plane Tree	5b

TABLE 4-16   LARGE OVAL TREES WITH MAPLE-LIKE LEAVES

		Cold Hardy to Zone
Acer x freemanii 'Autumn Blaze'	Autumn Blaze Maple	4
Acer x freemanii 'Autumn Fantasy'	Autumn Fantasy Maple	4
Acer x freemanii 'Celebration'	Celebration Maple	4
Acer x freemanii 'Marmo'	Marmo Maple	4
Acer x freemanii 'Morgan'	Morgan Maple	4
Acer x freemanii 'Scarlet Sentinel'	Scarlet Sentinel Maple	4
Acer pseudoplatanus 'Spaethii'	Spaethii Sycamore Maple	5b
Acer platanoides 'Cleveland'	Cleveland Norway Maple	5b
Acer platanoides 'Parkway'	Parkway Norway Maple	4a
Acer rubrum 'Red Sunset'	Red Sunset Maple	3b
Acer saccharum 'Caddo'	Caddo Sugar Maple	3b
Acer saccharum 'Commemoration'	Commemoration Sugar Maple	3b
Acer saccharum 'Green Mountain'	Green Mountain Sugar Maple	3b
Acer saccharum 'Legacy'	Legacy Sugar Maple	3b
Acer saccharum 'Majesty'	Majesty Sugar Maple	3b
Liquidambar styraciflua	Sweetgum	5b
Liquidambar styraciflua 'Moraine'	Moraine Sweetgum	5b
Liriodendron tulipifera	Tulip Poplar	5a

root plants come with no soil around their roots. Container or boxed plants are grown in a container, and all the soil and roots come with the plant. Balled and burlapped (B&B) plants are harvested from the field with a tree spade that removes a large part of the root system but retains the remaining roots with soil they were grown in within a burlap–covered ball.

Technical comments related to plant specifications are used only to call

TABLE 4-17   LARGE OVAL TREES WITH HEART-SHAPED LEAVES

		Cold Hardy to Zone
Cercidiphyllum japonicum	Katsura Tree	5a
Corylus columa	Turkish Filbert	5a
Tilia cordata 'Chancellor'	Chancellor Littleleaf Linden	3b
Tilia cordata 'Glenleven'	Glenleven Littleleaf Linden	3b
Tilia cordata 'Greenspire'	Greenspire Littleleaf Linden	3b
Tilia cordata 'Olympic'	Olympic Littleleaf Linden	3b
Tilia cordata 'Rancho'	Rancho Littleleaf Linden	3b
Tilia x euchlora	Crimean Linden	4b

TABLE 4-18   SMALL TREES WITH LOBED LEAVES

		Cold Hardy to Zone
Acer buergeranum	Trident Maple	6a
Acer campestre	Hedge Maple	5a
Acer tataricum ssp. ginnala	Amur Maple	3a
Acer tataricum	Tatarian Maple	3a
Acer truncatum	Shantung Maple	4a
Crataegus phaenopyrum	Washington Hawthorn	4b
Crataegus punctata inermis 'Ohio Pioneer'	Thornless Ohio Pioneer Hawthorn	4a
Crataegus viridis 'Winter King'	Winter King Hawthorn	5a
Sorbus intermedia	Swedish Mountain Ash	5

for something that is not standard, such as a greater than normal number of stems, a special pruning type, or a specific height to first branch.

Minimum-quality standards for root size, plant height, and branching of nursery-grown plants have been codified by the American Nursery and Landscape Association (ANLA) in *The American Standard for Nursery Stock* (ANSI Z60.1). All plants should be specified as adhering to ANLA standards as a minimum. This standard provides a uniform national specification with which the nursery trade is familiar. In addition, it is often worthwhile to specify other plant characteristics you feel are desirable to ensure good plant quality (see Appendix III). This allows you to reject a plant at the job site if it does not meet your stated specification. Many designers and municipalities have developed their own specifications to supplement the ANLA standards. The states of California and Florida have developed excellent statewide specifications that are worth evaluating.

Important features of the specification should include reasons a plant

TABLE 4-19   SELECTION FACTORS

Factors to Consider	Recommendations
Spatial constraints such as overhead wires, narrow setbacks, signage, frequent truck traffic	May require small trees or narrower crown shapes such as oval or columnar
Limited soil volume	Small trees
Screening of sight, sounds, wind, or heavy shade desired	Dense branching, possibly large trees
Trees growing with or near other plants such as turf grass or flower beds	Open branching
Canopy effect desired	Vase-shaped crowns
Formal effect desired	Columnar crowns

may be rejected, such as the presence of insects or disease, damage to the trunk or branches, a circling root system, poor crown symmetry, inadequate moisture in the root system upon delivery, or and desiccation.

REFERENCE CITED

Trowbridge, P., L. Mudrak et al. 1988. Landscape forms for mitigating winds on shoreline sites. National Endowment for the Arts and Cornell University, Ithaca, N.Y.

CHAPTER 5

TRANSPLANTING AND INITIAL CARE IN THE LANDSCAPE

A final stage in landscape establishment is when plants are installed or transplanted into the prepared site. All too often, little attention is paid to this crucial step compared with overall site design and plant selection. Even if all the preceding steps in landscape establishment (site assessment, plant selection, site remediation, and preparation) are carried out properly, transplanting practices and initial aftercare can make or break the eventual success of the landscape.

Although trees and shrubs often exhibit a remarkable ability to survive environmental stresses, transplanting can involve removing approximately 90 percent of the plants' root system (Watson and Himelick, 1997). The removal of so many roots makes the plant especially sensitive to water deficits until a reasonable regrowth of roots has occurred. Even a tree that is normally drought-tolerant may be susceptible to water deficits in some cases for several years after transplanting because its reduced root system will be unable to supply water to the leaves of the tree as efficiently as before.

After transplanting, the tree or shrub is said to be in a state of transplant shock, which can be seen as a drastically reduced growth of shoots and leaves. The shoot growth is reduced, as is the leaf area. First-season shoot growth after transplanting is often minimal—perhaps only a few centimeters—and new leaves may be less than half their normal size. This occurs because water uptake is reduced—but perhaps as important, the shoots may be responding to the lack of shoot-promoting hormones and nutrients synthesized and taken up by the root system. We know that new active white root growth is where most of the essential nutrients are taken up from the soil and where some plant hormones are produced. Until the root growth is reestablished and translocates its products to the shoots, their growth will remain stunted. Conversely, active shoot growth is necessary for continued root growth. Shoots and leaves produce sugars and hormones that nourish root growth. This interplay of root and shoot growth is severely disrupted during transplanting. Often it takes several years for a normal balance to be reestablished. Only then will normal shoot growth return and the plant can be said to be over transplant shock (Harris and Bassuk, 1993).

The purpose of using the best transplanting practices is to minimize this period of transplant shock. Only when the plant can be said to be established in the landscape will it fully exhibit the environmental tolerances it was selected for. Many factors influence transplant shock. Understanding these can help the landscape professional minimize this stressful period.

PLANT QUALITY AND NURSERY PRODUCTION PRACTICES

In Chapter 4, on page 133, criteria for good-quality plant materials were discussed. A well-grown plant showing a high degree of vigor, as evidenced by long annual increments of growth and healthy leaves, will recover from transplanting sooner than a slowly growing tree (Struve et al., 2000). Wherever possible, plants should be personally inspected and tagged at the nursery to ensure that well-grown specimens can be delivered. In addition, plants should be reinspected with the right to refuse them written into the specification, should they arrive at the planting site in unsatisfactory condition.

Individual plants should be selected that exhibit the characteristic form and canopy for the species and cultivar. Branch spacing and connections to the trunk should allow for the widest possible angles between the branch and the trunk and avoid clustering of branches emanating from one location. This branch clustering typically results in weak branch attachments to the trunk. If the characteristic form of the plant has a central leader, this should be in evidence. New pruning cuts that have not healed may be cause for rejecting a plant. The sample nursery stock specification below (Figure 5-1) provides a more detailed description of good-quality nursery stock.

METHODS OF PRODUCTION AND HARVEST

Most woody plants are available in one or more of three production methods: container-grown, balled and burlapped, and bare-root (Figures 5-2 and 5-3). The advantages of a container-grown or box-grown plant are that all the roots are intact during transplanting. The plants are typically grown in

Figure 5-1 SAMPLE NURSERY STOCK SPECIFICATION FOR SHADE TREES
(Source: Edward F. Gilman, 1997)

- Trees shall be freshly dug. No tree dug in a prior season or heeled-in trees will be accepted.
- The genus, species, and cultivar of all trees shall be clearly and legibly labeled in weather-resistant ink or embossed tag on the plant list and on each plant.
- Tree and ball or root size shall conform to ANSI Z60.1 (American Standard for Nursery Stock).
- Trees indicated as Balled and Burlapped (B&B) shall be wrapped in natural burlap only and jute twine. Wire baskets are acceptable.
- There shall be no roots greater than one-tenth the diameter of the trunk circling more than one-third the way around in the top half of the root ball. Roots larger than this may be cut provided they are smaller than one-third the trunk diameter. There shall be no kinked roots greater than one-fifth the trunk diameter. Roots larger than this can be cut provided they are less than one-third the trunk diameter.
- Trees should be rooted into the root ball so that soil or media remains intact and trunk and root ball move as one when lifted. The trunk should bend when gently pushed and not pivot at or below soil line.
- The point where the topmost root in the root ball emerges from the trunk shall be visible at the soil surface.
- There should be one dominant leader more or less straight to the top of the tree, with the largest branches spaced at least 6 inches apart. There can be a double leader in the top 10 percent of the tree.
- The tree canopy should be symmetrical, free of large voids, and typical of the species or cultivar. Crown ratio (distance from bottom of canopy to tree top/tree height) should be at least 60 percent.
- Branches should be less than two-thirds the trunk diameter, free of bark inclusions, and more or less radially distributed around the trunk.
- Trees greater than 1½ inches in caliper should be able to stand erect without a supporting stake.
- The trunk and main branches shall be free of wounds (except for properly made pruning wounds), damaged areas, scrapes, knots, bleeding, and signs of insects or disease. Trees shall not be pruned immediately prior to delivery.
- The [client or client's agent] has the right to select and tag trees at the nursery prior to the digging of any trees. If any of the above conditions are not met, trees may be rejected.

the same container they are shipped in so no root loss occurs. Generally, container plants are grown in a lightweight soilless medium such as composted bark or a mixture of peat and perlite that is easier to handle than field soil and encourages good aeration and root development. Theoretically, container-grown plants may be planted at any time the soil can be dug, even while the plants are actively growing, because all the roots are moved with the plant. Some plants that are initially harvested as bare-root plants are later grown as container plants once they are potted up.

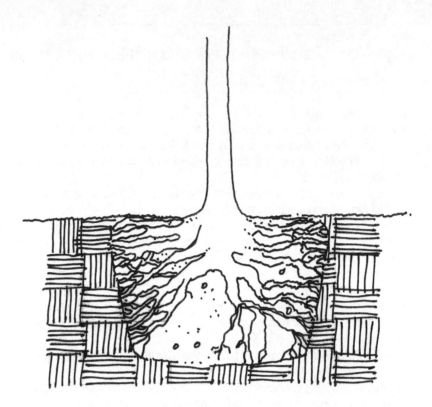

Figure 5-2 Sketch of the root flare in the root ball, visible at the soil surface at the time of transplanting.

Container-grown plants present several limitations. Too often, plants are grown for too long in the container and the root system becomes deformed with masses of pot-bound circling roots (Figure 5-4). When transplanted, these roots will continue to grow in a circular direction rather than into the soil adjacent to the planting bed. This will eventually reduce the plant's stability but, more importantly, reduce the soil volume that the roots may explore to take up water and nutrients. If possible, inspect a few sample root systems by removing plants from the containers to make sure this is not the case. Should the roots be deformed, they *may* be teased out of their circular pattern or the most intransigent ones cut to encourage rooting outward from the root ball upon transplanting (Watson and Himelick, 1997).

When possible, plants grown in containers should be transplanted while dormant to minimize water stress until new roots can grow into the surrounding soil. The lightweight planting mix that encourages aeration and root growth in an irrigated nursery yard holds comparatively little water when transplanted into soil. The large pores of the container medium hold little water, while the smaller pores of field soil hold onto water more readily. Container-grown root systems need to grow into field soil if they are to survive without constant watering. This is a good reason to minimize water stress for container plants and plant them when dormant. Although it is possible to transplant a container-grown plant while it is in full leaf and actively growing, it will need nearly daily monitoring for water status until

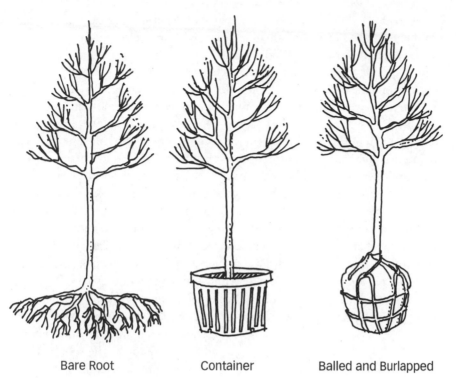

| Bare Root | Container | Balled and Burlapped |

Figure 5-3 Sketches of balled and burlapped, bare-root, and container planting stock.

the roots have grown into the surrounding soil. This puts a large burden on the landscape manager to guard against water deficits in newly planted trees and shrubs (Gilman et al., 1998).

Finally, many larger-size trees and shrubs may not be available as container-grown specimens. It is more common to find large container-grown

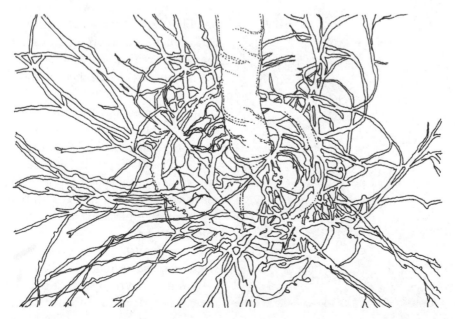

Figure 5-4 Sketch of circling roots caused by poorly grown container stock.

trees in the western and southern parts of North America, while smaller container-grown trees and shrubs are available in every region.

Balled and burlapped (B&B) plants are commonly grown in most of the country, aside from the far West. B&B harvesting means digging a tree or shrub from the field with a packed ball of earth around the roots. Although B&B trees may be dug by hand, more commonly a mechanical digger called a *tree spade* is used to dig them (Figure 5-5). These plants typically lose as much as 90 percent of the root system in the digging process and must be dug while plants are dormant to minimize stress (Figure 5-6). The advantages of B&B trees and shrubs are that large plants may be harvested this way. In specialized nurseries, trees up to 10 inches in caliper may be found B&B, although the great majority of trees are harvested below 4 inches in caliper. The roots are grown in and protected with field soil so there is less of a problem of root balls drying out than is found with containerized plants. Likewise, deformed root systems are less prevalent, although, increasingly, B&B plants are being dug with soil on top of where the true trunk-root connection exists. This sometimes occurs during cultivation in the nursery, when soil can be thrown up on top of the root system, or during the digging process itself, when several

Figure 5-5 Vermeer spade method of balled and burlapped plant materials.

inches of soil may be inadvertently added to the top of the root ball. This is a problem to check for, as few roots are taken in the digging process. If not corrected, roots may be stunted until they have grown closer to the surface (Gilman, 1997).

B&B trees may be stored at the job site if precautions are taken to prevent the root balls from drying out (Figure 5-7). The best way to do this is to group the trees with root balls touching, cover the root systems with bark mulch, and thoroughly irrigate them. It is critical that the root balls not dry out. Grouping the trees helps them shade each other and centralizes the storage and irrigation operations. Storage at the job site should be for the short term only or, preferably, not at all. Trees that experience water stress at this point are set back, more susceptible to attack from boring insects, and less able to overcome transplant shock.

Trees dug B&B are prone to water stress because so much of their root system is removed. It is best to plant them when dormant in early spring

Figure 5-6 Diagram showing the loss of the majority of tree roots when digging from the nursery to be balled and burlapped.

or in autumn (Watson and Himelick, 1982). Although properly stored B&B plants may be planted while in leaf, the risk of their experiencing water deficits is greater because of their limited root systems. Of course, evergreen trees are always in leaf, but they are in a more or less dormant state (no longer actively growing) in early autumn.

Trees dug B&B are extremely heavy, making handling difficult. A tree with a 24-inch-diameter root ball weighs approximately 300 pounds, while one with a 30-inch-diameter ball weighs 550 pounds. Moving these trees between nursery and job site requires heavy equipment and an experienced

Figure 5-7 Photograph of balled and burlapped plant materials stored at a construction site.

crew. ANLA standards for B&B trees specify minimum root ball diameter and depth for every tree height or caliper (Figure 5-8).

It is easy to plant B&B trees too deeply in the planting hole. You should always see the flare of the trunk where it meets the tree's root system above the ground after it has been planted. Because B&B trees may have additional soil placed over their roots in digging, the trunk flare may be hidden. This soil should be uncovered so that the roots at the top of the ball are at the new site grade. They may also be planted too deep because they are heavy. If the hole is dug and the tree found to be too low, it is difficult to place it a second time because of the tremendous weight of the tree ball. Always measure the depth of the root ball first and then check it against the depth of the hole before placing the tree. If the hole is too deep, replace soil and tamp it to eliminate the possibility of the tree settling in the hole.

Wire baskets and root ball coverings and ties also need to be considered when planting B&B trees. Wire baskets make B&B trees easier to handle and keep the balls more secure. However, once the tree is placed in the planting hole and secured with soil, the top half of the wired basket should be removed to prevent the possibility of the wires girdling the thick roots that will buttress the trunk of the tree as it grows (Figure 5-9). It is also possible to remove the entire wire basket if care is taken when doing so not to fracture the root ball. Once the wire basket is removed, repositioning the tree is

Figure 5-8	EXCERPT FROM AMERICAN STANDARD FOR NURSERY STOCK
	(ANSI Z60.1)

Purpose: Provide buyers and sellers with a common terminology in order to specify a minimum standard for nursery stock. The standard defines standard measurement techniques, proper relationships between tree height and caliper, and whether the root system is large enough for a particular size plant.

It does not provide buyers with any assurance of the health or quality of the nursery stock being specified or sold. The following is a synopsis of just part of ANSI standards as they apply to trees. For a more complete listing, the ANSI Z60.1 Standard is published by the American Nursery and Landscape Association, 1000 Vermont Avenue SW, Suite 300, Washington, D.C. 20005-4914.

Please note that caliper is measured at 6 inches from grade on trees equal to or less than 4 inches in caliper, whereas trees over 4 inches are measured at 12 inches from grade.

BARE-ROOT CALIPER, TREE HEIGHT, AND ROOT SPREAD

Caliper (inches)	Height (feet)	Minimum Root Spread (inches)
0.5	5–6	12
0.75	6–8	16
1.0	8–10	18
1.25	8–10	20
1.5	10–12	22
1.75	10–12	24
2.0	12–14	28
2.5	12–14	32
3.0	14–16	38

HEIGHT-TO-CALIPER RELATIONSHIP FOR MOST SHADE TREES

Caliper (inches)	Average Height Range (feet)	Maximum Height (feet)
0.5	5–6	8
0.75	6–8	10
1.0	8–10	11
1.25	8–10	12
1.5	10–12	14
1.75	10–12	14
2.0	12–14	16
2.5	12–14	16
3.0	14–16	18
3.5	14–16	18
4.0	16–18	22
5.0	18 and up	26

Figure 5-8 *(Continued)*

BALL DIAMETER FOR MULTISTEMMED TREES

Average Height (feet)	Minimum Diameter Ball (inches)	Average Height (feet)	Minimum Diameter Ball (inches)
4	14	12	28
5	16	14	32
6	18	16	38
7	20	18	42
8	22	20	48
10	24		

HEIGHT AND ROOT SPREAD FOR BARE-ROOT TREES

Caliper (inches)	Average Height Range (feet)	Minimum Root Spread (inches)
0.5	5–6	12
0.75	6–8	16
1.0	8–10	18
1.25	8–10	20
1.5	10–12	22
1.75	10–12	24
2.0	12–14	28
2.5	12–14	32
3.0	14–16	38

BALL SIZES FOR NURSERY-GROWN SHADE TREES

Caliper (inches)	Minimum Diameter Ball (inches)	Caliper (inches)	Minimum Diameter Ball (inches)
0.5	12	3.5	38
0.75	14	4.0	42
1.0	16	4.5	48
1.25	18	5.0	54
1.5	20	5.5	57
1.75	22	6.0	60
2.0	24	7.0	70
2.5	28	8.0	80
3.0	32		

Figure 5-8 *(Continued)*

CONTAINER SIZES FOR TREES

Tree Height or Caliper	Container Size
12 inches	#1
18 inches	#1
2 feet	#1
3 feet	#1
4 feet	#2
5 feet	#5
6 feet	#5
7 feet	#7
8 feet or 1.25 inches caliper	#10
1.5 inches	#15
1.75 inches	#25
2.0 inches	#25
2.5 inches	#25

BOX SIZES FOR TREES

Caliper* (inches)	Box size (inches)
1.25–1.5	20
1.5–2.0	24
2.0–3.0	30
2.5–3.5	36
3.0–4.0	42
3.5–4.5	48
4.0–5.0	60

*Caliper varies according to specific tree characteristics.

difficult. Other root coverings such as twine and excess burlap at the top of the ball should be removed as well so as not to hinder root or trunk growth (Figure 5-10). Never accept a B&B tree in anything other than natural biodegradable burlap. Synthetic tree ball coverings may severely hinder root development.

Bare-root trees and shrubs are limited to smaller sizes, generally less than 2 inches in caliper for trees and under 36 inches in height or spread for shrubs. Bare-root plants are dug without soil around their roots, so the biggest constraint is preventing the roots from drying out. Bare-root plants are relatively inexpensive, lightweight, and easy to ship and store. When they are dug with an undercutting U blade, as much as 200 percent more roots are harvested in a bare root plant than in a plant dug with a tree spade, B&B (Figure 5-11). It is easy to plant bare-root plants at their proper depth because there is no soil to visually obscure the root-trunk flare interface.

However, the risk of the roots drying out requires knowledgeable handling for bare-root planting to be successful. Bare-root deciduous trees should be planted only in the dormant state, either before leafing out in the spring or after leaf fall in the autumn. Evergreens are rarely specified to be planted bare root, except for small seedlings. Recent work done at

Figure 5-9 Photograph of root flare, girdled by wire basket left on at transplanting.

Cornell University shows that fall-planted bare-root trees grow better during their first growing season than spring-planted bare-root trees. A new method for ensuring that bare-root trees don't dry out between the nursery and planting site was also developed at Cornell. Many communities are trying bare-root tree planting because these trees are lightweight—about 25 pounds—and lend themselves to planting by volunteers (Buckstrup and Bassuk, 2000).

Figure 5-10 Non-biodegradable twine left on at transplanting, girdling tree.

(a)

(b)

Figure 5-11 Bare-root trees (a) under-cut and lifted with a *U* blade and the resulting larger root system, (b) with an example of bare roots after digging.

SOME TREES ARE MORE DIFFICULT
TO TRANSPLANT SUCCESSFULLY THAN OTHERS

It has long been noted that some trees are easier to transplant than others, and it is no surprise that easy transplanters are found more often in the planted landscape. The reason trees differ in this way is unclear. Part of the issue relates to the type of root system the plant has. A highly fibrous rooted system with many thin, branched roots has greater surface area and more potential for water uptake than a coarsely branched root system. Most nurseries manage their plants to produce a more fibrous root system by either root pruning or transplanting. This may reduce overall root weight but does produce a root system with greater numbers of fine roots. This has been found to aid in transplanting success (Figure 5-12). There are undoubtedly other reasons for the differences in transplanting success between species. Some trees may have greater difficulty taking up enough water to meet the leaves' demand after roots have been cut. Whatever the reason, good water management in the root zone after transplanting is the key factor in plant survival. Tree size or age has also been shown to be an important factor in determining transplant success, with the smaller or younger trees establishing more easily (Harris and Bassuk, 1994; Watson and Himelick, 1997).

The trees in Table 1-5 have been found difficult to transplant regardless of planting methods.

TREE SIZE

As a rule, smaller trees transplant more successfully than larger trees. Growth rate is not generally affected by plant size until the tree is mature and moving into old age, when the growth rate slows. For trees of a size that is typically transplanted, growth rate is not unduly different in a 1-inch- or 4-inch-caliper tree. Trees also have a characteristic ratio of root growth to shoot growth. This balance is upset during the transplanting process, when much of the root system is lost. Watson and Himelick (1997), using a root growth rate of 18 inches per year, calculated that a 4-inch-caliper tree and a 10-inch-caliper tree planted at the same time will be the same size 13 years after planting, all environmental conditions being equal. The 10-inch tree needs to replace much more root system to achieve root and shoot balance than does the 4-inch tree, even though similar percentages of roots were initially removed. The 4-inch tree should have reestablished its original root to shoot ratio in 5 years and thereafter put on a significant amount of growth, whereas the 10-inch tree will take 13 years to replace the roots lost in transplanting. Not only will the smaller tree catch up with the larger tree but also the 10-inch tree will be more subject to drought stress because of its impaired root system during those 13 years.

A reasonable rule of thumb can be given as 1 year of reestablishment for every inch of caliper until a tree is said to be no longer in transplant shock. Therefore, a 1½-inch-caliper tree will probably overcome transplant shock

Figure 5-12 CORNELL BARE ROOT TRANSPLANTING METHOD
(Adapted from Buckstrup et al., 1999)

WHY TRANSPLANTING IS TRAUMATIC

Whether from a nursery field to the city tree lawn or just from one place in your yard to another, it's the roots that suffer when trees are transplanted. Consider this: Shade tree roots are found primarily in the top 12 inches of soil. Tiny absorbing roots, responsible for most of the tree's intake of water and nutrients, are in the top several inches of soil. Roots not only grow horizontally beyond the drip line; there often is a higher percentage of them beyond the drip line than within it.

An unbelievable 90 percent of tree roots are routinely left behind in the nursery at the time of harvest. The fine absorbing roots that are harvested are easily broken off, damaged, and desiccated. Water stress, resulting in part from the tremendous reduction in root mass, is the main reason transplanted trees fail.

WHY BARE ROOT?

The three main nursery production methods are balled and burlapped (B&B), bare root, and container grown. Container nurseries are less common in the northern United States, where low winter temperatures restrict their use to smaller-sized plant material. Container-grown trees are generally the most expensive of the three methods and are subject to circling roots that can reduce a tree's vigor. While the lightweight media used in containers is useful for free drainage out of pots, once in the ground the medium may lose its water too readily to the surrounding native soil.

Conventional wisdom says that B&B production is superior to bare root because a protective ball of soil surrounds the roots at harvest. However, we find that for many species the positive attributes of bare root planting outweigh the perceived B&B edge. The three best arguments for the bare-root method:

1. *You can plant more trees more cheaply.* Bare-root trees are one-third to one-half less expensive than B&B trees. Because they are so much lighter and many more can fit on the bed of a truck, they are cheaper to ship. Planting a bare-root tree costs virtually nothing when done by volunteers with shovels (Figure 5-13). The cost of planting a B&B tree, by con-

Figure 5-13
Volunteers picking up and carrying bare-root trees, prepared in plastic bags, to planting sites.

Figure 5-12 *(Continued)*

trast, is markedly higher because the sheer weight of the ball requires machinery and machinery operators to load the tree, unload it, and to get it in the ground.

2. *You will take more roots along.* A simple study was done at Cornell to compare the amount of roots in a B&B ball with the root mass on a bare-root harvested tree of the same size and species. The bare-root trees had 200 percent more roots. The reason for this? The harvesting machinery for bare-root trees digs a much larger root system than the tree spade used for B&B digging.

3. *You'll avoid the deadly planting-too-deep syndrome.* Frequently, when a newly transplanted B&B tree dies, it is because it was planted too deep. When the fine absorbing roots are buried too far down, they can't access oxygen and the tree suffocates. Trees should be planted so their root flare begins just at the soil line. With B&B trees, the soil may be mounded on the trunk, making it difficult to see the buried root flare. On the other hand, the root flare of bare-root trees is obvious and the proper planting depth easy to determine.

Figure 5-14 Bare-root trees being dipped into a hydro-gel slurry, then placed in plastic bags for shipping.

Figure 5-12 *(Continued)*

When you plant bare root, you can spot girdling roots and remove them before you plant; with B&B trees, girdled roots can be buried. With bare-root trees you won't rob nurseries of their valuable field soil, and there is no ball of nursery soil meeting the city soil with potential interface problems in terms of water movement. For municipalities with limited tree budgets, the low cost of the bare-root method is the most critical factor. *With a budget of $500, volunteers can plant eight to ten trees a year.* So why hasn't everyone switched to bare-root planting? With municipal tree planting there is an inevitable holding period between digging the trees and planting them. During this period, root desiccation is the most critical disadvantage to planting bare-root trees. In the past, people put wet straw around the roots or coated them in a mud slurry. These methods did not prove satisfactory or practical; the straw did not protect fine roots adequately, and the mud slurry tended to dry out and chip off.

We use a synthetic, nontoxic product called *hydrogel* to solve the desiccation problem for that critical time between digging and replanting. Hydrogels are polymers that look like table sugar when dry but can hold several hundred times their weight in water. Fine grades and coarse grades are available; be sure to use the fine grades because they give much better coverage of the absorbing roots. We dip tree roots in a hydrogel slurry and immediately bag them in plastic to protect the roots from drying out until the tree is planted no more than a week later (Figure 5-14).

AT LEAST THREE MONTHS BEFORE PLANTING DAY

- Contact your local wholesale nursery growers. Find out who does bare-root digging and request that they let you set up a dipping operation the day the trees are dug. Some nurseries, such as Schichtel's near Buffalo, New York, are equipped to do the dipping themselves. Our hope is that consumer-driven demand will prompt more nurseries to offer this service.
- Place an order for 1½- to 2-inch-caliper trees that are good bare-root prospects. Caliper size greater than 2 inches is not recommended for bare-root transplanting. The digging should occur during the dormant season for your area. In the northeast United States, we feel dormant bare-root trees can be dug in late October or early November for fall planting, mid-April for spring planting. Trees should not be leafed out. In fall, most dormant trees have lost their leaves; in spring, dormant trees have not yet broken bud.
- Order and gather the supplies: fine-grade hydrogel, plastic bags, tree tags, shovels. Consider investing in tree irrigation bags. They hold 20 gallons of water and slowly release it to the roots, saving watering time and aiding in tree establishment.
- Assess available planting sites. The more comprehensive your site assessment, the better your tree will be matched and will thrive in its location. If overhead wires are present, consider planting a small species, one that matures no taller than 30 feet. Make sure there is adequate soil volume for the mature tree size.
- Cluster sites for ease of planting. Select 20 percent more sites than you need, since some sites will not work out. Write or speak to the property owners near the sites (including those near the alternate sites) and get their OK. Inform them of what's going to happen and invite their participation.

Figure 5-12 *(Continued)*

THE WEEK BEFORE PLANTING DAY

- Call to have underground utilities marked for the sites you plan to use. Call directory assistance and ask for your state's underground locating service.
- Prepare aluminum marking tags for your trees. Label each tree with its intended address before it gets dipped and bagged so that when volunteers pick up the trees to plant, they can simply go to the address on the label.
- Work with the nursery to have your trees dug within 24 hours of your arrival. If they absolutely must be dug earlier, they should be kept in a cool, dark place and watered frequently. Bare-root trees should never be allowed to dry out! Verify that the nursery will tie the branches with twine to prevent breakage in transit.

DIPPING DAY AT THE NURSERY

- Take an enclosed truck or a truck that can be tarped to transport the trees after dipping. Bring hydrogel, buckets, metal tags, and plastic bags. If the nursery can't supply a large (50–100-gallon) plastic vat for mixing the hydrogel and water, bring a vat and something to stir with. The vat should be much wider than it is tall to allow for the wide-spreading root system of bare-root trees. We use durable plastic horse troughs.
- Follow the manufacturer's recommendations for root dips; we use about 15 ounces of hydrogel per 25 gallons of water. Allow 30 minutes to an hour for the hydrogel to become fully hydrated in the water; it should be the consistency of thick gravy when you start dipping.
- Dip the root system in the slurry. Don't shake the hydrogel off the roots; you want to leave as much coating on the roots as possible. Immediately slip the roots into a large, pleated plastic bag and tie to the trunk.
- After bagging, trees should be stored in a cool, shaded place until ready to be transported. Stack trees in the truck bed, being careful not to injure bark or break branches. Water down the bagged trees to create humidity in the truck bed. Close the truck bed or securely tarp it for your trip back to the city. Upon arrival, trees should be stored in a cool, shaded building until ready to plant.

PLANTING DAY

On the day of planting, bring trees out of storage and lay them down in a central, shady staging area. Keep them out of the sun. Remind volunteers about underground utility considerations and instruct them on proper planting.

Figure 5-12   *(Continued)*

- Carry the tree, with roots still bagged, to the planting site. Lay the tree on its side and remove all string and nursery plastic flags. Leave only the aluminum marking tag; make sure it is attached loosely to prevent girdling.
- Prune only dead or broken branches. At this stage, the tree needs all the potential leaves it can get.
- Dig the planting hole wide and shallow. Do not loosen the soil that will be underneath the root system; instead, concentrate on creating loose soil horizontally for the spreading roots. The hole should be 2 to 3 times wider in all directions than the root spread. A hint for loosening soil: Use the hole you are digging as a bowl to first break up the soil clods, then shovel the loosened soil out.
- Turf surrounding the tree should be completely removed so it doesn't compete with the newly planted tree for water.
- Remove the tree from the plastic bag and stand it upright in the hole. Plant the tree so that the beginning of the root flare is visible at soil level. It is critical not to plant the tree too deep. Lay your shovel across the hole to see where the shovel meets the root flare and adjust the planting depth accordingly. If you anticipate settling of the soil, plant a little high. It is better to plant too high than too deep.
- Check to see that the tree is plumb, then backfill with the soil you removed. When you've replaced half of the backfill, water the hole to help collapse air pockets. Alternatively, use the opposite, wood end of your shovel to gently poke out air pockets. Finish backfilling and gently firm soil. Make sure the soil is not mounded against the trunk and that the beginning of the root flare is showing above ground.
- Mulch over the entire rooting area with 3 to 4 inches of wood chips or shredded bark mulch. The farther out you mulch, the better. Don't let mulch mound against the trunk, as this could create a favorable environment for fungi.
- Attach a tree gator bag, making sure the tape has been removed from all trickle holes. Fill bags at least once a week during dry spells. Fertilizer is not recommended for newly planted trees.
- Staking is not necessary and can even be detrimental for most young trees. The exceptions: an extremely windy site, a tree with an unusually small root system, an unusually large sail/canopy relative to a tree's root system, or a tree whose trunk is seriously bowed. A final reason to stake is to protect trees in high traffic areas where vandalism is feared. Young trees are less likely to be victimized when staked.
- Initial maintenance: Mulch should be maintained at a depth of 3 to 4 inches. If you employ stakes or guy wires, remove these devices after one or two years to prevent girdling of the tree.

Figure 5-12 *(Continued)*

Good success has occurred transplanting bare-root the following trees (both spring and fall):

TREES WE HAVE SUCCESSFULLY PLANTED USING THIS METHOD

Acer campestre	Hedge Maple
Acer x freemanii	Freeman Maple
Acer platanoides	Norway Maple
Acer pseudoplatanus	Sycamore Maple
Acer rubrum	Red Maple
Acer saccharum	Sugar Maple
Acer truncatum	Shantung Maple
Alnus glutinosa	European Alder
Amelanchier spp.	Serviceberry
Catalpa speciosa	Northern Catalpa
Cercidiphyllum japonicum	Katsura Tree
Cladrastis kentukea	Yellow Wood
Cornus mas	Cornelian Cherry
Cornus racemosa	Gray Dogwood
Fraxinus spp.	Ash
Gleditsia triacanthos	Honey Locust
Gymnocladus dioicus	Kentucky Coffee Tree
Malus spp.	Crabapple
Parrotia persica	Ironwood
Platanus x acerifolia	London Plane Tree
Prunus 'Accolade'	Accolade Flowering Cherry
Prunus virginiana 'Canada Red'	Canada Red Chokecherry
Pyrus calleryana	Callery Pear
Pyrus ussuriensis	Ussurian Pear
Quercus bicolor	Swamp White Oak
Quercus rubra	Red Oak
Robinia pseudoacacia cultivars 'Purple Robe,' 'Pyramidalis,' 'Globosum,' 'Bessoniana,' 'Twisty Baby'	Black Locust
Sophora japonica	Scholar Tree
Syringa reticulata	Japanese Tree Lilac
Tilia cordata	Littleleaf Linden
Ulmus americana and elm hybrids except 'Frontier'	Elm
Zelkova serrata	Japanese Zelkova

Figure 5-12 *(Continued)*

The following trees were better transplanted only in the fall. These trees are moderately difficult to transplant bare-root.

Alnus glutinosa	European Alder
Betula spp.	Birch
Celtis occidentalis	Hackberry
Cercis canadensis	Redbud
Corylus colurna	Turkish Filbert
Crataegus crus-galli inermis	Thornless Cockspur Hawthorn
Crataegus viridis 'Winter King'	Winter King Hawthorn
Prunus subhirtella var. autumnalis	Flowering Cherry
Quercus robur	English Oak
Quercus velutina	Black Oak
Tilia tomentosa	Silver Linden

These trees are difficult to successfully transplant with the bare-root method.

Carpinus spp.	Hornbeam
Crataegus phaenopyrum	Washington Hawthorn
Ginkgo biloba	Ginkgo
Liriodendron tulipifera	Tulip Poplar
Ostrya virginiana	American Hop Hornbeam
Quercus coccinea	Scarlet Oak
Quercus imbricaria	Shingle Oak
Quercus macrocarpa	Bur Oak
Quercus prinus	Chestnut Oak
Taxodium distichum	Bald Cypress
Ulmus 'Frontier'	Frontier Elm

in about 2 years. In its third year in the ground, it will begin to grow more strongly if environmental conditions are favorable. In warm climates with a year-round growing season, the time to reestablishment is reduced. Tree species also interacts with tree age to determine transplant success. An easy-to-transplant 1½-inch tree may take 2 years to establish; a difficult-to-transplant tree may take an additional year or more (Lauderdale et al., 1995; Struve et al., 2000; Harris and Bassuk, 1993).

Transplanting objectives are to minimize water deficits or waterlogging and to encourage new root growth while the tree is reestablishing a normal root–to–shoot ratio (Gilman, 1990) (Figure 5-15).

TABLE 5-1   TREES DIFFICULT TO TRANSPLANT

Scientific Name	Common Name
Acer buergeranum	Trident Maple
Amelanchier spp.	Serviceberry
Asimina triloba	Pawpaw
Betula spp.	Birch
Carpinus betulus	European Hornbeam
Carpinus caroliniana	Musclewood
Carya spp.*	Hickory
Corylus colurna	Turkish Filbert
Crataegus spp.	Hawthorn
Diospyros virginiana*	Persimmon
Fagus spp.	Beech
Juglans spp.*	Walnut
Liriodendron tulipifera	Tulip Poplar
Liquidambar styraciflua	Sweetgum
Magnolia spp.	Magnolia
Nyssa sylvatica*	Tupelo
Ostrya virginiana	American Hop Hornbeam
Oxydendrum arboreum	Sourwood
Quercus alba*	White Oak
Quercus coccinea	Scarlet Oak
Quercus imbricaria	Shingle Oak
Quercus macrocarpa	Bur Oak
Quercus prinus	Chestnut Oak
Quercus rubra	Red Oak
Quercus velutina	Black Oak
Sassafras albidum*	Sassafras
Taxodium distichum	Bald Cypress
Tilia tomentosa	Silver Linden

* Particularly difficult to transplant

THE PROCESS OF HANDLING AND STORAGE

Much can go wrong for the tree before it ever gets to the landscape site. The tree should be handled by the root ball or container, never by the trunk, as the flexing of the trunk with the heavy root ball can sever root-trunk connections that cannot be seen. Trunk protectors on B&B trees help minimize

Figure 5-15 New white root growth from roots severed during transplanting.

the potential for scrapes during shipping. Plants should always be delivered in closed or tarped trucks to reduce desiccation to the tree. Even in the dormant state, trees can lose a significant amount of water through the bark if left uncovered. For the same reason, it is also important to avoid overheating the trees in transit. At the job site, plants must be kept well watered until planting. Store them in a shaded area if possible (see Figure 5-7).

Plants should be inspected before they are accepted. All plants should be labeled with species and cultivar. Plants that are damaged or unhealthy after transit should not be accepted, and plant sizes and conformation to ANLA specifications should be checked.

PLANTING PROCEDURE

The site should be prepared as discussed in Chapter 3 to correct any soil problems if necessary. Compaction and poor drainage are the two most important issues to correct in order for the tree to get off to a good start. Dig a planting area no deeper than the root ball (Figure 5-16) but 2 to 3 times wider than the spread of the root ball or bare roots (Figure 5-17). If establishing a bed of shrubs, work the entire site and plant into the prepared soil at the desire spacing.

If the soil drains poorly and cannot be further ameliorated, plant the tree or shrub high, with approximately one-third of the root ball above existing and surrounding grade. Feather the backfill soil to form a gradual slope back to grade.

Make sure that surface drainage does not collect in the planting hole in a poorly draining site. Avoid low spots for planting unless you are planting into an exceptionally well-draining sandy soil. Make sure the bottom of the hole

is firm and level or even slightly raised so as not to encourage excess water to pool there. A firm base at the bottom of the planting hole prevents sinking and shifting of the tree after planting. The wider the soil can be prepared prior to transplanting to encourage root growth, the more successful the eventual plant reestablishment.

SUMMARY OF TRANSPLANTING TECHNIQUES

Consider amending the entire planting site or bed before planting, as was covered in Chapter 3. Amendments should never be limited to the planting hole. For B&B plants, loosen the twine around the trunk and check that the trunk-root connection is just under the surface. If the roots cannot be felt, gently remove soil from the top of the root ball until the topmost roots are just under the surface. Once the hole is dug and its depth checked, place the plant in it, making sure it is not too deep. Place a shovel handle across the planting hole and make sure the trunk-root connection is at or slightly above the shovel handle. Remove at least the top half of the wire basket for a B&B plant after the bottom of the root ball has been

Figure 5-16 Measuring depth of planting pit relative to tree ball.

secured with soil. Fill in with loose, crumbly soil around the remainder of the root system, tamping gently as it is being filled to remove air pockets. Good soil-root contact and a few air pockets are essential to maximizing water uptake. The best way to settle the soil is to thoroughly water the plant in, regardless of season.

Any excess burlap and all ties should be removed before finishing the backfilling process, as well as twine and any ties associated with the B&B process. Materials that are not quickly biodegradable carry the potential for girdling, especially on fast-growing trees (see Figure 5-10).

In a container-grown plant, the procedure is much the same except that the container is removed with the least disruption to the root system

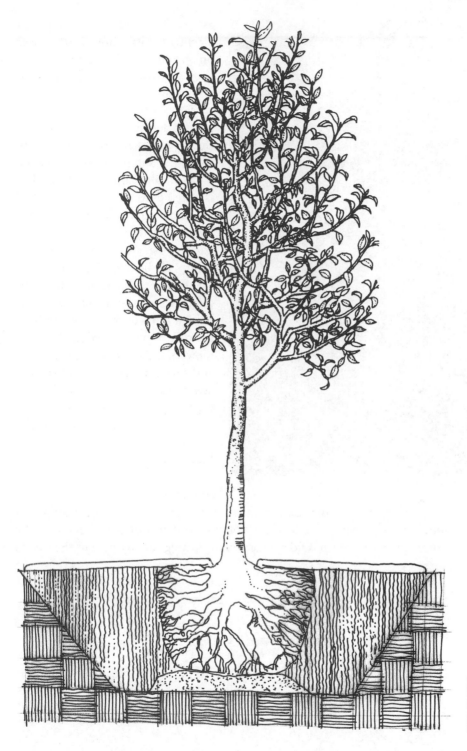

Figure 5-17 Planting pit 3 times the width of root spread at time of transplanting.

Figure 5-18
Appropriate guying techniques.

as possible. Before planting, any circling roots should be teased out or cut to change their direction of growth. Reorient the circling roots away from the stem.

For a bare-root plant, dig the hole to accommodate 2 to 3 times the spread of the root system and the tree planted, as in Figure 5-17.

With all plants, after the plant is watered in, a 3- to 4-inch layer of organic mulch should be added at least to the dimensions of the prepared hole. When planting in a group or bed, mulch the entire planting area. No mulch should be piled against the trunk of the tree. Mulch reduces moisture loss from the soil, provides a barrier between mowers and the tree, reduces weed and turf competition, and moderates soil temperatures. In time, an organic mulch breaks down to add organic matter to the soil, which improves soil structure, increases beneficial microorganisms, and provides a better balance of moisture retention and aeration.

Prune only dead, diseased, broken, or crossing branches at planting. It is important to leave as much of the potential leaf area of the tree to feed the regrowing root system. Old advice about pruning the top part of the tree to

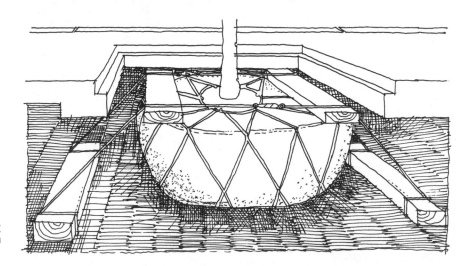

Figure 5-19
Below-grade guying using the dead men method.

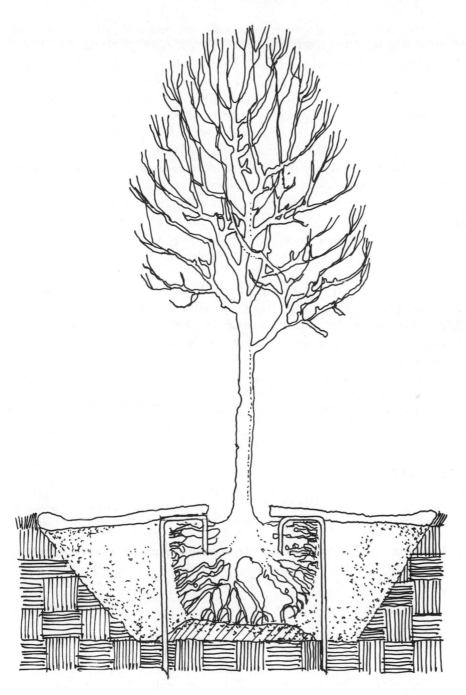

Figure 5-20
Below-grade guying
using tree staples.

compensate for root loss during transplanting only slows tree establishment further (Ranney et al., 1989). The most critical thing that can be done for the plant after transplanting is preventing the root system from becoming too dry or waterlogged. Usually, 1 inch of water per week during the grow-ing season is adequate in other than a very sandy soil. In a sandy site, 1 inch twice a week would be better.

Staking and guying of trees is necessary only where the tree cannot stand on its own, in a particularly windy site, or where the branches are out of proportion to the root ball and the sail effect might move the trunk away from being perpendicular to grade. Trees should never be rigidly staked but rather a stake and guy system should allow the trunk to move somewhat (Figure 5-18). This movement has been shown to strengthen the trunk when compared to one rigidly staked. Guy wires should be removed after one growing season (Watson and Himelick, 1997).

Underground guying is also possible where some support is necessary, but an aboveground system would cause a potential tripping hazard. One system for underground guying includes installing two 2×4 pieces of lumber over the root ball and placing two anchoring guy wires over the boards and anchored deep in the adjacent soil (Figure 5-19). Another method of stabilizing the root ball is to use a technique that staples the ball into the ground (Figure 5-20).

Wrapping tree trunks to reduce frost cracking or to prevent sunscald has not been shown to be effective with materials currently on the market. Temperature fluctuations under tree wrap have been shown to be greater than trunks with no wrap. In addition, insect infestations can be a problem under tree wraps.

In summary, write a good specification for planting at the site that covers the acceptance of plant material and includes a guarantee for at least one year (see Appendix III for sample specification).

REFERENCES CITED

Barton, A.J., and C.S. Walsh. 2000. Effects of transplanting on water relations and canopy development in *Acer*. *Journal of Environmental Horticulture* 189(4): 202–206.

Buckstrup, M., and N. Bassuk. 2000. Transplanting success of balled and burlapped versus bare-root trees in the urban landscape. *Journal of Arboriculture* 26(6): 298–308.

Buckstrup, M., N.L. Bassuk, and A. Hillman. 1999. Creating the urban forest: The BareRoot method. http://www.hort.cornell.edu/department/faculty/bassuk/uhi/bareroot.htm

Gilman, E.F. 1990. Tree root growth and development: Response to culture, management and planting. *Journal of Environmental Horticulture* 8(4): 220–227.

———. 1997. Sample nursery stock specification for shade trees. Adapted from *Trees for urban and suburban landscapes*. Albany, N.Y.: Delmar. http://hort.ifas.ufl.edu/woody/planting/

Gilman, E.F., R.J. Black, and B. Dehgan. 1998. Irrigation volume and frequency and tree size affect establishment rate. *Journal of Arboriculture* 24(1): 1–9.

Harris, J.R., and N. Bassuk. 1993. Tree planting fundamentals. *Journal of Arboriculture* 19(2): 64–70.

———. 1994. Seasonal effects on transplantability of scarlet oak, green ash, Turkish hazelnut and tree lilac. *Journal of Arboriculture* 20(6): 310–317.

———. 1995. The effect of drought and phenological stage at transplanting on root hydraulic conductivity, growth indices and photosynthesis of Turkish hazelnut. *Journal of Environmental Horticulture* 13(1): 11–14.

Harris, J.R., N.L., Bassuk, R.W. Zobel, and T.H. Whitlow. 1995. Root and shoot growth periodicity of green ash, scarlet oak, Turkish hazelnut and tree lilac. *Journal of the American Society of Horticultural Science* 120(3): 211–216.

Lauderdale, D.M., C.H. Gilliam, D.J. Eakes, G.J. Keever, and A.H. Chappelka. 1995. Tree transplant size influences post-transplant growth, gas exchange, and leaf water potential of 'October Glory' red maple. *Journal of Environmental Horticulture* 13(4): 178–181.

Ranney, T.G., N.L. Bassuk, and T.H. Whitlow. 1989. Effect of transplanting practices on growth and water relations of 'Colt' cherry trees during reestablishment. *Journal of Environmental Horticulture* 7(1): 41–45.

Struve, D.K., L. Burchfield, and C. Maupin. 2000. Survival and growth of transplanted large- and small-caliper red oaks. *Journal of Arboriculture* 26(30): 162–169.

Watson, G.W., and E.B. Himelick. 1982. Seasonal variation in root regeneration of transplanted trees. *Journal of Arboriculture* 8(12): 304–310.

———. 1997. *Principles and practice of planting trees and shrubs.* Savoy, Ill.: International Society of Arboriculture.

CHAPTER 6

SITE PRESERVATION AND MANAGEMENT

One area of landscape construction that is rarely documented well as part of the construction document development is site preparation and landscape preservation. Even when good site preservation methods and techniques are incorporated into construction drawings, on-site methods and management must be employed to save vegetation and reduce impacts on related site features.

PRESERVING EXISTING TREES

Despite the high level of failure in preserving on-site trees and vegetation during construction processes, vegetation preservation and building activities can be compatible. To successfully preserve vegetation during construction, a variety of site-specific analyses and resultant protective strategies must be employed. The strategies for the preservation of trees during construction require the coordinated efforts of developers, landscape architects, architects, and municipal officials as well as contractors.

Vegetation protection and preservation must start well before construction begins. Prior to any site design, vegetation communities as well as individual trees should be evaluated relative to the construction activities planned. A site survey that specifically locates all vegetation being considered for preservation as well as for removal is essential. Far too often, offering only general locations of vegetation can unintentionally put it in the path of construction. Vegetation should also be considered relative to its rare, unique, and scarce designations. This is important not only for ethical reasons and environmental concerns but also because such vegetation will require identification and documentation in state and local environment impact review as well as local site plan evaluations.

Vegetation should also be documented when it occurs on steep slopes, especially when it helps hold soil in place. Removing such vegetation may increase stormwater runoff volumes and simultaneously cause soil erosion. Vegetation should also be considered as it contributes to wildlife habitat and food sources. This may be difficult to assess, as habitat is not usually restricted to a specific site or to any particular time of day or month of the year. Habitat assessment should be developed by a specialist or confirmed from prior documentation. Habitat documentation should occur, when practicable, over an entire year.

Views and vistas that vegetation helps create should also be considered. It is well documented that we value mature vegetation, which adds real monetary value to a site. Consequently, the quality and views that existing trees create must be evaluated both for real estate values and environmental review. Vegetation can also have cultural and historic value. It is essential to understand the historical development of any site under consideration to determine the significance of existing vegetation. Local, regional, and state records should be reviewed to determine vegetation significance as well as documented unique natural areas.

The considerations outlined above are essential when developing a vegetation assessment for any site prior to design and related construction activities. The health, vigor, and significance of vegetation are essential to document at the beginning of a design and construction review process. These assessment criteria and associated methods are covered in greater depth later in this chapter.

An overview of tree protection techniques should be considered to establish as thorough an assessment as possible of plant impacts relative to construction. See Figure 6-1 for detailed information on this topic.

POSSIBLE CONSTRUCTION ACTIVITIES AND RELATED DAMAGE TO TREES

Most of the more serious damage to trees occurs below the soil surface. Below-grade impacts on vegetation regularly include the general compaction of soils; stripping of the surface soil layer; subsurface excavations that sever roots; changes in surface stormwater flow that increase or decrease soil moisture and, potentially, the local water table; changes in soil chemistry and toxicity due to truck washouts and on-site material spills; and loading soils with heavy piles of construction materials that crush and kill roots. The aboveground damage to trees is much more obvious but no less deadly. Mechanical damage to trees, including bark removal, broken branches, and scorched foliage, is quite common. Adding soil above the existing soil surface and above roots, both in the short term and permanently, reduces oxygen to the root system and may create a layer impervious to water and oxygen above the roots. Removing large amounts of vegetation from a tree grove or forested area can leave the remaining vegetation weak and unsupported; then it can bend and be easily damaged by wind and solar exposure.

The likely damage to vegetation due to construction activities should be thought about in some detail. The most insidious damage to trees comes from the compaction of soil around the root zone. As described earlier in this text, tree roots are, in general, superficial in the soil, often in the top 2 feet and extending well beyond the canopy of the tree. The only way to significantly and economically eliminate soil compaction is to fence the zone of root extension beyond the area of the tree canopy or tree protection zone, as described in Figure 6-1. Fencing should be structurally significant—wood posts and timbers or chain link—so it is not easily taken down or moved during the construction process (Figure 6-2). Commercially available plastic fencing, widely used in the construction trade, is generally unacceptable. While it is easy to install and inexpensive, it is also easily moved or removed during construction, leaving trees vulnerable to equipment and materials storage under canopies; this crushes and destroys roots, although this is not apparent or visible during a site inspection (Figures 6-3 and 6-4). While other documented methods for root protection include placing 12 inches or more of wood chips over tree roots to distribute construction compaction, this surface treatment is unsatisfactory for traction of heavy equipment and must be replenished during the construction process. It also allows for the possibility of mechanical damage to tree trunks and branches (Figure 6-5).

Regrading around trees, both removing soil from and adding soil to the root zone, can damage roots mechanically. The stripping of soil, even a few inches around trees, can remove important superficial roots (Figure 6-6). In fact, removing soil anywhere near a tree canopy or adjacent to plant masses can remove critical roots. Technical grading plans should account for not only trees but also tree root location. Understory vegetation to be removed under tree canopies should be dug out by hand. Adding soil over tree roots reduces oxygen and is one of the activities that causes the quickest decline and death of trees. While there are many documented mitigating measures such as inserting aeration pipes, that may be undertaken when filling over tree roots, the process is expensive and shows limited documented success except with species that tolerate low oxygen levels in the soil.

Excavation such as trenching for utilities, construction footers, and foundation walls should occur outside the area of roots. Severing roots to any great degree causes stress to trees. Utilities can be tunneled under tree roots without severing them (Figure 6-7). While this technique is not inexpensive, it is widely used and should be specified where trees are to be preserved. When possible, footers and foundation walls should span over tree roots. The use of

Figure 6-1 DETERMINING PROTECTION ZONES AROUND TREES PRIOR
TO CONSTRUCTION

A protection zone is one in which no soil disturbance (grading, digging, storage, or compaction) may take place around a tree. Most roots are within the first 12 to 18 inches of the soil surface. That is why soil disturbance can cause severe problems with tree health. A protection zone must be fenced off and the importance of this barrier made clear to people working on site.

Trees have varying abilities to tolerate root zone disturbance. In general, a younger, actively growing tree will be better able to withstand some damage to its root zone than a slowly growing older tree or one that is already under some stress.

Trees that can tolerate a wide variation in soil moisture (see Appendix I) and are actively growing will be more resilient. Those that require a narrow range of more exacting soil moisture conditions or are growing slowly due to age or less than adequate conditions will tolerate less. Where possible, it is always best to protect a group of trees with a larger shared root zone than to protect individual trees on a site.

Many people have used the imaginary line where the edge of the canopy meets the ground, or drip line, as the area to be protected. This may be adequate for vigorously growing trees with wide, round canopies. However, oval or columnar shaped trees will generally be short-changed if this method is used.

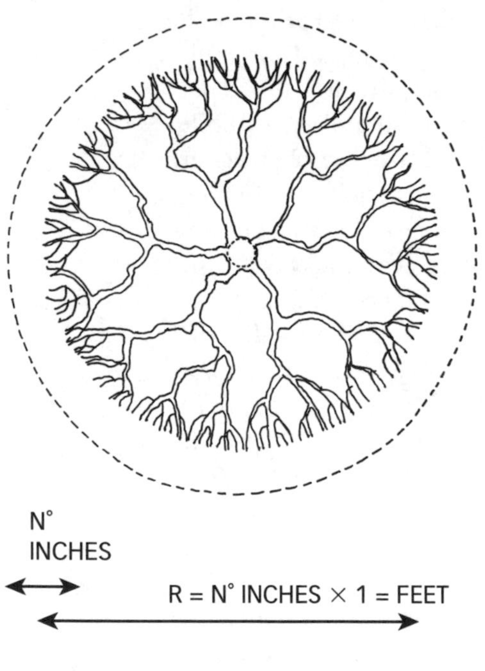

Another method of determining the tree protection zones is to base it on tree trunk diameter. Measuring the diameter of the tree in inches or centimeters and multiplying that by either 1 foot (for trees measured in inches) or 0.12 meters (for those measured in centimeters) will provide a reasonable radius with which to create a tree protection zone.

For example: A sugar maple with a trunk diameter of 20 inches would require a tree protection zone with a radius of 20 or 40 feet, with the tree in the center of the protective circle. The same tree of 51 centimeters will require a tree protection zone with a radius of 6.1 meters.

If this method is used for a tree with average tree health and resilience, tree protection zones can be enlarged or reduced slightly for older and stressed trees as well as younger, more vigorously growing trees.

N°
INCHES

R = N° INCHES × 1 = FEET

Figure 6-2 Temporary tree protection fence detail, beyond edge of canopy.

grade beams that do not require deep excavation or footers should also be considered when encountering significant tree roots.

When soil is saturated with water, oxygen is displaced. Consequently, when surface stormwater flow is redirected toward vegetation or when water table levels rise, roots can be deprived of needed oxygen. Certain species that depend on well-drained soils decline rapidly when soils are saturated with water or surface flow is redirected at vegetation, especially if the vegetation occurs naturally in a topographically low area.

Soil chemistry can be abruptly changed. Soil pH is altered when concrete trucks are washed out on the construction site or liquid construction waste is spilled on soil and surrounding vegetation. Special attention must be paid to developing construction specifications that strictly forbid such dumping and disposal on site. After a spill occurs on a site, soil remediation, while sometimes possible, is costly. Remediation can only occur when spilling and disposal is noticed. Such disposal near trees can cause catastrophic death, especially if the spill displaces oxygen in the soil and if the liquid volatilizes.

The damage easiest to eliminate on a construction site is mechanical

Figure 6-3 Superficial roots of Norway Maple under a sidewalk.

damage to tree trunks and branches. Trees should be pruned, or, in some cases, removed if they are by necessity in the path of construction and equipment. The pruning of branches to allow for the minimum height of machinery and the ultimate built elements should occur prior to the commencement of construction and should be done by a trained forester, arborist, or tree care specialist. This will eliminate the ripping and breakage of branches during construction and provide for professional pruning of vegetation.

Finally, saving trees and vegetation in clusters or groups not only maintains the natural shape of the plants but also increases their chances for survival. Trees that have grown up in a forested condition or in a group get structural support from surrounding trees. Removing too many trees from a cluster may cause the remaining trees to fail at a later date, especially during a storm event. Foliage and bark can also be sun-scorched when newly exposed to solar radiation.

The assessment of existing vegetation as outlined above, when considered in conjunction with anticipated construction activities, provides the information necessary to develop strategies to preserve vegetation during the construction process.

WRITING SPECIFICATIONS FOR VEGETATION PROTECTION DURING CONSTRUCTION

The quality of specifications written for vegetation assessment and protection during construction is important, and the enforcement of their prescriptive aspects is vital. It is essential to have frequent site inspections, especially during the demolition and project staging periods of construction. This will ensure that protective fencing, material stockpiling, design layout, and staking is consistent with specifications and related plans. Regular site visits are important to be sure fencing that protects trees

Figure 6-4 Easily removable construction fencing being relocated.

remains in place and that contractors are reminded regularly of the value and importance of keeping vegetation healthy. In order to keep contractors from damaging trees during construction, penalties or other repercussions for not following specifications must be spelled out. The International Society of Arboriculture (ISA) spells out an excellent protocol for establishing penalties for damage to vegetation in its publication *The Guidelines for Evaluating Landscape Trees*. However, to enforce the ISA guidelines, you must establish the quality and conditions of the existing vegetation as a baseline against

Figure 6-5 Construction materials stored under a tree canopy.

Figure 6-6
Mechanical damage
to a tree trunk.

which any future possible arbitration can be reviewed. This is best done by a certified arborist but can be accomplished by anyone who has demonstrated horticultural knowledge.

To be sure that the general contractor and the subcontractors understand the significance of vegetation protection in the specifications, it is important to make it part of the agenda for the pre-bid conference and pre-construction meetings as well as part of periodic site inspections.

Even with well-developed specifications for plant protection, roots are inevitably cut, as they usually extend well beyond the canopy drip line of trees. Specifications should be written so that, when encountered, significant tree roots are cut squarely and kept moist. When backfilling, well-draining soil should be placed around roots. If a granular material is used as a backfill material, structural soil may be used (see page 65). Typical excavations where roots are encountered occur in utility trenches and excavations for footers for retaining walls and foundations. When large roots are encountered during construction, root prune only as necessary and cover exposed roots with wet burlap or, when practicable, moist organic matter or soil. When backfilling around severed roots, use soil materials that allow root regeneration. When a well-drained, compacted backfill is required, utilize structural soil. Do not thin the top growth of trees when roots are removed. Trees should be frequently watered to compensate for root loss instead of removing top growth. Keeping as many branches and leaves as possible will assist in plant root regeneration. Top growth pruning should only occur when so many roots are removed that wind throw may become a problem. If excessive root removal is anticipated, consider whether the tree should be retained as part of the overall design. If top pruning does occur, specifications should indicate that the work be done by a certified arborist. This should ensure that the aesthetic value and canopy balance of the tree is maintained. When soil is cut away

Figure 6-7 Tunneling utilities below an existing tree root system.

permanently on one or more sides of a tree, it is possible to construct a tree well or tree wall to cover roots and retain soil (Figure 6-8). Use the tree protection zone calculation outlined in Figure 6-1 to determine optimum tree well–wall locations.

In general, no more than one-third of tree roots should ever be removed. Once more than this amount of root area is removed, the overall

Figure 6-8 Illustration of constructed wall with root pruning.

design should be reconsidered with a view to alternatives. On some occasions, it may be best to remove the affected vegetation and replant. Tree wells and other remedial actions are expensive and require considerable attention to tree care during construction (Figure 6-9). Consequently, they should only be used when tree survival is certain or the tree(s) have determined significance.

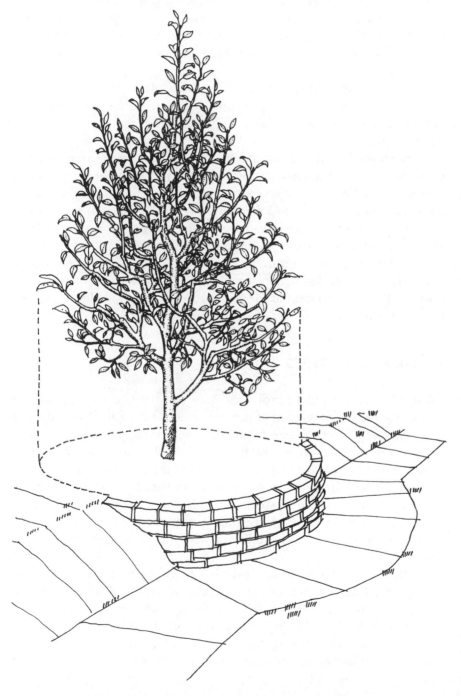

Figure 6-9 Partial tree well using unit masonry construction.

IMPACT OF SOIL COMPACTION DURING CONSTRUCTION

As previously mentioned, soil compaction has the most significant impact on vegetation during the construction process. Soil compaction is measured as bulk density. At certain levels of bulk density, not only is oxygen and water limited in the soil but also tree roots and plant growth are inhibited. Once soil structure is destroyed, it is difficult to recreate good structure and soil peds. Natural freezing and/or drying cycles do little to recreate acceptable soil structure. Other than soil protection from construction activities, surface treatments of mulch, geo-textiles, gravel, and plywood applied over tree roots and associated soil have proved unsatisfactory in preventing soil compaction.

Existing on-site soil texture can be variable. Heavy clay soils are more readily compacted under construction loading than sandy soils. Consequently, greater care must be taken to protect heavy clay soils during construction processes.

When topsoil is stripped and stockpiled for reuse on a site, it must not be compacted. Even when topsoil is respread on the construction site without compaction, subsoil is often severely compacted. Compacted soil should be remediated to a depth of 2 to 3 feet. Typical topsoil placement and remediation in the first 4 to 6 inches is satisfactory for lawn grasses but not for trees and woody plants with roots at a depth of 2 feet or more.

It is clear from the literature that it is better to prevent soil compaction than to rely on postconstruction remediation. In addition to protecting vegetation, all areas not essential for construction staging should be securely fenced to reduce the total area of soil compaction.

PAVING AROUND TREES

Once trees are adequately protected from construction damage and are considered viable, installation of new pavements, especially in urban areas, can cause significant damage to root systems. Most rigid and semirigid pavement profiles require several inches of granular base course before the pavement can be installed. The options are to excavate into the soil, removing many superficial roots, or to install base course above the roots, effectively filling over the root system. Pervious nonrigid pavement can allow for oxygen and water to reach the root system in a limited manner. Rigid pavement severely limits the ability of water or air to move through the paving profile.

Mitigation for paving around existing trees can be achieved using permeable pavement over a granular base such as structural soil. Leaving as large an area as practicable around the tree without pavement is desirable. If rigid pavement is a design requirement, leaving as large an opening as possible around the existing tree may partially mitigate the pavement requirement. Once again, structural soil may be used under the pavement to allow for desired compaction of the base course while allowing the oxygen, water, and root expansion that results in good tree growth. Pavement installation typically results in the most common construction damage to tree roots, limiting soil aeration. All roots must be provided with an adequate supply of oxygen for respiration and necessary metabolic activities. While tree species vary in their tolerance for construction practices related to pavement installation, all trees are affected by the reduction in soil aeration. In temperate climates, Sugar Maples, many of the oaks and lindens, and almost all conifers are affected by even the smallest change in soil aeration. Other typical street trees such as the Red Maple, Ash, Honey Locust, Sycamore, and Elm are slightly less troubled by changes in soil aeration brought on by soil compaction and paving. A good way to think about tree tolerance to soil aeration is to consider their naturally occurring physiological tolerance to wet and saturated soils, which can be inherently oxygen deprived.

Leaving as large an area as possible free of pavement and the resultant compacted subgrade improves soil aeration and tree viability and longevity. The area left open to pavement should be mulched to retain soil moisture as well as reduce the potential for compaction due to foot traffic around the tree. Organic mulch as a top dressing has the added benefit of promoting the development of soil structure as it breaks down and is replenished over time.

REMEDIATION TECHNIQUES FOR TREES SITUATED IN RECENTLY COMPACTED SOILS

If soil does become compacted within the root zone of trees to be preserved on a site, remediation techniques can be undertaken. Treatments using compressed air, augering and water-jetting, or the installation of perforated pipe have been found to offer limited benefit for tree growth and vigor (Lichter and Lindsey, 1994).

Creating breakout zones with a backhoe or mechanical trencher in a radial pattern moving out from the edge of the existing root system has shown to be effective in remediating, to some degree, soil compaction around existing vegetation as outlined in Chapter 3, page 97. The soil removed from these radial trenches is subsequently amended with organic matter at a rate of 50 percent or more by volume and replaced in the trenches. The bottom of the excavated trenches should allow for subsurface water to flow away from the root system.

An organic mulch should be applied over radial breakout trenches as well as around the tree to reduce the potential for recompaction of amended soil. Surface treatments such as organic mulch are successful in both the prevention and recompaction of soils. Mulch requires periodic replenishment over the life of the tree. A maintenance schedule is needed to keep the mulch area free of weeds and grass.

CONCLUDING REMARKS

Understanding and utilizing site assessment methods and related design options greatly expands the possibilities for the establishment of trees in urban environments. Knowing the complex and heterogeneous aspects of the urban environment, including above- and belowground factors, soil conditions, legal jurisdictions, structural limitations, microclimate conditions, the history of a site, and conditions of existing vegetation as related to design intentions, is fundamental to planting and establishing trees successfully. The synthesis of this information acquired through site assessment will help determine the intervention strategies needed, including modification or replacement of soils and site conditions and plant selection as required.

Innovative materials, including structural soils and pervious pavements, enhance the conditions that allow for success in plant establishment. Credibly determining the soil volumes needed for trees to reach their design intentions is now possible. This soil volume knowledge, combined with design strategies such as continuous planting trenches, clustered trees with shared rooting space, and increased soil volumes due to raising soil above surrounding grades, is part of the kit of tools needed for contemporary planting design. The value and impact of various surface treatments around trees—turf grass, mulch, pavements, tree grates, and the like—must all be considered. Using techniques for raising and lowering grades around trees, and remediating compacted, poorly drained soils, will solve many problems frequently encountered when installing trees in the urban landscape.

Perhaps the most important aspect of planting design is plant selection—matching trees to planting sites through site assessment and possible related modification. Ultimately, the protection of existing trees on the site and early maintenance installation techniques and follow-up maintenance practices of weed control, watering, fertilizing, and pruning affect the health of the planting and long-term landscape value.

Urban horticulture and plant establishment is an evolving field with new methods, techniques, and research continually being documented. This text represents the best new thinking and substantiated empirical work. The challenges are to not only utilize what we now know but also to incorporate the best horticultural and design practices as they become known and are documented.

REFERENCES CITED

Anderson, L.M., and Jane Barrows-Broaddus. January 1989. Inexpensive ways to improve home builders tree survival. *Journal of Arboriculture* 15(1): 13–16.

Ball, John. 15 August 1990. Insights on on-site tree preservation. *American Nurseryman* 180(8): 93–111.

Britton, Denise F., and Gene P. Snyder. December 1992. Construction Damage: Correction begins with prevention. *Arbor Age* 12(2): 10–12.

Fazio, James R., ed. 1994a. A systematic approach to building with trees. *Tree City USA Bulletin No. 20*. The National Arbor Day Foundation. 8 pp.

————. 1994b. How to protect trees during underground work. *Tree City USA Bulletin No. 35*. The National Arbor Day Foundation. 8 pp.

————. 1993. Tree protection ordinances. *Tree City USA Bulletin No. 31*. The National Arbor Day Foundation. 8 pp.

————. 1992. Trees and parking lots. *Tree City USA Bulletin No. 24*. The National Arbor Day Foundation. 8 pp.

————. 1991a. How to save trees during construction. *Tree City USA Bulletin No. 7*. The National Arbor Day Foundation. 8 pp.

————. 1991b. Resolving tree-sidewalk conflicts. *Tree City USA Bulletin No. 3*. The National Arbor Day Foundation.

Lichter, John M., and Patricia A. Lindsey. July 1994. The use of surface treatments for the prevention of soil compaction during site construction. *Journal of Arboriculture* 20(4): 205–209.

Mayne, Leslie S. November 1982. Specifications for construction around trees. *Journal of Arboriculture* 8 (11): 27–29.

Miller, Nancy L., David M. Rathke, and Gary R. Johnson. 1993. *Protecting trees from construction damage: A homeowner's guide*. Saint Paul, Minn.: Minnesota Extension Service.

Morell, John D. May 1984. Parkway tree augering specifications. *Journal of Arboriculture* 10(5): 129–132.

O'Brien, Patrick, Tracy Martin, and Barbara Colony. June 1998. *How to protect tree roots while replacing sidewalks and curbs*. Urban and Community Assistance Program, USDA Forest Service, Forestry Report R8–FR63, Technology Bulletin 5.

Randrup, Thomas B., and Kim Dralle. 1997. Influence of planning and design on soil compaction in construction sites. *Landscape and Urban Planning* 403, 1–6, Elsevier Science BV.

Schoeneweiss, Donald F. July 1982. Prevention and treatment of construction damage to shade trees. *Journal of Arboriculture* 8(7): 169–175.

Yingling, Earl L., Charles A. Keeley, Silas Little, and James Burtis. May 1979. Reducing damage to shade and woodland trees from construction activities. *Journal of Arboriculture* 5(5): 97–105.

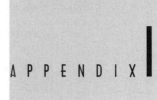

Tree and Large Shrub Tolerance of Varying Soil Moisture, Soil pH, and Salt Conditions

The following lists of trees from USDA Hardiness Zone 6 (minimum winter temperature of 0° to −5°F) and colder will help you choose appropriate trees for a variety of urban situations. However, there is no one perfect tree for every situation. The best approach is to select trees to match site conditions based on a thorough site assessment. Diversity is one key to a successful tree-planting program. Overplanting of one species in an area can result in monocultures that encourage the buildup of insect populations and diseases that can destroy the entire planting.

A reasonable strategy for most urban plantings is to limit any one species to 5 percent of a total urban population for small to midsize cities. Consequently, if a disease or insect infestation should occur, 95 percent of the tree population would remain unaffected.

There is no one perfect tree because there is no one homogeneous urban environment or site. The urban environment is a conglomeration of soils, microclimates, and other site conditions. Both aboveground and below-grade conditions can change dramatically in the space of 10 feet. Needless to say, the lists of trees that follow are provided only as a guide for selection. A comprehensive site assessment should be undertaken to identify plant requirements such as:

1. Moisture
   a. Tolerates poorly drained or intermittently flooded soils
   b. Requires moist but well-drained soils
   c. Tolerates moderate drought
   d. Tolerates more severe drought

2. pH
   a. Requires acid soil pH 5.0 to 7.0
   b. Can tolerate acid to neutral soil pH 5.0 to 7.5
   c. Can tolerate acid to alkaline soil pH 5.0 to 8.2

3. Salt Tolerance
   a. Tolerates salt
   b. Is sensitive to salt

Two Notes of Caution

It is important to note that some trees are adaptable to a fairly wide range of environmental conditions, while others have a narrow range in which they grow well. By presenting the following lists, we are providing information about adaptability. All trees will grow well under near-optimal conditions of a pH of 6.8 and soil consistently moist but well drained. However, we rarely find these conditions in the urban environment. It is our purpose to highlight those trees that tolerate broader, less ideal conditions while still providing the benefits for which we planted them. These more adaptable plants don't *prefer* poorer conditions, but they can still grow adequately in them. This important information is key to making informed plant selections.

Another consideration: Trees become acclimated to less than ideal conditions *after they have become established* in the landscape. Newly transplanted trees are not as acclimated as their established counterparts. It is critical to give newly transplanted trees several years of supplemental watering to hasten their establishment before expecting them to tolerate a wide range of soil moisture conditions.

TABLE I-1

Botanical Name	Common Name	Very Wet ———→ Very Dry											
		1	2	3	4	5	6	7	8	9	10	11	12
		OCCASIONALLY SATURATED OR VERY WET			CONSISTENTLY MOIST, WELL DRAINED			OCCASIONAL PERIODS OF DRY SOIL			PROLONGED PERIODS OF DRY SOIL		
Abies spp.	Firs				▓	▓	▓						
Acer buergeranum	Trident Maple				▓	▓	▓	▓	▓	▓	▓	▓	
Acer campestre	Hedge Maple				▓	▓	▓	▓	▓	▓	▓	▓	▓
Acer griseum	Paperbark Maple				▓	▓							
Acer miyabei	Miyabei Maple				▓	▓	▓	▓	▓	▓			
Acer nigrum	Black Maple				▓	▓	▓	▓	▓	▓			
Acer palmatum	Japanese Maple				▓	▓	▓						
Acer pensylvanicum	Moosewood				▓	▓	▓						
Acer platanoides	Norway Maple			▓	▓	▓	▓	▓	▓	▓			
Acer pseudoplatanus	Sycamore Maple			▓	▓	▓	▓	▓	▓	▓			
Acer rubrum	Red Maple												
	'Red Sunset,' 'Bowhall'		▓	▓	▓	▓	▓						
	'Autumn Flame,' 'October Glory'	▓	▓	▓	▓	▓	▓						
	'Northwood,' 'Karpick'				▓	▓	▓						
Acer saccharinum	Silver Maple	▓	▓	▓	▓	▓	▓	▓	▓	▓			
Acer saccharum	Sugar Maple				▓	▓	▓						
Acer tataricum ssp. ginnala	Amur Maple			▓	▓	▓	▓	▓	▓	▓			
Acer truncatum	Shantung Maple				▓	▓	▓	▓	▓	▓			
Acer x freemanii	Freeman Maple			▓	▓	▓	▓	▓	▓	▓			
Aesculus hippocastanum	Common Horse Chestnut				▓	▓	▓	▓	▓	▓			
Aesculus parviflora	Bottlebrush Buckeye		▓	▓	▓	▓	▓	▓	▓	▓			
Aesculus x carnea	Red Horse Chestnut				▓	▓	▓	▓	▓	▓			
Alnus glutinosa	European Alder			▓	▓	▓	▓						
Amelanchier spp.	Serviceberry			▓	▓	▓	▓	▓	▓				
Aralia spinosa	Devil's Walking Stick				▓	▓	▓	▓	▓	▓	▓	▓	▓
Asimina triloba	Pawpaw			▓	▓	▓	▓	▓	▓				
Betula alleghaniensis	Yellow Birch			▓	▓	▓	▓	▓					
Betula lenta	Sweet Birch			▓	▓	▓	▓	▓					
Betula nigra	River Birch	▓	▓	▓	▓	▓	▓	▓					
Betula papyrifera	Paper Birch				▓	▓	▓	▓	▓				
Betula pendula	Weeping Birch				▓	▓	▓	▓	▓	▓			
Betula platyphylla	Asian White Birch				▓	▓	▓	▓	▓	▓			
Betula populifolia	Gray Birch				▓	▓	▓	▓	▓	▓			
Caragana arborescens	Siberian Pea Tree				▓	▓	▓	▓	▓	▓	▓	▓	▓
Carpinus betulus	European Hornbeam				▓	▓	▓	▓	▓	▓	▓		
Carpinus caroliniana	Musclewood			▓	▓	▓	▓	▓	▓	▓			
Carya glabra	Pignut Hickory				▓	▓	▓	▓	▓	▓	▓	▓	
Carya ovata	Shagbark Hickory				▓	▓	▓	▓	▓	▓	▓		

TABLE I-1 *(Continued)*

Botanical Name	Common Name	Very Wet 1	2	3	4	5	6	7	8	9	10	11	Very Dry 12
		OCCASIONALLY SATURATED OR VERY WET			CONSISTENTLY MOIST, WELL DRAINED			OCCASIONAL PERIODS OF DRY SOIL			PROLONGED PERIODS OF DRY SOIL		
Castanea mollissima	Chinese Chestnut				▓	▓	▓	▓	▓				
Catalpa speciosa	Northern Catalpa		█	█	█	█	█	█	█	█	█		
Cedrus libani	Lebanese Cedar			▓	▓	█	█	█	█				
Celtis laevigata	Sugar Hackberry		█	█	█	█	█	█	█	▓			
Celtis occidentalis	Hackberry			▓	▓	▓	▓	▓	▓	▓	▓		
Cercidiphyllum japonicum	Katsura Tree		█	█	█	█	█						
Cercis canadensis	Redbud				▓	▓	▓	▓	▓				
Chamaecyparis nootkatensis	Alaska Cedar				▓	█	█	█	█				
Chamaecyparis obtusa	Hinoki False Cypress				▓	▓	▓	▓					
Chamaecyparis pisifera	Sawara False Cypress		█	█	█	█	█	▓					
Chamaecyparis thyoides	Atlantic White Cedar			▓	▓	▓	▓	▓					
Chionanthus virginicus	Fringetree		█	█	█	█	█	▓					
Cladrastis kentukea	Yellow Wood				▓	▓	▓	▓	▓				
Cornus alternifolia	Pagoda Dogwood					█	█	█					
Cornus florida	Flowering Dogwood				▓	▓	▓	▓	▓				
Cornus kousa	Kousa Dogwood				▓	█	█	█	▓				
Cornus mas	Cornelian Cherry				▓	▓	▓	▓	▓	▓			
Cornus racemosa	Gray Dogwood		█	█	█	█	█	█	█				
Corylus colurna	Turkish Filbert					▓	▓	▓	▓	▓			
Cotinus coggygria	Smokebush					█	█	█	█	█	█	█	█
Cotinus obovatus	American Smokebush					▓	▓	▓	▓	▓	▓		
Crataegus crus-galli	Cockspur Hawthorn					█	█	█	█	█	█	█	█
Crataegus laevigata	English Hawthorn			▓	▓	▓	▓	▓	▓	▓			
Crataegus phaenopyrum	Washington Hawthorn					█	█	█	█	█	█	█	█
Crataegus punctata	Thicket Hawthorn				▓	▓	▓	▓	▓	▓	▓		
Crataegus viridis	Green Hawthorn			█	█	█	█	█	█	█	█	█	█
Cryptomeria japonica	Japanese Cryptomeria					▓	▓	▓	▓				
Davidia involucrata	Handkerchief Tree					█	█	█	█				
Eucommia ulmoides	Hardy Rubber Tree				▓	▓	▓	▓	▓	▓			
Elaeagnus angustifolia	Russian Olive					█	█	█	█	█	█	█	█
Fagus grandifolia	American Beech				▓	▓	▓	▓	▓				
Fagus sylvatica	European Beech				█	█	█	█	▓				
Franklinia alatamaha	Franklinia				▓	▓	▓	▓					
Fraxinus americana	White Ash			█	█	█	█	█	█	▓			
Fraxinus excelsior	European Ash			█	█	█	█	█	█				
Fraxinus pennsylvanica	Green Ash			█	█	█	█	█	█	█	█		
Ginkgo biloba	Ginkgo				▓	▓	▓	▓	▓	▓	▓	▓	▓
Gleditsia triacanthos	Honey Locust		█	█	█	█	█	█	█	█	█	█	
Gymnocladus dioicus	Kentucky Coffee Tree				▓	▓	▓	▓	▓	▓	▓		
Halesia tetraptera	Carolina Silverbell				▓	▓	▓	▓					
Hamamelis mollis	Chinese Witch Hazel				▓	▓	▓	▓					

TABLE I-1   (Continued)

Botanical Name	Common Name	Very Wet → Very Dry

Botanical Name	Common Name	1	2	3	4	5	6	7	8	9	10	11	12
		OCCASIONALLY SATURATED OR VERY WET			CONSISTENTLY MOIST, WELL DRAINED			OCCASIONAL PERIODS OF DRY SOIL			PROLONGED PERIODS OF DRY SOIL		
Hamamelis virginiana	Common Witch Hazel			■	■	■	■	■	■	■			
Hibiscus syriacus	Rose of Sharon				■	■	■	■	■	■	■		
Ilex opaca	American Holly				■	■	■	■	■	■			
Juglans nigra	Black Walnut		■		■	■	■	■	■	■			
Juniperus spp.	Junipers				■	■	■	■	■	■		■	■
Koelreuteria paniculata	Goldenrain Tree				■	■	■	■	■	■	■	■	
Laburnum anagyroides	Goldenchain Tree				■	■	■						
Lagerstromia indica	Crapemyrtle												
Larix decidua	European Larch			■	■	■	■						
Larix laricina	American Larch		■	■	■	■	■						
Liquidambar styraciflua	Sweetgum			■	■	■	■	■	■	■			
Liriodendron tulipifera	Tulip Poplar				■	■	■	■	■				
Maackia amurensis	Maackia				■	■	■	■	■	■			
Maclura pomifera	Osage Orange		■	■	■	■	■	■	■	■	■	■	■
Magnolia acuminata	Cucumber Tree					■	■	■	■	■			
Magnolia grandiflora	Southern Magnolia				■	■	■	■	■	■			
Magnolia macrophylla	Bigleaf Magnolia			■	■	■	■	■	■				
Magnolia stellata	Star Magnolia				■	■	■	■	■	■			
Magnolia virginiana	Sweet Bay		■	■	■	■	■	■					
Magnolia x soulangiana	Saucer Magnolia				■	■	■	■	■				
Malus spp.	Crabapple				■	■	■	■	■	■	■	■	
Metasequoia glyptostroboides	Dawn Redwood			■	■	■	■	■	■	■			
Morus alba	White Mulberry		■	■	■	■	■	■	■	■	■	■	
Nyssa sylvatica	Tupelo		■	■	■	■	■	■	■				
Ostrya virginiana	American Hop Hornbeam					■	■	■	■	■			
Oxydendrum arboreum	Sourwood				■	■	■	■	■				
Parrotia persica	Ironwood				■	■	■	■	■	■	■		
Phellodendron amurense	Amur Cork Tree				■	■	■	■	■	■			
Picea abies	Norway Spruce				■	■	■	■	■	■			
Picea glauca	White Spruce				■	■	■	■	■	■			
Picea omorika	Serbian Spruce				■	■	■	■	■	■			
Picea orientalis	Oriental Spruce				■	■	■	■	■	■			
Picea pungens	Colorado Blue Spruce				■	■	■	■	■	■			
Pinus aristata	Bristlecone Pine				■	■	■	■	■	■	■	■	
Pinus bungeana	Lacebark Pine				■	■	■	■	■	■			
Pinus cembra	Swiss Stone Pine				■	■	■	■	■	■			
Pinus densiflora	Japanese Red Pine				■	■	■	■	■	■			
Pinus flexilis	Limber Pine					■	■	■	■	■	■		
Pinus mugo	Mugo Pine				■	■	■	■	■	■	■		
Pinus nigra	Austrian Pine			■	■	■	■	■	■	■			
Pinus parviflora	Japanese White Pine				■	■	■	■	■	■	■		

TABLE I-1 (Continued)

Botanical Name	Common Name	Very Wet 1	2	3	4	5	6	7	8	9	10	11	Very Dry 12
		OCCASIONALLY SATURATED OR VERY WET			CONSISTENTLY MOIST, WELL DRAINED			OCCASIONAL PERIODS OF DRY SOIL			PROLONGED PERIODS OF DRY SOIL		
Pinus ponderosa	Ponderosa Pine				■	■	■	■	■	■			
Pinus resinosa	Red Pine				■	■	■	■	■	■	■	■	
Pinus rigida	Pitch Pine				■	■	■	■	■	■	■	■	■
Pinus strobus	Eastern White Pine				■	■	■	■	■	■			
Pinus sylvestris	Scotch Pine				■	■	■	■	■	■	■	■	
Pinus thunbergiana	Japanese Black Pine				■	■	■	■	■	■	■	■	
Platanus occidentalis	Eastern Sycamore		■	■	■	■	■	■	■	■	■	■	
Platanus x acerifolia	London Plane Tree		■	■	■	■	■	■	■	■	■	■	
Populus alba	White Poplar		■	■	■	■	■	■	■	■	■	■	
Populus deltoides	Northern Cottonwood		■	■	■	■	■	■	■	■			
Populus tremuloides	Quaking Aspen			■	■	■	■	■	■	■			
Prunus cerasifera	Cherry Plum				■	■	■	■	■	■			
Prunus sargentii	Sargent Cherry				■	■	■	■	■				
Prunus serotina	Black Cherry				■	■	■	■	■	■			
Prunus serrulata	Japanese Flowering Cherry				■	■	■	■	■				
Prunus subhirtella	Higan Cherry				■	■	■	■	■				
Prunus virginiana	Chokecherry				■	■	■	■	■	■			
Pseudotsuga menziesii	Douglas Fir				■	■	■	■	■	■			
Pyrus calleryana	Callery Pear		■	■	■	■	■	■	■	■	■	■	
Quercus acutissima	Sawtooth Oak						■	■	■	■	■	■	
Quercus alba	White Oak				■	■	■	■	■	■	■	■	
Quercus bicolor	Swamp White Oak		■	■	■	■	■	■	■	■	■	■	
Quercus coccinea	Scarlet Oak				■	■	■	■	■	■	■	■	
Quercus falcata	Southern Red Oak				■	■	■	■	■	■	■	■	
Quercus imbricaria	Shingle Oak				■	■	■	■	■	■	■	■	■
Quercus lyrata	Overcup Oak		■	■	■	■	■	■	■	■			
Quercus macrocarpa	Bur Oak		■	■	■	■	■	■	■	■	■	■	■
Quercus michauxii	Swamp Chestnut Oak		■	■	■	■	■	■	■	■			
Quercus muehlenbergii	Chinkapin Oak				■	■	■	■	■	■	■	■	■
Quercus palustris	Pin Oak		■	■	■	■	■	■	■	■	■	■	
Quercus phellos	Willow Oak				■	■	■	■	■	■	■	■	■
Quercus prinus	Chestnut Oak				■	■	■	■	■	■	■	■	
Quercus robur	English Oak				■	■	■	■	■	■	■	■	
Quercus rubra	Red Oak				■	■	■	■	■	■			
Quercus virginiana	Live Oak				■	■	■	■	■	■	■	■	■
Robinia pseudoacacia	Black Locust			■	■	■	■	■	■	■	■	■	■
Salix alba 'Tristis'	Weeping Willow	■	■	■	■	■	■	■	■	■			
Sciadopitys verticillata	Umbrella Pine				■	■	■	■	■				
Sequoiadendron giganteum	Sierra Redwood				■	■	■	■	■	■			
Sophora japonica (Styphnolobium japonicus)	Scholar Tree				■	■	■	■	■	■	■	■	■

TABLE I-1   (Continued)

Botanical Name	Common Name	Very Wet ◄———————————————► Very Dry											
		1	2	3	4	5	6	7	8	9	10	11	12
		OCCASIONALLY SATURATED OR VERY WET			CONSISTENTLY MOIST, WELL DRAINED			OCCASIONAL PERIODS OF DRY SOIL			PROLONGED PERIODS OF DRY SOIL		
Sorbus alnifolia	Korean Mountain Ash				▓	▓	▓	▓	▓	▓			
Sorbus aucuparia	European Mountain Ash				▓	▓	▓	▓	▓				
Sorbus thuringiaca	Oak-Leafed Mountain Ash				▓	▓	▓	▓	▓	▓			
Stewartia pseudocamellia	Japanese Stewartia				▓	▓							
Styrax japonicus	Japanese Snowbell				▓	▓							
Syringa reticulata	Japanese Tree Lilac				▓	▓	▓	▓	▓	▓	▓	▓	
Taxodium distichum	Bald Cypress	▓	▓	▓	▓	▓	▓	▓	▓	▓	▓		
Thuja occidentalis	Eastern Arborvitae			▓	▓	▓	▓	▓	▓	▓			
Thuja plicata	Western Arborvitae			▓	▓	▓	▓	▓	▓	▓			
Tilia americana	Basswood			▓	▓	▓	▓	▓	▓	▓			
Tilia cordata	Littleleaf Linden				▓	▓	▓	▓	▓	▓			
Tilia tomentosa	Silver Linden				▓	▓	▓	▓	▓	▓	▓		
Tilia x euchlora	Crimean Linden				▓	▓	▓	▓	▓	▓			
Tsuga canadensis	Eastern Hemlock			▓	▓	▓	▓	▓	▓	▓			
Tsuga caroliniana	Carolina Hemlock			▓	▓	▓	▓	▓	▓	▓			
Ulmus americana	American Elm		▓	▓	▓	▓	▓	▓	▓	▓	▓		
Ulmus carpinifolia	Smooth-Leaf Elm		▓	▓	▓	▓	▓	▓	▓	▓	▓	▓	
Ulmus parvifolia	Lace Bark Elm			▓	▓	▓	▓	▓	▓	▓	▓	▓	
Viburnum lentago	Nannyberry			▓	▓	▓	▓	▓	▓	▓			
Viburnum sieboldii	Siebold Viburnum				▓	▓	▓	▓	▓	▓			
Zelkova serrata	Japanese Zelkova				▓	▓	▓	▓	▓	▓			

TABLE I-2   SOIL pH TOLERANCES OF SELECTED TREES AND LARGE SHRUBS: REQUIRES ACID SOIL <7.0

Botanical Name	Common Name
Abies spp.	Firs in general
Acer rubrum	Red Maple
Betula nigra	River Birch
Chionanthus virginicus	Fringetree
Cornus alternifolia	Pagoda Dogwood
Cornus florida	Flowering Dogwood
Fagus grandifolia	American Beech
Franklinia alatamaha	Franklinia
Halesia tetraptera	Carolina Silverbell
Ilex opaca	American Holly
Magnolia virginiana	Sweet Bay
Oxydendrum arboreum	Sourwood
Pinus rigida	Pitch Pine
Quercus palustris	Pin Oak
Sassafras albidum	Sassafras
Stewartia pseudocamellia	Japanese Stewartia
Styrax japonicus	Japanese Snowbell

TABLE I-3   SOIL pH TOLERANCES OF SELECTED TREES AND LARGE SHRUBS: CAN TOLERATE INTO THE NEUTRAL OR SLIGHTLY ALKALINE ZONE <7.5

Botanical Name	Common Name
Abies concolor	White Fir
Acer buergeranum	Trident Maple
Acer griseum	Paperbark Maple
Acer pensylvanicum	Moosewood
Acer saccharum	Sugar Maple
Acer tataricum ssp. ginnala	Amur Maple
Acer x freemanii	Freeman Maple
Amelanchier spp.	Serviceberry
Asimina triloba	Pawpaw
Betula alleghaniensis	Yellow Birch
Betula lenta	Sweet Birch
Betula papyrifera	Paper Birch
Betula pendula	Weeping Birch
Betula platyphylla	Asian White Birch
Betula populifolia	Gray Birch
Carpinus caroliniana	Musclewood

TABLE I-3 *(Continued)*

Botanical Name	Common Name
Chamaecyparis obtusa	Hinoki False Cypress
Chamaecyparis pisifera	Sawara False Cypress
Chamaecyparis thyoides	Atlantic White Cedar
Cornus kousa	Kousa Dogwood
Davidia involucrata	Handkerchief Tree
Hamamelis mollis	Chinese Witch Hazel
Hamamelis virginiana	Common Witch Hazel
Liquidambar styraciflua	Sweetgum
Magnolia macrophylla	Bigleaf Magnolia
Nyssa sylvatica	Tupelo
Pinus strobus	Eastern White Pine
Prunus cerasifera	Cherry Plum
Prunus sargentii	Sargent Cherry
Prunus serotina	Black Cherry
Prunus serrulata	Japanese Flowering Cherry
Prunus subhirtella	Higan Cherry
Prunus virginiana	Chokecherry
Quercus acutissima	Sawtooth Oak
Quercus alba	White Oak
Quercus bicolor	Swamp White Oak
Quercus coccinea	Scarlet Oak
Quercus falcata	Southern Red Oak
Quercus imbricaria	Shingle Oak
Quercus lyrata	Overcup Oak
Quercus michauxii	Swamp Chestnut Oak
Quercus phellos	Willow Oak
Quercus prinus	Chestnut Oak
Quercus rubra	Red Oak
Quercus virginiana	Live Oak
Sciadopitys verticillata	Umbrella Pine
Sequoiadendron giganteum	Sierra Redwood
Taxodium distichum	Bald Cypress

TABLE I-4   SOIL pH TOLERANCES OF SELECTED TREES AND LARGE
SHRUBS: CAN TOLERATE HIGHLY ALKALINE SOIL <8.2

Botanical Name	Common Name
Acer campestre	Hedge Maple
Acer miyabei	Miyabei Maple
Acer nigrum	Black Maple
Acer platanoides	Norway Maple
Acer pseudoplatanus	Sycamore Maple
Acer truncatum	Shantung Maple
Aesculus hippocastanum	Common Horse Chestnut
Aesculus parviflora	Bottlebrush Buckeye
Aesculus x carnea	Red Horse Chestnut
Alnus glutinosa	European Alder
Aralia spinosa	Devil's Walking Stick
Caragana arborescens	Siberian Pea Tree
Carpinus betulus	European Hornbeam
Carya glabra	Pignut Hickory
Carya ovata	Shagbark Hickory
Castanea mollissima	Chinese Chestnut
Catalpa speciosa	Northern Catalpa
Cedrus libani	Lebanese Cedar
Celtis laevigata	Sugar Hackberry
Celtis occidentalis	Hackberry
Cercidiphyllum japonicum	Katsura Tree
Cercis canadensis	Redbud
Cladrastis kentukea	Yellow Wood
Cornus mas	Cornelian Cherry
Cornus racemosa	Gray Dogwood
Corylus colurna	Turkish Filbert
Cotinus coggygria	Smokebush
Cotinus obovatus	American Smokebush
Crataegus crus-galli	Cockspur Hawthorn
Crataegus laevigata	English Hawthorn
Crataegus phaenopyrum	Washington Hawthorn
Crataegus punctata	Thicket Hawthorn
Crataegus viridis	Green Hawthorn
Cryptomeria japonica	Japanese Cryptomeria
Eucommia ulmoides	Hardy Rubber Tree
Elaeagnus angustifolia	Russian Olive
Fraxinus americana	White Ash
Fraxinus excelsior	European Ash
Fraxinus pennsylvanica	Green Ash
Ginkgo biloba	Ginkgo

TABLE I-4 *(Continued)*

Botanical Name	Common Name
Gleditsia triacanthos	Honey Locust
Gymnocladus dioicus	Kentucky Coffee Tree
Hibiscus syriacus	Rose of Sharon
Juglans nigra	Black Walnut
Koelreuteria paniculata	Goldenrain Tree
Laburnum anagyroides	Goldenchain Tree
Lagerstromia indica	Crapemyrtle
Liriodendron tulipifera	Tulip Poplar
Maackia amurensis	Maackia
Maclura pomifera	Osage Orange
Magnolia acuminata	Cucumber Tree
Magnolia grandiflora	Southern Magnolia
Magnolia stellata	Star Magnolia
Magnolia x soulangiana	Saucer Magnolia
Malus spp.	Crabapple
Metasequoia glyptostroboides	Dawn Redwood
Morus alba	White Mulberry
Ostrya virginiana	American Hop Hornbeam
Parrotia persica	Ironwood
Phellodendron amurense	Amur Cork Tree
Picea abies	Norway Spruce
Picea glauca	White Spruce
Picea omorika	Serbian Spruce
Picea orientalis	Oriental Spruce
Picea pungens	Colorado Blue Spruce
Pinus aristata	Bristlecone Pine
Pinus bungeana	Lacebark Pine
Pinus cembra	Swiss Stone Pine
Pinus densiflora	Japanese Red Pine
Pinus flexilis	Limber Pine
Pinus mugo	Mugo Pine
Pinus nigra	Austrian Pine
Pinus parviflora	Japanese White Pine
Pinus ponderosa	Ponderosa Pine
Pinus resinosa	Red Pine
Pinus sylvestris	Scotch Pine
Pinus thunbergiana	Japanese Black Pine
Platanus occidentalis	Eastern Sycamore
Platanus x acerifolia	London Plane Tree
Populus alba	White Poplar
Populus deltoides	Northern Cottonwood

TABLE I-4   *(Continued)*

Botanical Name	Common Name
Populus tremuloides	Quaking Aspen
Pseudotsuga menziesii	Douglas Fir
Pyrus calleryana	Callery Pear
Quercus macrocarpa	Bur Oak
Quercus muehlenbergii	Chinkapin Oak
Quercus robur	English Oak
Robinia pseudoacacia	Black Locust
Salix alba 'Tristis'	Weeping Willow
Sophora japonica (Styphnolobium japonicus)	Scholar Tree
Sorbus alnifolia	Korean Mountain Ash
Sorbus aucuparia	European Mountain Ash
Sorbus thuringiaca	Oak-Leafed Mountain Ash
Syringa reticulata	Japanese Tree Lilac
Thuja occidentalis	Eastern Arborvitae
Thuja plicata	Western Arborvitae
Tilia americana	Basswood
Tilia cordata	Littleleaf Linden
Tilia tomentosa	Silver Linden
Tilia x euchlora	Crimean Linden
Tsuga canadensis	Eastern Hemlock
Tsuga caroliniana	Carolina Hemlock
Ulmus americana	American Elm
Ulmus carpinifolia and hybrids	Smooth-Leaf Elm and hybrids
Ulmus parvifolia	Lace Bark Elm
Viburnum lentago	Nannyberry
Viburnum sieboldii	Siebold Viburnum
Zelkova serrata	Japanese Zelkova

TABLE I-5   PLANTS OBSERVED TO HAVE SOME SALT TOLERANCE

Botanical Name	Common Name
Acer buergeranum	Trident Maple
Acer campestre	Hedge Maple
Acer platanoides	Norway Maple
Acer tataricum ssp. ginnala	Amur Maple
Acer pseudoplatanus	Sycamore Maple
Alnus glutinosa	European Alder
Caragana arborescens	Siberian Pea Tree
Crataegus crus-galli	Cockspur Hawthorn
Crataegus laevigata	English Hawthorn
Crataegus phaenopyrum	Washington Hawthorn
Crataegus punctata	Thicket Hawthorn
Crataegus viridis	Green Hawthorn
Elaeagnus angustifolia	Russian Olive
Fraxinus americana	White Ash
Fraxinus excelsior	European Ash
Fraxinus pennsylvanica	Green Ash
Ginkgo biloba	Ginkgo
Gleditsia triacanthos	Honey Locust
Juniperus spp.	Junipers
Koelreuteria paniculata	Goldenrain Tree
Larix laricina	American Larch
Maclura pomifera	Osage Orange
Morus alba	White Mulberry
Picea glauca	White Spruce
Picea pungens	Colorado Blue Spruce
Pinus mugo	Mugo Pine
Pinus nigra	Austrian Pine
Pinus ponderosa	Ponderosa Pine
Pinus rigida	Pitch Pine
Pinus thunbergiana	Japanese Black Pine
Platanus occidentalis	Eastern Sycamore
Platanus x acerifolia	London Plane Tree
Populus alba	White Poplar
Populus deltoides	Northern Cottonwood
Populus tremuloides	Quaking Aspen
Prunus sargentii	Sargent Cherry
Pyrus calleryana	Callery Pear
Quercus robur	English Oak
Quercus rubra	Red Oak
Quercus virginiana	Live Oak
Robinia pseudoacacia	Black Locust
Sophora japonica (Styphnolobium japonicus)	Scholar Tree
Taxodium distichum	Bald Cypress
Ulmus americana	American Elm
Ulmus carpinifolia	Smooth-Leaf Elm
Ulmus parvifolia	Lace Bark Elm

TABLE I-6   PLANTS SENSITIVE TO SALT

Botanical Name	Common Name
Abies spp.	Firs
Acer nigrum	Black Maple
Acer rubrum	Red Maple
Acer saccharum	Sugar Maple
Amelanchier spp.	Serviceberry
Carpinus betulus	European Hornbeam
Carpinus caroliniana	Musclewood
Cornus florida	Flowering Dogwood
Chionanthus virginicus	Fringetree
Hamamelis mollis	Chinese Witch Hazel
Hamamelis virginiana	Common Witch Hazel
Liriodendron tulipifera	Tulip Poplar
Pinus aristata	Bristlecone Pine
Pinus cembra	Swiss Stone Pine
Pinus densiflora	Japanese Red Pine
Pinus parviflora	Japanese White Pine
Pinus resinosa	Red Pine
Pinus sylvestris	Scotch Pine
Pinus strobus	Eastern White Pine
Pseudotsuga menziesii	Douglas Fir
Ostrya virginiana	American Hop Hornbeam
Quercus palustris	Pin Oak
Tilia americana	Basswood
Tilia cordata	Littleleaf Linden
Tilia x euchlora	Crimean Linden

Model Soil Specifications

The following material presents general considerations for the development of soil specifications. This is not provided in a standard specifications format but does reflect general performance considerations when developing soils characteristics. The descriptions can be attributed to new soil that is intended to be brought to a site as well as characteristics of soil modification and/or amendment of soils that have been stripped and stockpiled on a site for reuse.

Specification considerations include:

1. Soil classification
2. Particle size distribution
3. Organic amendments
4. Soluble salts
5. Chemical analysis

The contractor shall submit representative samples of topsoil to bring onto the site and samples of topsoil that was stockpiled from on-site stripping to a Soil Plant Testing Laboratory. All reports shall be sent to the Landscape Architect or owners' representative for approval. Samples of the topsoil to be brought to the site must be approved prior to delivery. Deficiencies in the topsoil shall be corrected by the Contractor as directed after review of the testing agency report. Testing reports shall include the following tests and recommendations:

1. Particle size analysis of the topsoil determined by ASTM F-1632 shall be performed and compared to the USDA Soil Classification System.
2. Percent organic matter shall be determined by a Loss on Ignition or Walkley/Black Test (ASTM F-1647).
3. Tests for gradation and organics shall be performed by a private test-

ing laboratory. Tests for soil chemistry and pH may be performed by a public extension service agency or a private testing laboratory.

4. Chemical analysis shall be undertaken for phosphorous, potassium, calcium, magnesium, cation exchange capacity, base saturation percentages, micronutrients, and acidity (pH).

5. Soil analysis tests shall show recommendations for soil additives or fertilizers to correct soil deficiencies as necessary.

6. All tests shall be performed in accordance with the current standards of the Association of Official Agricultural Chemists (AOAC).

Off-site topsoil shall be natural, fertile friable loam or sandy loam as classified by the U.S. Department of Agriculture Soil Classification System. The soil shall contain not less than 3 percent or more than 8 percent by weight of decayed organic matter (humus) as determined by ASTM F-1647. The topsoil shall be free of stones 1 inch (25 millimeters) or larger and other extraneous materials harmful to plant growth. Topsoil shall not have a pH of less than 6.0 or greater than 7.5, and shall not be delivered or used for planting while in a frozen or muddy condition.

If organic amendments are needed to obtain the specific organic matter content of the topsoil, the organic matter source may be a peat or compost material. The peat shall be sphagnum peat having an ash content not exceeding 15 percent, as determined by ASTM D-2974. Composts may be used provided that the material has an ash content not exceeding 40 percent.

Particle size specification varies for soil types defined by the USDA Soil Classification System. The following is *an example* of a particle size specification for a sandy loam. Particle size analysis will vary for other specified soil types.

PARTICLE SIZE	ANALYSIS	SIEVE #	% RETAINED
0–5%	gravel	8	0–5%
0–5%	very coarse sand	20	0–15%
60–75%	medium to coarse sand	60	60–75%
10–25%	silt	pan	pan 15–40%
5–15%	clay	pan	pan 15–40%

Another example of particle size analysis for a specified sandy loam topsoil and definition of sizes might be as follows:

	APPROXIMATE PARTICLE DISTRIBUTION	SIZE
Gravel	Less than 10%	+2 mm
Coarse to medium sand	60–75%	0.25–2 mm
Fine sand	5–10%	0.1–0.25 mm
Very fine sand	0–5%	0.05–0.1 mm
Silt	10–30%	0.0002–0.05 mm
Clay	15–20%	minus 0.002 mm

Soluble salts in soil and, especially, organic amendments should be analyzed at an accepted testing laboratory. Soluble salts in parts per million (ppm) can be converted as follows:

$$1 \text{ mmho/cm} = 1000 \text{ ppm} = 1.5\,6 \text{ d S/m}$$

If laboratory testing provides a ppm analysis, the following thresholds for concentrations and acceptable levels should be taken into consideration:

CONCENTRATION	LEVEL
0–1000	low (normal)
1000–2000	medium
3000–4000	high
>5000	very high

Low to normal levels of soluble salts in the soil, measured in ppm, are in the range of 0 to 1000 where plants with low tolerance of soluble salts can be recommended. With a ppm of 1000 to 2000, only plants sensitive to salts would be affected. With a ppm of 2000 to 4000, plants with salt tolerance should be used. When greater than 5000 ppm soluble salts are detected in soils, few plants will survive.

When soluble salts are measured as mmho/cm, the following restrictions would occur:

SOLUBLE SALTS (MMHO/CM)
0–2	nonsaline
3–4	slightly saline; sensitive plants might be restricted
4–8	moderately saline; many plants will be restricted
8–16	strongly saline; only tolerant plants will grow
>16	very strongly saline; very few plants will grow

Chemical analysis of soils should occur in accordance with standards of the AOAC. Based on the results of the chemical analysis for the types of plantings proposed, the following products may need to be added to the soil specification as amendments:

Lime: ASTM C-602, Class T, agricultural limestone containing a minimum 80 percent calcium carbonate equivalent, with a minimum 99 percent passing a No. 8 (2.36 mm) sieve and a minimum 75 percent passing a No. 60 (250 micrometer) sieve. Provide lime in the form of dolomitic limestone.

Aluminum sulfate: Commercial grade, unadulterated.

Nitrogen, phosphorous, and potassium in amounts recommended in soil analysis results from a qualified soil testing laboratory.

Developing an exact specification for soils to be used in planting areas on a site, whether from on-site or off-site sources, is critical to plant survival and establishment.

Depth of Planting Hole

Do *not* dig the hole deeper than the depth of the roots or container.

Placing the Tree

Trees should be planted with the root collar at ground level or slightly above. Protect the crown at all times.

Paraphernalia

The container for container trees shall not be removed until the time of planting. After placing balled and burlapped plants, all inorganic, plastic, or treated burlap and all strings, ropes, twines, or wire lacing shall be completely removed. At least the top third of the wire basket should be removed once the ball is stabilized in the ground. If the complete removal of untreated burlap from a large-size-caliper tree would severely disturb the root ball, the burlap should be pulled down so it is below the upper third of the ball. No burlap shall emerge from the soil or be near the soil surface after the hole is backfilled.

Backfilling and Amendments

Backfill the hole with the soil dug from the hole. Cover all roots with soil. Tamp out the air pockets with a shovel handle or the heel of the planter's foot without using full body weight. Care should be taken not to crush the roots on bare root trees.

Watering

The root zone around the plant to the drip line shall be thoroughly and deeply watered at the time of planting.

IMMEDIATE AFTERCARE SPECIFICATIONS

Mulching

To retain water and prevent lawn mower damage, all trees shall be mulched to a 3-inch depth in a ring extending to the drip line. Organic material such as wood chips, not sawdust, shall be used. Mulch should be kept 3 to 6 inches away from the trunk. This program should be maintained for at least three years after completion of the contract.

Model Landscape/Planting Specification

QUALITY

All plant material furnished shall meet the grades of the latest edition of the *American Standard for Nursery Stock*, ANSI Z60.1-1996, and the latest edition of the *American Joint Committee of Horticulture Nomenclature: Standard Plant Names*, and be free of all foreign plant material.

All plants shall be healthy, uniformly branched, and with well-developed fibrous root systems. The plants shall be free from dead or broken branches, lichens, scars, broken bark or wounds, and damage caused by insects or disease. All pruning wounds must be well healed, with no evidence of decay.

The contractor shall reject all plant materials not meeting the above specifications and trees having damaged or missing leaders, multiple leaders, Y-crotches, or indications of "topping" or "heading back."

HANDLING AND SHIPPING

Handling, shipping, and hauling shall be done in a careful manner that emphasizes the survival of the plant material. Roots should be kept moist and protected at all times from sun, wind, heat, drying, and excessive cold and freezing.

All container-grown plants shall be handled by the container. All balled and burlapped plants shall be handled by the ball.

Plant material shall be packed for transporting in accordance with prevailing practice for the type of plant shipped. Where necessary, plant material shall be temporarily heeled in. When transported in closed vehicles, plants shall receive adequate ventilation to prevent sweating. When transported in open vehicles, plants shall be protected by tarpaulins or other suitable cover material.

Root balls shall be kept moist during transit and protected from extreme weather conditions by insulating with mulch, soil, or other approved materials. Bare-root material must always be transported in closed vehicles.

ACCEPTANCE OF NURSERY TREES AND DELIVERY

1. All trees shall be nursery grown and true to type and name as ordered or shown on the plans and shall be individually tagged by species and cultivar (variety).

2. All trees shall be healthy, well-rooted, and have a form typical for the species or cultivar.

3. All trees shall comply with federal and state laws requiring inspection for plant diseases and pest infestations. Inspection certificates required by law shall accompany each shipment of plants.

4. The root ball of all trees shall be moist throughout and show no signs of moisture stress.

5. *Tree crown:* Deciduous
   a. A single, straight trunk that has not been headed or that could be pruned to a leader.
      Potential lateral scaffolds (height of lowest scaffold depends on landscape use):
         Radially distributed around the trunk.
         Not more than two-thirds the diameter of the trunk measured 25 millimeters (1 inch) above the branch.
         Free of included bark at attachments (bark embedded between trunk and lateral).
   b. The minimum acceptable length of the most recent season's shoots of small-growing trees (i.e., Red Maple, Red Oak, Ginkgo) might be 300 millimeters (12 inches), and for large-growing trees the minimum acceptable length night be 450 millimeters (18 inches).
   c. It is necessary that the tree stand upright without support.

6. *Tree crown:* Coniferous
   a. Crown has a single, straight trunk with no double leaders (codominant stems) or vigorous, upright branches competing with the leader.
   b. Radial and vertical distribution of branches forms a symmetrical crown.

7. *Roots:* Container, boxed, or balled and burlapped trees regardless of species or mature size.
   a. If in a container, the root ball should be slipped out and inspected; the root ball periphery shall be free of circling roots and a bottom mat of roots.
   b. Tip the root ball or container on its side and, with a small jet of water, expose the roots within 50 millimeters (2 inches) of the trunk to a depth of 65 millimeters (2.5 inches) below the topmost root

attached to the trunk. The trunk and main roots should be free of circling and kinks. Replace soil washed from around the trunk with a similar soil mix.

8. In case sample trees inspected are found to be defective, the buyer reserves the right to reject the entire lot or lots of trees represented by the defective samples.

9. The buyer shall be notified when plants are to be shipped at least ten days prior to the actual shipment date, or the buyer may request to select the plants at the nursery before delivery.

SITE SPECIFICATIONS

Location

Site characteristics such as overhead power lines, existing vegetation, and infrastructure items such as curbs and sidewalks shall be considered.

Minimum Distance Standards

In the absence of municipal codes to the contrary, the following minimum placing distance standards are recommended for street trees:

- Centered between curb and sidewalk, at least 2 feet from curb
- At least 10 feet from driveways, wheelchair ramps, and fire hydrants
- At least 5 feet from underground utility branches
- At least 10 feet from streetlights, farther for larger trees
- At least 15 feet from storm sewer inlets
- At least 30 feet from intersections

PLANTING SPECIFICATIONS

Planting shall be performed by a licensed and bonded contractor.

Planting Seasons

Shade and ornamental trees should be planted when dormant. Careful attention should be given to weather conditions, such as avoiding planting in hot, dry weather.

Width of Planting Hole

The planting hole shall be saucerlike and 3 times wider than the root diameter, ball, or container.

Pruning

Plants shall *not* be pruned at the time of planting except to remove broken or crossing branches. Broken or crossing branches shall be pruned with a sharp tool in a manner to retain and encourage the plant's natural growth characteristics. The crown of a young tree should *not* be cut back to compensate for root loss. Wound paint or dressing shall not be used.

Staking/Guying

Staking shall be done only if the tree requires support in strong winds or protection from equipment, vehicles, or vandals. If staking is necessary, stakes of nonrusting metal or untreated wood shall be driven outside the root ball and attached to the tree with broad straps or hoses (not wires). *The contractor shall be responsible for removing staking and guying materials no later than one year after planting.*

Watering and Care

The contractor shall water the plants deeply at least weekly during the dry season. The contractor shall keep the area immediately surrounding the tree free of weeds and turf.

INDEX

Adhesion, 30
Aeration systems, 55
Amending soils, 52, 53. *See also* Soil
American Standard for Nursery Stock, 133, 143
Atmospheric demand, 74
Available water-holding capacity, 77

Balled and burlaped, 136, 140
Bare-root, 136
Bed dimensions, 78
   calculating, 80
Biological diversity, 20
Bulk density, 35
   two methods for determining, 36

Carbon dioxide, 5, 10
Cation exchange capacity, 41
Climate, 7
Cohesion, 30
Container-grown, 136
Crown projection, 76
CU-Soil, 68

Desiccation, 25
Design intentions, 20
Development guidelines, 17
Die-back, 21, 22
Drainage, 55
   characteristics, 7
   principles, 99
Dry density, 35

Envisioned design size, 74
Erosion and runoff, 110
Evaporation:
   pan, 75
   ratio, 76

Fertilizer burn, 42
Field capacity, 31
French drain, 56

Genetic potential, 10
Grade, around trees, 94
Guying techniques, 160

Habitat, 111
Hardiness, 44
Heat Islands, 5

Included bark, 22
Increment of growth, 22
Interveinal chlorosis, 21
Irrigation, 7

Land form, 50
Landscape, human-impacted, 2
Leaf area index, 75
Leaf scorch, 25
Light, 10

Macronutrients, 39, 40
Macropores, 30
Maintenance easements, 17
Mechanical damage, 13
Microclimate, 5, 7, 20, 44
Micronutrients, 39, 40
Micropores, 30
Mulch, 86

Native species, non-native plants, 18, 118
Noise, 110
Nursery:
    stock specification, 137
    production practices, 136
Nutrients, 10
    availability, 40
    essential, 39

Organic:
    amendment, 12
    matter, 53
Oxygen, 5, 10

Penetrometer, 39
Percolation test, 32
Permanent wilting point, 31
Pervious pavements, 87
Pests and diseases, 116
Photosynthesis, 5
Plant-available water, 31
Plant establishment, 6, 8
Planting design, 16
Planting key, 129
Plant selection, 10, 15
Proctor density, 63, 64
Production and harvest, 136
Protection zones, 168

Radial trenching, 95, 98
Remediation techniques, 177. *See also* Soil
Root:
    shared space, 84
    type, 131
    zone temperatures, 6. *See also* Soil

Salt: 47. *See also* Soil
    damage, 25
    de-icing, 42
Saturated flow, 100
Sieve designations and openings, 54

Site assessment: 6
    checklist, 7
    method, 15
Site constraints, 8
Site modification, 10
Site preservation, 165
Soil:
    amendment, 15
    assessment, 27
    chemical properties, 38
    compaction, 11, 176
    density, 35, 45, 47, 62
    determining an adequate volume, 80
    factors, 7
    intrapedal conditions, 30
    modification, 11, 15, 49
    moisture, 113
    nutrients and salts, 60
    peds, 29
    penetrometer, 36
    pH, 4, 41, 46, 57, 58, 115
    physical properties, 27
    profile, 11
    protection, 176
    remediating poor drainage, 98
    restricting volume, 4, 5
    specification, 50
    structure, 29, 61, 65, 68, 69, 100, 176
    temperature, 42
    tests for fertility, 43
    texture, 29, 33, 34, 45
    volume, 64, 73
    volume calculations, 73, 74, 80
Spatial limitations, 16. *See also* Soil;
        Utilities
Species:
    composition, 18
    diversity, 119
    varieties, and cultivars, 126
Structural factors, 7, 72
Subsurface drainage, 56
Subsurface soil sculpting, 52
Suckering, 22
Sump drains, 101
Sun and shade, 112
Surface treatment, 85

Temperature, 10
    modification, 106
Texture-by-feel, 32
Topsoil, 27, 50
Transplanting, 117
    methods, bare root, 149
    techniques, 158

Tree protection, 169
Tree spade, 140

Underdrainage, 55, 101
Unsaturated flow, 100
Urban landscapes, 3, 4
Urban soil, 3, 28. *See also* Soil
Utilities:
   overhead, 16
   underground, 44

Vegetation protection, 171
Vegetative screen, 18
Visual assessment, 8
Visual similarity of trees, 121, 123
Visual uniformity, 119

Water, 10
Water-holding capacity, 31
Whole tree water use, 80
Wind mitigation, 106, 109

Model Landscape/Planting Specification

QUALITY

All plant material furnished shall meet the grades of the latest edition of the *American Standard for Nursery Stock*, ANSI Z60.1-1996, and the latest edition of the *American Joint Committee of Horticulture Nomenclature: Standard Plant Names*, and be free of all foreign plant material.

All plants shall be healthy, uniformly branched, and with well-developed fibrous root systems. The plants shall be free from dead or broken branches, lichens, scars, broken bark or wounds, and damage caused by insects or disease. All pruning wounds must be well healed, with no evidence of decay.

The contractor shall reject all plant materials not meeting the above specifications and trees having damaged or missing leaders, multiple leaders, Y-crotches, or indications of "topping" or "heading back."

HANDLING AND SHIPPING

Handling, shipping, and hauling shall be done in a careful manner that emphasizes the survival of the plant material. Roots should be kept moist and protected at all times from sun, wind, heat, drying, and excessive cold and freezing.

All container-grown plants shall be handled by the container. All balled and burlapped plants shall be handled by the ball.

Plant material shall be packed for transporting in accordance with prevailing practice for the type of plant shipped. Where necessary, plant material shall be temporarily heeled in. When transported in closed vehicles, plants shall receive adequate ventilation to prevent sweating. When transported in open vehicles, plants shall be protected by tarpaulins or other suitable cover material.

Root balls shall be kept moist during transit and protected from extreme weather conditions by insulating with mulch, soil, or other approved materials. Bare-root material must always be transported in closed vehicles.

ACCEPTANCE OF NURSERY TREES AND DELIVERY

1. All trees shall be nursery grown and true to type and name as ordered or shown on the plans and shall be individually tagged by species and cultivar (variety).

2. All trees shall be healthy, well-rooted, and have a form typical for the species or cultivar.

3. All trees shall comply with federal and state laws requiring inspection for plant diseases and pest infestations. Inspection certificates required by law shall accompany each shipment of plants.

4. The root ball of all trees shall be moist throughout and show no signs of moisture stress.

5. *Tree crown:* Deciduous
   a. A single, straight trunk that has not been headed or that could be pruned to a leader.
      Potential lateral scaffolds (height of lowest scaffold depends on landscape use):
      Radially distributed around the trunk.
      Not more than two-thirds the diameter of the trunk measured 25 millimeters (1 inch) above the branch.
      Free of included bark at attachments (bark embedded between trunk and lateral).
   b. The minimum acceptable length of the most recent season's shoots of small-growing trees (i.e., Red Maple, Red Oak, Ginkgo) might be 300 millimeters (12 inches), and for large-growing trees the minimum acceptable length night be 450 millimeters (18 inches).
   c. It is necessary that the tree stand upright without support.

6. *Tree crown:* Coniferous
   a. Crown has a single, straight trunk with no double leaders (codominant stems) or vigorous, upright branches competing with the leader.
   b. Radial and vertical distribution of branches forms a symmetrical crown.

7. *Roots:* Container, boxed, or balled and burlapped trees regardless of species or mature size.
   a. If in a container, the root ball should be slipped out and inspected; the root ball periphery shall be free of circling roots and a bottom mat of roots.
   b. Tip the root ball or container on its side and, with a small jet of water, expose the roots within 50 millimeters (2 inches) of the trunk to a depth of 65 millimeters (2.5 inches) below the topmost root

attached to the trunk. The trunk and main roots should be free of circling and kinks. Replace soil washed from around the trunk with a similar soil mix.

8. In case sample trees inspected are found to be defective, the buyer reserves the right to reject the entire lot or lots of trees represented by the defective samples.

9. The buyer shall be notified when plants are to be shipped at least ten days prior to the actual shipment date, or the buyer may request to select the plants at the nursery before delivery.

SITE SPECIFICATIONS

Location

Site characteristics such as overhead power lines, existing vegetation, and infrastructure items such as curbs and sidewalks shall be considered.

Minimum Distance Standards

In the absence of municipal codes to the contrary, the following minimum placing distance standards are recommended for street trees:

- Centered between curb and sidewalk, at least 2 feet from curb
- At least 10 feet from driveways, wheelchair ramps, and fire hydrants
- At least 5 feet from underground utility branches
- At least 10 feet from streetlights, farther for larger trees
- At least 15 feet from storm sewer inlets
- At least 30 feet from intersections

PLANTING SPECIFICATIONS

Planting shall be performed by a licensed and bonded contractor.

Planting Seasons

Shade and ornamental trees should be planted when dormant. Careful attention should be given to weather conditions, such as avoiding planting in hot, dry weather.

Width of Planting Hole

The planting hole shall be saucerlike and 3 times wider than the root diameter, ball, or container.

Depth of Planting Hole

Do *not* dig the hole deeper than the depth of the roots or container.

Placing the Tree

Trees should be planted with the root collar at ground level or slightly above. Protect the crown at all times.

Paraphernalia

The container for container trees shall not be removed until the time of planting. After placing balled and burlapped plants, all inorganic, plastic, or treated burlap and all strings, ropes, twines, or wire lacing shall be completely removed. At least the top third of the wire basket should be removed once the ball is stabilized in the ground. If the complete removal of untreated burlap from a large-size-caliper tree would severely disturb the root ball, the burlap should be pulled down so it is below the upper third of the ball. No burlap shall emerge from the soil or be near the soil surface after the hole is backfilled.

Backfilling and Amendments

Backfill the hole with the soil dug from the hole. Cover all roots with soil. Tamp out the air pockets with a shovel handle or the heel of the planter's foot without using full body weight. Care should be taken not to crush the roots on bare root trees.

Watering

The root zone around the plant to the drip line shall be thoroughly and deeply watered at the time of planting.

IMMEDIATE AFTERCARE SPECIFICATIONS

Mulching

To retain water and prevent lawn mower damage, all trees shall be mulched to a 3-inch depth in a ring extending to the drip line. Organic material such as wood chips, not sawdust, shall be used. Mulch should be kept 3 to 6 inches away from the trunk. This program should be maintained for at least three years after completion of the contract.

Pruning

Plants shall *not* be pruned at the time of planting except to remove broken or crossing branches. Broken or crossing branches shall be pruned with a sharp tool in a manner to retain and encourage the plant's natural growth characteristics. The crown of a young tree should *not* be cut back to compensate for root loss. Wound paint or dressing shall not be used.

Staking/Guying

Staking shall be done only if the tree requires support in strong winds or protection from equipment, vehicles, or vandals. If staking is necessary, stakes of nonrusting metal or untreated wood shall be driven outside the root ball and attached to the tree with broad straps or hoses (not wires). *The contractor shall be responsible for removing staking and guying materials no later than one year after planting.*

Watering and Care

The contractor shall water the plants deeply at least weekly during the dry season. The contractor shall keep the area immediately surrounding the tree free of weeds and turf.

INDEX

Adhesion, 30
Aeration systems, 55
Amending soils, 52, 53. *See also* Soil
American Standard for Nursery Stock, 133, 143
Atmospheric demand, 74
Available water-holding capacity, 77

Balled and burlaped, 136, 140
Bare-root, 136
Bed dimensions, 78
   calculating, 80
Biological diversity, 20
Bulk density, 35
   two methods for determining, 36

Carbon dioxide, 5, 10
Cation exchange capacity, 41
Climate, 7
Cohesion, 30
Container-grown, 136
Crown projection, 76
CU-Soil, 68

Desiccation, 25
Design intentions, 20
Development guidelines, 17
Die-back, 21, 22
Drainage, 55
   characteristics, 7
   principles, 99
Dry density, 35

Envisioned design size,
   74
Erosion and runoff, 110
Evaporation:
   pan, 75
   ratio, 76

Fertilizer burn, 42
Field capacity, 31
French drain, 56

Genetic potential, 10
Grade, around trees, 94
Guying techniques, 160

Habitat, 111
Hardiness, 44
Heat Islands, 5

Included bark, 22
Increment of growth, 22
Interveinal chlorosis, 21
Irrigation, 7

Land form, 50
Landscape, human-impacted, 2
Leaf area index, 75
Leaf scorch, 25
Light, 10

Macronutrients, 39, 40
Macropores, 30
Maintenance easements, 17
Mechanical damage, 13
Microclimate, 5, 7, 20, 44
Micronutrients, 39, 40
Micropores, 30
Mulch, 86

Native species, non-native plants, 18, 118
Noise, 110
Nursery:
    stock specification, 137
    production practices, 136
Nutrients, 10
    availability, 40
    essential, 39

Organic:
    amendment, 12
    matter, 53
Oxygen, 5, 10

Penetrometer, 39
Percolation test, 32
Permanent wilting point, 31
Pervious pavements, 87
Pests and diseases, 116
Photosynthesis, 5
Plant-available water, 31
Plant establishment, 6, 8
Planting design, 16
Planting key, 129
Plant selection, 10, 15
Proctor density, 63, 64
Production and harvest, 136
Protection zones, 168

Radial trenching, 95, 98
Remediation techniques, 177. *See also* Soil
Root:
    shared space, 84
    type, 131
    zone temperatures, 6. *See also* Soil

Salt: 47. *See also* Soil
    damage, 25
    de-icing, 42
Saturated flow, 100
Sieve designations and openings, 54

Site assessment: 6
    checklist, 7
    method, 15
Site constraints, 8
Site modification, 10
Site preservation, 165
Soil:
    amendment, 15
    assessment, 27
    chemical properties, 38
    compaction, 11, 176
    density, 35, 45, 47, 62
    determining an adequate volume, 80
    factors, 7
    intrapedal conditions, 30
    modification, 11, 15, 49
    moisture, 113
    nutrients and salts, 60
    peds, 29
    penetrometer, 36
    pH, 4, 41, 46, 57, 58, 115
    physical properties, 27
    profile, 11
    protection, 176
    remediating poor drainage, 98
    restricting volume, 4, 5
    specification, 50
    structure, 29, 61, 65, 68, 69, 100, 176
    temperature, 42
    tests for fertility, 43
    texture, 29, 33, 34, 45
    volume, 64, 73
    volume calculations, 73, 74, 80
Spatial limitations, 16. *See also* Soil;
        Utilities
Species:
    composition, 18
    diversity, 119
    varieties, and cultivars, 126
Structural factors, 7, 72
Subsurface drainage, 56
Subsurface soil sculpting, 52
Suckering, 22
Sump drains, 101
Sun and shade, 112
Surface treatment, 85

Temperature, 10
    modification, 106
Texture-by-feel, 32
Topsoil, 27, 50
Transplanting, 117
    methods, bare root, 149
    techniques, 158

Tree protection, 169
Tree spade, 140

Underdrainage, 55, 101
Unsaturated flow, 100
Urban landscapes, 3, 4
Urban soil, 3, 28. *See also* Soil
Utilities:
    overhead, 16
    underground, 44

Vegetation protection, 171
Vegetative screen, 18
Visual assessment, 8
Visual similarity of trees, 121, 123
Visual uniformity, 119

Water, 10
Water-holding capacity, 31
Whole tree water use, 80
Wind mitigation, 106, 109